Big Data Analytics

A handy reference guide for data analysts and data
scientists to help to obtain value from big data analytics
using Spark on Hadoop clusters

Venkat Ankam

BIRMINGHAM - MUMBAI

Big Data Analytics

First published: September 2016

Production reference: 12309016

Published by Packt Publishing Ltd.
Livery Place
35 Livery Street
Birmingham B3 2PB, UK.

ISBN 978-1-78588-469-6

www.packtpub.com

Credits

Author
Venkat Ankam

Reviewers
Sreekanth Jella
De Witte Dieter

Commissioning Editor
Akram Hussain

Acquisition Editors
Ruchita Bhansali
Tushar Gupta

Content Development Editor
Sumeet Sawant

Technical Editor
Pranil Pathare

Copy Editors
Vikrant Phadke
Vibha Shukla

Project Coordinator
Shweta H Birwatkar

Proofreader
Safis Editing

Indexer
Mariammal Chettiyar

Graphics
Kirk D'Penha

Production Coordinator
Arvindkumar Gupta

Cover Work
Arvindkumar Gupta

About the Author

Venkat Ankam has over 18 years of IT experience and over 5 years in big data technologies, working with customers to design and develop scalable big data applications. Having worked with multiple clients globally, he has tremendous experience in big data analytics using Hadoop and Spark.

He is a Cloudera Certified Hadoop Developer and Administrator and also a Databricks Certified Spark Developer. He is the founder and presenter of a few Hadoop and Spark meetup groups globally and loves to share knowledge with the community.

Venkat has delivered hundreds of trainings, presentations, and white papers in the big data sphere. While this is his first attempt at writing a book, many more books are in the pipeline.

Acknowledgement

I would like to thank Databricks for providing me with training in Spark in early 2014 and an opportunity to deepen my knowledge of Spark.

I would also like to thank Tyler Allbritton, principal architect, big data, cloud and analytics solutions at Tectonic, for providing me support in big data analytics projects and extending his support when writing this book.

Then, I would like to thank Mani Chhabra, CEO of Cloudwick, for encouraging me to write this book and providing the support I needed. Thanks to Arun Sirimalla, big data champion at Cloudwick, and Pranabh Kumar, big data architect at InsideView, who provided excellent support and inspiration to start meetups throughout India in 2011 to share knowledge of Hadoop and Spark.

Then I would like to thank Ashrith Mekala, solution architect at Cloudwick, for his technical consulting help.

This book started with a small discussion with Packt Publishing's acquisition editor Ruchita Bansali. I am really thankful to her for inspiring me to write this book. I am thankful to Kajal Thapar, content development editor at Packt Publishing, who then supported the entire journey of this book with great patience to refine it multiple times and get it to the finish line.

I would also like to thank Sumeet Sawant, Content Development Editor and Pranil Pathare, Technical Editor for their support in implementing Spark 2.0 changes.

I dedicate this book to my family and friends. Finally, this book would not have completed without the support from my wife, Srilatha, and my kids, Neha and Param, who cheered and encouraged me throughout the journey of this book.

About the Reviewers

Sreekanth Jella is a senior Hadoop and Spark developer with more than 11 years of IT industry development experience. He is a postgraduate from the University College of Engineering, Osmania University, with computer applications as major. He has worked in the USA, Turkey, and India and with clients such as AT&T, Cricket Communications, and Turk Telecom. Sreekanth has vast development experience with Java/J2EE technologies and web technologies as well. He is tech savvy and passionate about programming. In his words, *"Coding is an art and code is fun* ☺*"*.

De Witte Dieter received his master's degree in civil engineering (applied physics) from Ghent University in 2008. During his master's, he became really interested in designing algorithms to tackle complex problems.

In April 2010, he was recruited as the first bioinformatics PhD student at IBCN-iMinds. Together with his colleagues, he designed high-performance algorithms in the area of DNA sequence analysis using Hadoop and MPI. Apart from developing and designing algorithms, an important part of the job was data mining, for which he mainly used Matlab. Dieter was also involved in teaching activities around Java/Matlab to first-year bachelor of engineering students.

From May 2014 onwards, he has been working as a big data scientist for Archimiddle (Cronos group). He worked on a big data project with Telenet, part of Liberty Global. Working in a Hadoop production environment together with a talented big data team, he considered it really rewarding and it made him confident in using the Cloudera Hadoop stack. Apart from consulting, he also conducted workshops and presentations on Hadoop and machine learning.

In December 2014, Dieter joined iMinds Data Science Lab, where he was responsible for research activities and consultancy with respect to big data analytics. He is currently teaching a course on big data science to master's students in computer science and statistics and doing consultancy on scalable semantic query systems.

I would like to thank iMinds Data Science Lab for all the opportunities and challenges they offer me.

www.PacktPub.com

eBooks, discount offers, and more

Did you know that Packt offers eBook versions of every book published, with PDF and ePub files available? You can upgrade to the eBook version at www.PacktPub.com and as a print book customer, you are entitled to a discount on the eBook copy. Get in touch with us at customercare@packtpub.com for more details.

At www.PacktPub.com, you can also read a collection of free technical articles, sign up for a range of free newsletters and receive exclusive discounts and offers on Packt books and eBooks.

https://www2.packtpub.com/books/subscription/packtlib

Do you need instant solutions to your IT questions? PacktLib is Packt's online digital book library. Here, you can search, access, and read Packt's entire library of books.

Why subscribe?

- Fully searchable across every book published by Packt
- Copy and paste, print, and bookmark content
- On demand and accessible via a web browser

Table of Contents

Preface

Big Data Analytics aims at providing the fundamentals of Apache Spark and Hadoop, and how they are integrated together with most commonly used tools and techniques in an easy way. All Spark components (Spark Core, Spark SQL, DataFrames, Datasets, Conventional Streaming, Structured Streaming, MLLib, GraphX, and Hadoop core components), HDFS, MapReduce, and Yarn are explored in great depth with implementation examples on Spark + Hadoop clusters.

The Big Data Analytics industry is moving away from MapReduce to Spark. So, the advantages of Spark over MapReduce are explained in great depth to reap the benefits of in-memory speeds. The DataFrames API, the Data Sources API, and the new Dataset API are explained for building Big Data analytical applications. Real-time data analytics using Spark Streaming with Apache Kafka and HBase is covered to help in building streaming applications. New structured streaming concept is explained with an Internet of Things (IOT) use case. Machine learning techniques are covered using MLLib, ML Pipelines and SparkR; Graph Analytics are covered with GraphX and GraphFrames components of Spark.

This book also introduces web based notebooks such as Jupyter, Apache Zeppelin, and data flow tool Apache NiFi to analyze and visualize data, offering Spark as a Service using Livy Server.

What this book covers

Chapter 1, Big Data Analytics at a 10,000-Foot View, provides an approach to Big Data analytics from a broader perspective and introduces tools and techniques used on Apache Hadoop and Apache Spark platforms, with some of most common use cases.

Chapter 2, *Getting Started with Apache Hadoop and Apache Spark*, lays the foundation for Hadoop and Spark platforms with an introduction. This chapter also explains how Spark is different from MapReduce and how Spark on the Hadoop platform is beneficial. Then it helps you get started with the installation of clusters and setting up tools needed for analytics.

Chapter 3, *Deep Dive into Apache Spark*, covers deeper concepts of Spark such as Spark Core internals, how to use pair RDDs, the life cycle of a Spark program, how to build Spark applications, how to persist and cache RDDs, and how to use Spark Resource Managers (Standalone, Yarn, and Mesos).

Chapter 4, *Big Data Analytics with Spark SQL, DataFrames, and Datasets*, covers the Data Sources API, the DataFrames API, and the new Dataset API. There is a special focus on why DataFrame API is useful and analytics of DataFrame API with built-in sources (Csv, Json, Parquet, ORC, JDBC, and Hive) and external sources (such as Avro, Xml, and Pandas). Spark-on-HBase connector explains how to analyze HBase data in Spark using DataFrames. It also covers how to use Spark SQL as a distributed SQL engine.

Chapter 5, *Real-Time Analytics with Spark Streaming and Structured Streaming*, provides the meaning of real-time analytics and how Spark Streaming is different from other real-time engines such as Storm, trident, Flink, and Samza. It describes the architecture of Spark Streaming with input sources and output stores. It covers stateless and stateful stream processing and using receiver-based and direct approach with Kafka as a source and HBase as a store. Fault tolerance concepts of Spark streaming is covered when application is failed at driver or executors. Structured Streaming concepts are explained with an Internet of Things (IOT) use case.

Chapter 6, *Notebooks and Dataflows with Spark and Hadoop*, introduces web-based notebooks with tools such as Jupyter, Zeppelin, and Hue. It introduces the Livy REST server for building Spark as a service and for sharing Spark RDDs between multiple users. It also introduces Apache NiFi for building data flows using Spark and Hadoop.

Chapter 7, *Machine Learning with Spark and Hadoop*, aims at teaching more about the machine learning techniques used in data science using Spark and Hadoop. This chapter introduces machine learning algorithms used with Spark. It covers spam detection, implementation, and the method of building machine learning pipelines. It also covers machine learning implementation with H20 and Hivemall.

Chapter 8, *Building Recommendation Systems with Spark and Mahout*, covers collaborative filtering in detail and explains how to build real-time recommendation engines with Spark and Mahout.

Chapter 9, *Graph Analytics with GraphX*, introduces graph processing, how GraphX is different from Giraph, and various graph operations of GraphX such as creating graph, counting, filtering, degrees, triplets, modifying, joining, transforming attributes, Vertex RDD, and EdgeRDD operations. It also covers GraphX algorithms such as triangle counting and connected components with a flight analytics use case. New GraphFrames component based on DataFrames is introduced and explained some concepts such as motif finding.

Chapter 10, *Interactive Analytics with SparkR*, covers the differences between R and SparkR and gets you started with SparkR using shell scripts in local, standalone, and Yarn modes. This chapter also explains how to use SparkR with RStudio, DataFrames, machine learning with SparkR, and Apache Zeppelin.

What you need for this book

Practical exercises in this book are demonstrated on virtual machines (VM) from Cloudera, Hortonworks, MapR, or prebuilt Spark for Hadoop for getting started easily. The same exercises can be run on a bigger cluster as well.

Prerequisites for using virtual machines on your laptop:

- RAM: 8 GB and above
- CPU: At least two virtual CPUs
- The latest VMWare player or Oracle VirtualBox must be installed for Windows or Linux OS
- Latest Oracle VirtualBox, or VMWare Fusion for Mac
- Virtualization enabled in BIOS
- Browser: Chrome 25+, IE 9+, Safari 6+, or Firefox 18+ recommended (HDP Sandbox will not run on IE 10)
- Putty
- WinScP

The Python and Scala programming languages are used in chapters, with more focus on Python. It is assumed that readers have a basic programming background in Java, Scala, Python, SQL, or R, with basic Linux experience. Working experience within Big Data environments on Hadoop platforms would provide a quick jump start for building Spark applications.

Who this book is for

Though this book is primarily aimed at data analysts and data scientists, it would help architects, programmers, and Big Data practitioners.

For a data analyst: This is useful as a reference guide for data analysts to develop analytical applications on top of Spark and Hadoop.

For a data scientist: This is useful as a reference guide for building data products on top of Spark and Hadoop.

For an architect: This book provides a complete ecosystem overview, examples of Big Data analytical applications, and helps you architect Big Data analytical solutions.

For a programmer: This book provides the APIs and techniques used in Scala and Python languages for building applications.

For a Big Data practitioner: This book helps you to understand the new paradigms and new technologies and make the right decisions.

Conventions

In this book, you will find a number of text styles that distinguish between different kinds of information. Here are some examples of these styles and an explanation of their meaning.

Code words in text, database table names, folder names, filenames, file extensions, pathnames, dummy URLs, user input, and Twitter handles are shown as follows: "Spark's default OFF_HEAP (experimental) storage is Tachyon."

Most of the examples are executed in Scala, Python and Mahout shells. Any command-line input is written as follows:

```
[root@myhost ~]# pyspark --master spark://sparkmasterhostname:7077
--total-executor-cores 4
```

A block of Python code executed in PySpark shell is shown as follows:

```
>>> myList = ["big", "data", "analytics", "hadoop" , "spark"]
>>> myRDD = sc.parallelize(myList)
>>> myRDD.getNumPartitions()
```

A block of code written in Python Application is shown as follows:

```
from pyspark import SparkConf, SparkContext
conf = (SparkConf()
        .setMaster("spark://masterhostname:7077")
        .setAppName("My Analytical Application")
        .set("spark.executor.memory", "2g"))
sc = SparkContext(conf = conf)
```

New terms and **important words** are shown in bold. Words that you see on the screen, for example, in menus or dialog boxes, appear in the text like this: "In case of VMWare Player, click on **Open a Virtual Machine**, and point to the directory where you have extracted the VM."

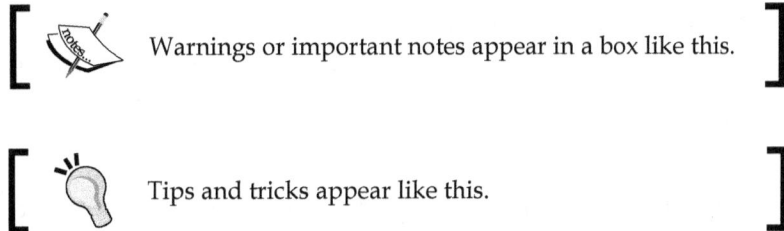

Warnings or important notes appear in a box like this.

Tips and tricks appear like this.

Reader feedback

Feedback from our readers is always welcome. Let us know what you think about this book—what you liked or disliked. Reader feedback is important for us as it helps us develop titles that you will really get the most out of.

To send us general feedback, simply e-mail feedback@packtpub.com, and mention the book's title in the subject of your message.

If there is a topic that you have expertise in and you are interested in either writing or contributing to a book, see our author guide at www.packtpub.com/authors.

Customer support

Now that you are the proud owner of a Packt book, we have a number of things to help you to get the most from your purchase.

Downloading the example code

You can download the example code files for this book from your account at
`http://www.packtpub.com`. If you purchased this book elsewhere, you can visit
`http://www.packtpub.com/support` and register to have the files e-mailed directly
to you.

You can download the code files by following these steps:

1. Log in or register to our website using your e-mail address and password.
2. Hover the mouse pointer on the **SUPPORT** tab at the top.
3. Click on **Code Downloads & Errata**.
4. Enter the name of the book in the **Search** box.
5. Select the book for which you're looking to download the code files.
6. Choose from the drop-down menu where you purchased this book from.
7. Click on **Code Download**.

You can also download the code files by clicking on the **Code Files** button on the
book's webpage at the Packt Publishing website. This page can be accessed by
entering the book's name in the **Search** box. Please note that you need to be logged in
to your Packt account.

Once the file is downloaded, please make sure that you unzip or extract the folder
using the latest version of:

- WinRAR / 7-Zip for Windows
- Zipeg / iZip / UnRarX for Mac
- 7-Zip / PeaZip for Linux

The code bundle for the book is also hosted on GitHub at `https://github.`
`com/PacktPublishing/big-data-analytics`. We also have other code bundles
from our rich catalog of books and videos available at `https://github.com/`
`PacktPublishing/`. Check them out!

Downloading the color images of this book

We also provide you with a PDF file that has color images of the
screenshots/diagrams used in this book. The color images will help you
better understand the changes in the output. You can download this file
from `http://www.packtpub.com/sites/default/files/downloads/`
`BigDataAnalyticsWithSparkAndHadoop_ColorImages.pdf`.

Errata

Although we have taken every care to ensure the accuracy of our content, mistakes do happen. If you find a mistake in one of our books—maybe a mistake in the text or the code—we would be grateful if you could report this to us. By doing so, you can save other readers from frustration and help us improve subsequent versions of this book. If you find any errata, please report them by visiting http://www.packtpub.com/submit-errata, selecting your book, clicking on the **Errata Submission Form** link, and entering the details of your errata. Once your errata are verified, your submission will be accepted and the errata will be uploaded to our website or added to any list of existing errata under the Errata section of that title.

To view the previously submitted errata, go to https://www.packtpub.com/books/content/support and enter the name of the book in the search field. The required information will appear under the **Errata** section.

Piracy

Piracy of copyrighted material on the Internet is an ongoing problem across all media. At Packt, we take the protection of our copyright and licenses very seriously. If you come across any illegal copies of our works in any form on the Internet, please provide us with the location address or website name immediately so that we can pursue a remedy.

Please contact us at copyright@packtpub.com with a link to the suspected pirated material.

We appreciate your help in protecting our authors and our ability to bring you valuable content.

Questions

If you have a problem with any aspect of this book, you can contact us at questions@packtpub.com, and we will do our best to address the problem.

1
Big Data Analytics at a 10,000-Foot View

The goal of this book is to familiarize you with tools and techniques using Apache Spark, with a focus on Hadoop deployments and tools used on the Hadoop platform. Most production implementations of Spark use Hadoop clusters and users are experiencing many integration challenges with a wide variety of tools used with Spark and Hadoop. This book will address the integration challenges faced with **Hadoop Distributed File System (HDFS)** and **Yet Another Resource Negotiator (YARN)** and explain the various tools used with Spark and Hadoop. This will also discuss all the Spark components—Spark Core, Spark SQL, DataFrames, Datasets, Spark Streaming, Structured Streaming, MLlib, GraphX, and SparkR and integration with analytics components such as Jupyter, Zeppelin, Hive, HBase, and dataflow tools such as NiFi. A real-time example of a recommendation system using MLlib will help us understand data science techniques.

In this chapter, we will approach Big Data analytics from a broad perspective and try to understand what tools and techniques are used on the Apache Hadoop and Apache Spark platforms.

Big Data analytics is the process of analyzing Big Data to provide past, current, and future statistics and useful insights that can be used to make better business decisions.

Big Data analytics is broadly classified into two major categories, data analytics and data science, which are interconnected disciplines. This chapter will explain the differences between data analytics and data science. Current industry definitions for data analytics and data science vary according to their use cases, but let's try to understand what they accomplish.

Data analytics focuses on the collection and interpretation of data, typically with a focus on past and present statistics. Data science, on the other hand, focuses on the future by performing explorative analytics to provide recommendations based on models identified by past and present data.

Figure 1.1 explains the difference between data analytics and data science with respect to time and value achieved. It also shows typical questions asked and tools and techniques used. Data analytics has mainly two types of analytics, descriptive analytics and diagnostic analytics. Data science has two types of analytics, predictive analytics and prescriptive analytics. The following diagram explains data science and data analytics:

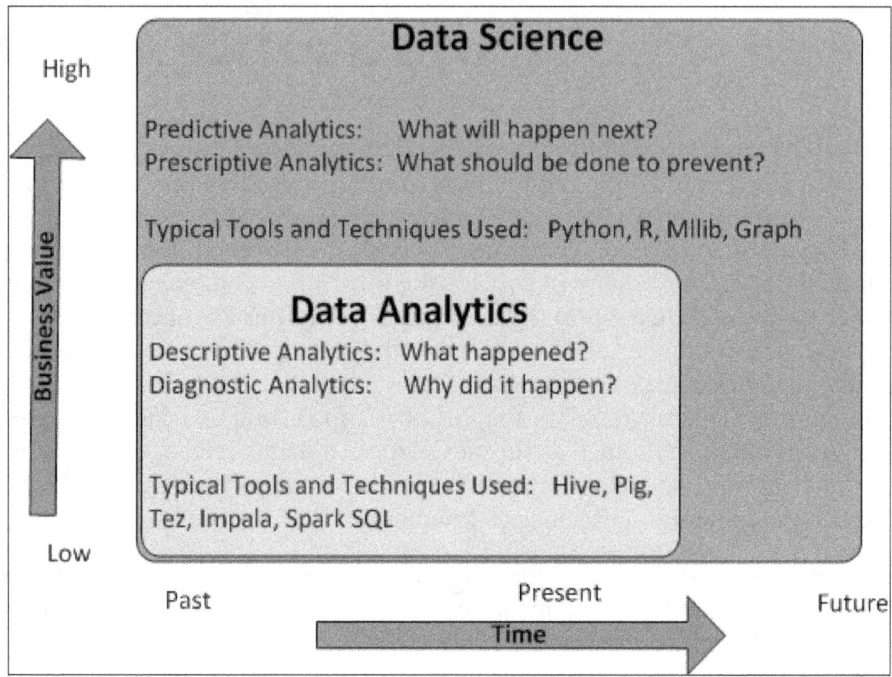

Figure 1.1: Data analytics versus data science

The following table explains the differences with respect to processes, tools, techniques, skill sets, and outputs:

	Data analytics	Data science
Perspective	Looking backward	Looking forward
Nature of work	Report and optimize	Explore, discover, investigate, and visualize
Output	Reports and dashboards	Data product

	Data analytics	Data science
Typical tools used	Hive, Impala, Spark SQL, and HBase	MLlib and Mahout
Typical techniques used	ETL and exploratory analytics	Predictive analytics and sentiment analytics
Typical skill set necessary	Data engineering, SQL, and programming	Statistics, machine learning, and programming

This chapter will cover the following topics:

- Big Data analytics and the role of Hadoop and Spark
- Big Data science and the role of Hadoop and Spark
- Tools and techniques
- Real-life use cases

Big Data analytics and the role of Hadoop and Spark

Conventional data analytics uses **Relational Database Management Systems (RDBMS)** databases to create data warehouses and data marts for analytics using business intelligence tools. RDBMS databases use the **Schema-on-Write** approach; there are many downsides for this approach.

Traditional data warehouses were designed to **Extract, Transform, and Load** (ETL) data in order to answer a set of predefined questions, which are directly related to user requirements. Predefined questions are answered using SQL queries. Once the data is transformed and loaded in a consumable format, it becomes easier for users to access it with a variety of tools and applications to generate reports and dashboards. However, creating data in a consumable format requires several steps, which are listed as follows:

1. Deciding predefined questions.
2. Identifying and collecting data from source systems.
3. Creating ETL pipelines to load the data into the analytic database in a consumable format.

If new questions arise, systems need to identify and add new data sources and create new ETL pipelines. This involves schema changes in databases and the effort of implementation typically ranges from one to six months. This is a big constraint and forces the data analyst to operate in predefined boundaries only.

Transforming data into a consumable format generally results in losing raw/atomic data that might have insights or clues to the answers that we are looking for.

Processing structured and unstructured data is another challenge in traditional data warehousing systems. Storing and processing large binary images or videos effectively is always a challenge.

Big Data analytics does not use relational databases; instead, it uses the **Schema-on-Read (SOR)** approach on the Hadoop platform using Hive and HBase typically. There are many advantages of this approach. *Figure 1.2* shows the Schema-on-Write and Schema-on-Read scenarios:

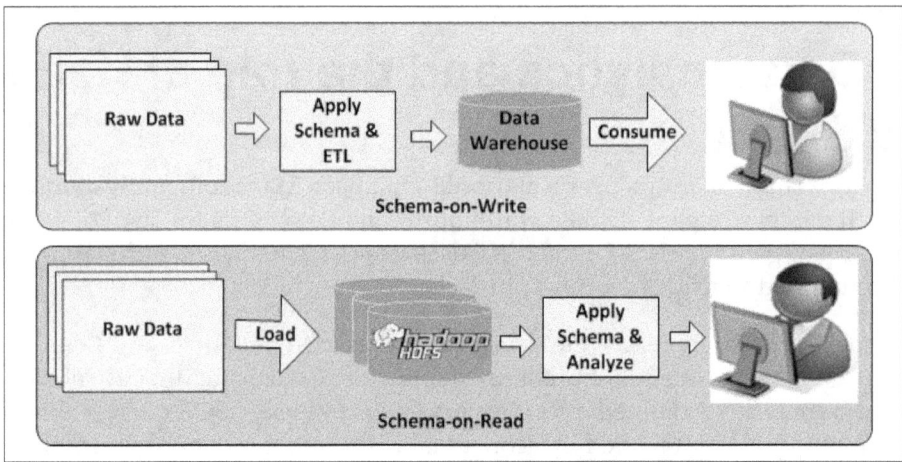

Figure 1.2: Schema-on-Write versus Schema-on-Read

The Schema-on-Read approach introduces flexibility and reusability to systems. The Schema-on-Read paradigm emphasizes storing the data in a raw, unmodified format and applying a schema to the data as needed, typically while it is being read or processed. This approach allows considerably more flexibility in the amount and type of data that can be stored. Multiple schemas can be applied to the same raw data to ask a variety of questions. If new questions need to be answered, just get the new data and store it in a new directory of HDFS and start answering new questions.

This approach also provides massive flexibility over how the data can be consumed with multiple approaches and tools. For example, the same raw data can be analyzed using SQL analytics or complex Python or R scripts in Spark. As we are not storing data in multiple layers, which is needed for ETL, so the storage cost and data movement cost is reduced. Analytics can be done for unstructured and structured data sources along with structured data sources.

A typical Big Data analytics project life cycle

The life cycle of Big Data analytics using Big Data platforms such as Hadoop is similar to traditional data analytics projects. However, a major paradigm shift is using the Schema-on-Read approach for the data analytics.

A Big Data analytics project involves the activities shown in *Figure 1.3*:

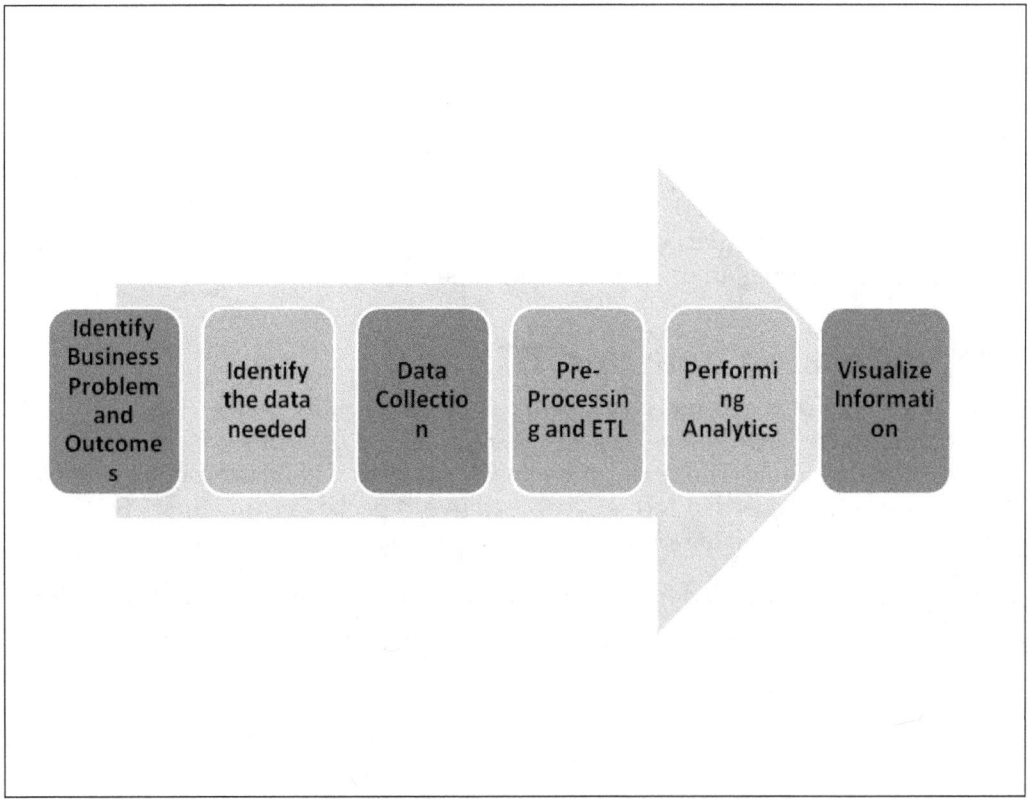

Figure 1.3: The Big Data analytics life cycle

Identifying the problem and outcomes

Identify the business problem and desired outcome of the project clearly so that it scopes in what data is needed and what analytics can be performed. Some examples of business problems are company sales going down, customers visiting the website but not buying products, customers abandoning shopping carts, a sudden rise in support call volume, and so on. Some examples of project outcomes are improving the buying rate by 10%, decreasing shopping cart abandonment by 50%, and reducing support call volume by 50% by the next quarter while keeping customers happy.

Identifying the necessary data

Identify the quality, quantity, format, and sources of data. Data sources can be data warehouses (OLAP), application databases (OLTP), log files from servers, documents from the Internet, and data generated from sensors and network hubs. Identify all the internal and external data source requirements. Also, identify the data anonymization and re-identification requirements of data to remove or mask **personally identifiable information (PII)**.

Data collection

Collect data from relational databases using the Sqoop tool and stream data using Flume. Consider using Apache Kafka for reliable intermediate storage. Design and collect data considering fault tolerance scenarios.

Preprocessing data and ETL

Data comes in different formats and there can be data quality issues. The preprocessing step converts the data to a needed format or cleanses inconsistent, invalid, or corrupt data. The performing analytics phase will be initiated once the data conforms to the needed format. Apache Hive, Apache Pig, and Spark SQL are great tools for preprocessing massive amounts of data.

This step may not be needed in some projects if the data is already in a clean format or analytics are performed directly on the source data with the Schema-on-Read approach.

Performing analytics

Analytics are performed in order to answer business questions. This requires an understanding of data and relationships between data points. The types of analytics performed are descriptive and diagnostic analytics to present the past and current views on the data. This typically answers questions such as what happened and why it happened. In some cases, predictive analytics is performed to answer questions such as what would happen based on a hypothesis.

Apache Hive, Pig, Impala, Drill, Tez, Apache Spark, and HBase are great tools for data analytics in batch processing mode. Real-time analytics tools such as Impala, Tez, Drill, and Spark SQL can be integrated into traditional business intelligence tools (Tableau, Qlikview, and others) for interactive analytics.

Visualizing data

Data visualization is the presentation of analytics output in a pictorial or graphical format to understand the analysis better and make business decisions based on the data.

Typically, finished data is exported from Hadoop to RDBMS databases using Sqoop for integration into visualization systems or visualization systems are directly integrated into tools such as Tableau, Qlikview, Excel, and so on. Web-based notebooks such as Jupyter, Zeppelin, and Databricks cloud are also used to visualize data by integrating Hadoop and Spark components.

The role of Hadoop and Spark

Hadoop and Spark provide you with great flexibility in Big Data analytics:

- Large-scale data preprocessing; massive datasets can be preprocessed with high performance
- Exploring large and full datasets; the dataset size does not matter
- Accelerating data-driven innovation by providing the Schema-on-Read approach
- A variety of tools and APIs for data exploration

Big Data science and the role of Hadoop and Spark

Data science is all about the following two aspects:

- Extracting deep meaning from the data
- Creating data products

Extracting deep meaning from data means fetching the value using statistical algorithms. A data product is a software system whose core functionality depends on the application of statistical analysis and machine learning to the data. Google AdWords or Facebook's *People You May Know* are a couple of examples of data products.

A fundamental shift from data analytics to data science

A fundamental shift from data analytics to data science is due to the rising need for better predictions and creating better data products.

Let's consider an example use case that explains the difference between data analytics and data science.

Problem: A large telecoms company has multiple call centers that collect caller information and store it in databases and filesystems. The company has already implemented data analytics on the call center data, which provided the following insights:

- Service availability
- The average speed of answering, average hold time, average wait time, and average call time
- The call abandon rate
- The first call resolution rate and cost per call
- Agent occupancy

Now, the telecoms company would like to reduce the customer churn, improve customer experience, improve service quality, and cross-sell and up-sell by understanding the customers in near real-time.

Solution: Analyze the customer voice. The customer voice has deeper insights than any other information. Convert all calls to text using tools such as CMU Sphinx and scale out on the Hadoop platform. Perform text analytics to derive insights from the data, to gain high accuracy in call-to-text conversion, create models (language and acoustic) that are suitable for the company, and retrain models on a frequent basis with any changes. Also, create models for text analytics using machine learning and **natural language processing** (**NLP**) to come up with the following metrics while combining data analytics metrics:

- Top reasons for customer churn
- Customer sentiment analysis
- Customer and problem segmentation
- 360-degree view of the customer

Notice that the business requirement of this use case created a fundamental shift from data analytics to data science implementing machine learning and NLP algorithms. To implement this solution, new tools and techniques are used and a new role, data scientist, is needed.

A data scientist has a combination of multiple skill sets — statistics, software programming, and business expertise. Data scientists create data products and extract value from the data. Let's see how data scientists differ from other roles. This will help us in understanding roles and tasks performed in data science and data analytics projects.

Data scientists versus software engineers

The difference between the data scientist and software engineer roles is as follows:

- Software engineers develop general-purpose software for applications based on business requirements
- Data scientists don't develop application software, but they develop software to help them solve problems
- Typically, software engineers use Java, C++, and C# programming languages
- Data scientists tend to focus more on scripting languages such as Python and R

Data scientists versus data analysts

The difference between the data scientist and data analyst roles is as follows:

- Data analysts perform descriptive and diagnostic analytics using SQL and scripting languages to create reports and dashboards.

- Data scientists perform predictive and prescriptive analytics using statistical techniques and machine learning algorithms to find answers. They typically use tools such as Python, R, SPSS, SAS, MLlib, and GraphX.

Data scientists versus business analysts

The difference between the data scientist and business analyst roles is as follows:

- Both have a business focus, so they may ask similar questions
- Data scientists have the technical skills to find answers

A typical data science project life cycle

Let's learn how to approach and execute a typical data science project.

The typical data science project life cycle shown in *Figure 1.4* explains that a data science project's life cycle is iterative, but a data analytics project's life cycle, as shown in *Figure 1.3*, is not iterative. Defining problems and outcomes and communicating phases are not in the iterations while improving the outcomes of the project. However, the overall project life cycle is iterative, which needs to be improved from time to time after production implementation.

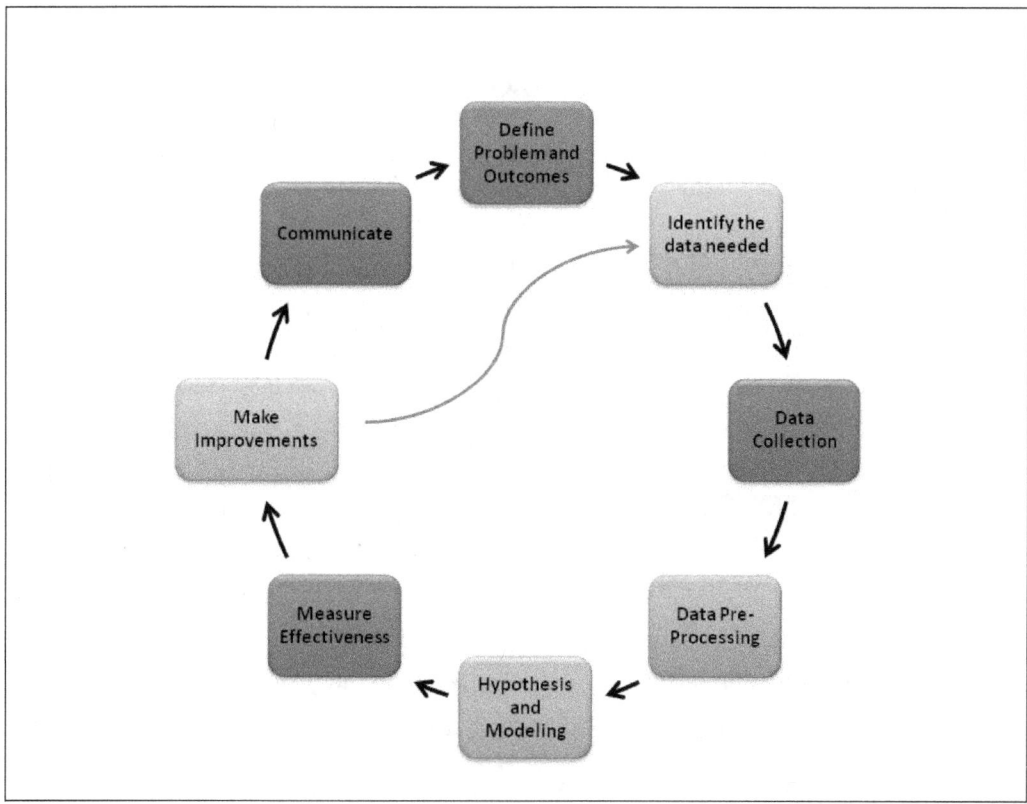

Figure 1.4: A data science project life cycle

Defining problems and outcomes in the data preprocessing phase is similar to the data analytics project, which is explained in *Figure 1.3*. So, let's discuss the new steps required for data science projects.

Hypothesis and modeling

Given the problem, consider all the possible solutions that could match the desired outcome. This typically involves a hypothesis about the root cause of the problem. So, questions around the business problem arise, such as why customers are canceling the service, why support calls are increasing significantly, and why customers are abandoning shopping carts.

A hypothesis would identify the appropriate model given a deeper understanding of the data. This involves understanding the attributes of the data and their relationships and building the environment for the modeling by defining datasets for testing, training, and production. Create the appropriate model using machine learning algorithms such as logistic regression, k-means clustering, decision trees, or Naive Bayes.

Measuring the effectiveness

Execute the model by running the identified model against the datasets. Measure the effectiveness of the model by checking the results against the desired outcome. Use test data to verify the results and create metrics such as **Mean Squared Error (MSE)** to measure effectiveness.

Making improvements

Measurements will illustrate how much improvement is required. Consider what you might change. You can ask yourself the following questions:

- Was the hypothesis around the root cause correct?
- Ingesting additional datasets would provide better results?
- Would other solutions provide better results?

Once you've implemented your improvements, test them again and compare them with the previous measurements in order to refine the solution further.

Communicating the results

Communication of the results is an important step in the data science project life cycle. The data scientist tells the story found within the data by correlating the story to business problems. Reports and dashboards are common tools to communicate the results.

The role of Hadoop and Spark

Apache Hadoop provides you with distributed storage and resource management, while Spark provides you with in-memory performance for data science applications. Hadoop and Spark have the following advantages for data science projects:

- A wide range of applications and third-party packages
- A machine learning algorithms library for easy usage
- Spark integrations with deep learning libraries such as H2O and TensorFlow

- Scala, Python, and R for interactive analytics using the shell
- A unification feature—using SQL, machine learning, and streaming together

Tools and techniques

Let's take a look at different tools and techniques used in Hadoop and Spark for Big Data analytics.

While the Hadoop platform can be used for both storing and processing the data, Spark can be used for processing only by reading data into memory.

The following is a tabular representation of the tools and techniques used in typical Big Data analytics projects:

	Tools used	Techniques used
Data collection	Apache Flume for real-time data collection and aggregation Apache Sqoop for data import and export from relational data stores and NoSQL databases Apache Kafka for the publish-subscribe messaging system General-purpose tools such as FTP/Copy	Real-time data capture Export Import Message publishing Data APIs Screen scraping
Data storage and formats	HDFS: Primary storage of Hadoop HBase: NoSQL database Parquet: Columnar format Avro: Serialization system on Hadoop Sequence File: Binary key-value pairs RC File: First columnar format in Hadoop ORC File: Optimized RC File XML and JSON: Standard data interchange formats Compression formats: Gzip, Snappy, LZO, Bzip2, Deflate, and others Unstructured Text, images, videos, and so on	Data storage Data archival Data compression Data serialization Schema evolution

	Tools used	Techniques used
Data transformation and enrichment	MapReduce: Hadoop's processing framework Spark: Compute engine Hive: Data warehouse and querying Pig: Data flow language Python: Functional programming Crunch, Cascading, Scalding, and Cascalog: Special MapReduce tools	Data munging Filtering Joining ETL File format conversion Anonymization Re-identification
Data analytics	Hive: Data warehouse and querying Pig: Data flow language Tez: Alternative to MapReduce Impala: Alternative to MapReduce Drill: Alternative to MapReduce Apache Storm: Real-time compute engine Spark Core: Spark core compute engine Spark Streaming: Real-time compute engine Spark SQL: For SQL analytics SolR: Search platform Apache Zeppelin: Web-based notebook Jupyter Notebooks Databricks cloud Apache NiFi: Data flow Spark-on-HBase connector Programming languages: Java, Scala, and Python	**Online Analytical Processing (OLAP)** Data mining Data visualization Complex event processing Real-time stream processing Full text search Interactive data analytics
Data science	Python: Functional programming R: Statistical computing language Mahout: Hadoop's machine learning library MLlib: Spark's machine learning library GraphX and GraphFrames: Spark's graph processing framework and DataFrame adoption to graphs.	Predictive analytics Sentiment analytics Text and Natural Language Processing Network analytics Cluster analytics

Real-life use cases

Let's take a look at different kinds of use cases for Big Data analytics. Broadly, Big Data analytics use cases are classified into the following five categories:

- **Customer analytics**: Data-driven customer insights are necessary to deepen relationships and improve revenue.

- **Operational analytics**: Performance and high service quality are the keys to maintaining customers in any industry, from manufacturing to health services.

- **Data-driven products and services**: New products and services that align with growing business demands.

- **Enterprise Data Warehouse (EDW) optimization**: Early data adopters have warehouse architectures that are 20 years old. Businesses modernize EDW architectures in order to handle the data deluge.

- **Domain-specific solutions**: Domain-specific solutions provide businesses with an effective way to implement new features or adhere to industry compliance.

The following table shows you typical use cases of Big Data analytics:

Problem class	Use cases	Data analytics or data science?
Customer analytics	A 360-degree view of the customer	Data analytics and data science
	Call center analytics	Data analytics and data science
	Sentiment analytics	Data science
	Recommendation engine (for example, the next best action)	Data science
Operational analytics	Log analytics	Data analytics
	Call center analytics	Data analytics
	Unstructured data management	Data analytics
	Document management	Data analytics
	Network analytics	Data analytics and data science
	Preventive maintenance	Data science
	Geospatial data management	Data analytics and data science
	IOT Analytics	Data analytics and data science

Problem class	Use cases	Data analytics or data science?
Data-driven products and services	Metadata management	Data analytics
	Operational data services	Data analytics
	Data/Big Data environments	Data analytics
	Data marketplaces	Data analytics
	Third-party data management	Data analytics
EDW optimization	Data warehouse offload	Data analytics
	Structured Big Data lake	Data analytics
	Licensing cost mitigation	Data analytics
	Cloud data architectures	Data analytics
	Software assessments and migrations	Data analytics
Domain-specific solutions	Fraud and compliance	Data analytics and data science
	Industry-specific domain models	Data analytics
	Data sourcing and integration	Data analytics
	Metrics and reporting solutions	Data analytics
	Turnkey warehousing solutions	Data analytics

Summary

Big Data analytics with Hadoop and Spark is broadly classified into two major categories: data analytics and data science. While data analytics focuses on past and present statistics, data science focuses on future statistics. While data science projects are iterative in nature, data analytics projects are not iterative.

Apache Hadoop provides you with distributed storage and resource management and Spark provides you with in-memory performance for Big Data analytics. A variety of tools and techniques are used in Big Data analytics depending on the type of use cases and their feasibility.

The next chapter will help you get started with Hadoop and Spark.

2
Getting Started with Apache Hadoop and Apache Spark

In this chapter, we will understand the basics of Hadoop and Spark, how Spark is different from MapReduce, and get started with the installation of clusters and setting up the tools needed for analytics.

This chapter is divided into the following subtopics:

- Introducing Apache Hadoop
- Introducing Apache Spark
- Discussing why we use Hadoop with Spark
- Installing Hadoop and Spark clusters

Introducing Apache Hadoop

Apache Hadoop is a software framework that enables distributed processing on large clusters with thousands of nodes and petabytes of data. Apache Hadoop clusters can be built using commodity hardware where failure rates are generally high. Hadoop is designed to handle these failures gracefully without user intervention. Also, Hadoop uses the *move computation to the data* approach, thereby avoiding significant network I/O. Users will be able to develop parallel applications quickly, focusing on business logic rather than doing the heavy lifting of distributing data, distributing code for parallel processing, and handling failures.

Apache Hadoop has mainly four projects: Hadoop Common, **Hadoop Distributed File System (HDFS)**, **Yet Another Resource Negotiator (YARN)**, and MapReduce.

In simple words, HDFS is used to store data, MapReduce is used to process data, and YARN is used to manage the resources (CPU and memory) of the cluster and common utilities that support Hadoop. Apache Hadoop integrates with many other projects, such as Avro, Hive, Pig, HBase, Zookeeper, and Apache Spark.

Hadoop mainly brings the following three components to the table:

- A framework for reliable distributed data storage: **HDFS**
- Multiple frameworks for parallel processing of data: **MapReduce, Crunch, Cascading, Hive, Tez, Impala, Pig, Mahout, Spark,** and **Giraph**
- A framework for cluster resource management: **YARN** and **Slider**

Let's take a look at Hadoop's adoption drivers with respect to the economy, business, and technical areas:

- **Economy**: Low cost per terabyte processing when compared to commercial solutions. This is because of its open source software and commodity hardware.
- **Business**: The ability to store and process all the data on a massive scale provides higher business value.
- **Technical**: The ability to store and process any Variety, Volume, Velocity, and Veracity (all four Vs) of Big Data.

The following list provides the typical characteristics of Hadoop:

- **Commodity**: Hadoop can be installed using commodity hardware on-premise or on any cloud provider.
- **Robust**: It can handle hardware failures at the software layer without user intervention and process failures gracefully without user intervention.
- **Scalable**: It can commission new nodes to scale out in order to increase the capacity of the cluster.
- **Simple**: Developers can focus on business logic only, and not on scalability, fault tolerance, and multithreading.
- **Data locality**: The data size is up to petabytes whereas code size is up to kilobytes. Moving code to the node where data blocks reside provides great reduction in network I/O.

Hadoop Distributed File System

HDFS is a distributed filesystem that provides high scalability and reliability on large clusters of commodity hardware.

HDFS files are divided into large blocks that are typically 128 MB in size and distributed across the cluster. Each block is replicated (typically three times) to handle hardware failures and block placement exposed by NameNode so that computation can be moved to data with the MapReduce framework, as illustrated in *Figure 2.1*:

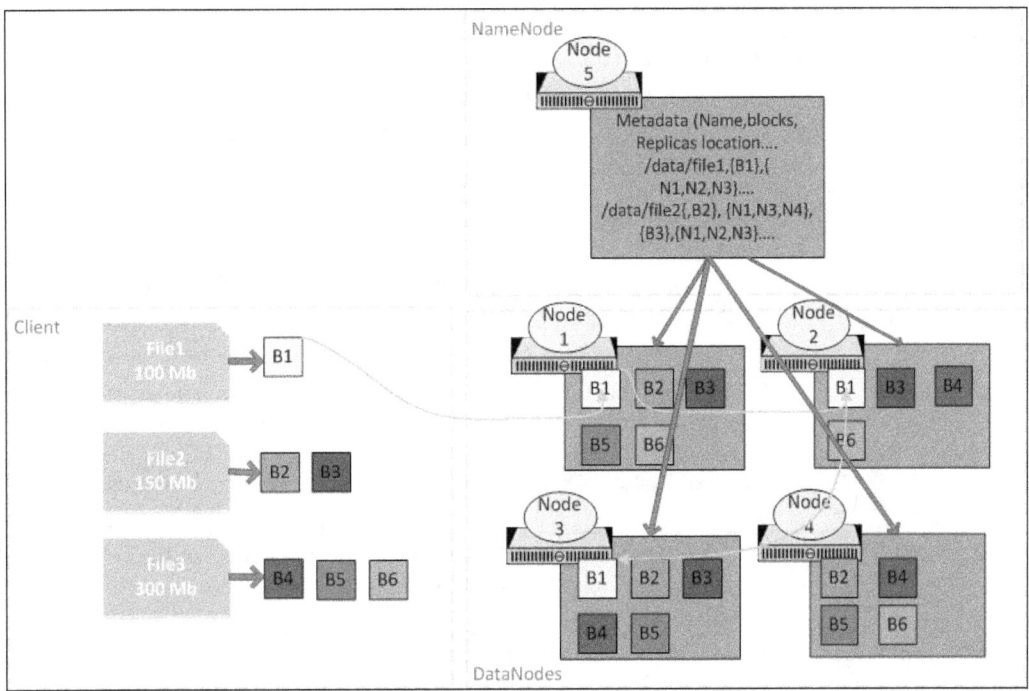

Figure 2.1: HDFS architecture

In the preceding image, when storing **File1**, it's divided into a single block (**B1**) as its size (100 MB) is less than the default block size (128 MB) and replicated on **Node 1**, **Node 2**, and **Node 3**. Block1 (**B1**) is replicated on the first node (**Node 1**) and then Node 1 replicates on Node 2 and Node 2 replicates on Node 3. **File2** is divided into two blocks as its size (150 MB) is greater than the block size, and block2 (**B2**) and block3 (**B3**) are replicated on three nodes (B2 on Node 1, Node 3, and Node 4 and B3 on Node 1, Node 2, and Node 3). Blocks' metadata (file name, blocks, location, date created, and size) is stored in **NameNode**, as shown in the preceding image. HDFS has a bigger block size to reduce the number of disk seeks needed to read the complete file.

The creation of a file seems like a single file to the user. However, it is stored as blocks on DataNodes and metadata is stored in NameNode. If we lose the NameNode for any reason, blocks stored on DataNodes become useless as there is no way to identify the blocks belonging to the file names. So, creating NameNode high availability and metadata backups is very important in any Hadoop cluster.

Features of HDFS

HDFS is becoming a standard enterprise Big Data storage system because of the unlimited scalability and yet provides most features needed for enterprise-grade Big Data applications. The following table explains the important features of HDFS:

Feature	Description
High availability	Enabling high availability is done by creating a standby NameNode.
Data integrity	When blocks are stored on HDFS, computed checksums are stored on the DataNodes as well. Data is verified against the checksum.
HDFS ACLs	HDFS implements POSIX-style permissions that enable an owner and group for every file with read, write, and execute permissions. In addition to POSIX permissions, HDFS supports POSIX **Access Control Lists (ACLs)** to provide access for specific named users or groups.
Snapshots	HDFS Snapshots are read-only point-in-time copies of the HDFS filesystem, which are useful to protect datasets from user or application errors.
HDFS rebalancing	The HDFS rebalancing feature will rebalance the data uniformly across all DataNodes in the cluster.
Caching	Caching of blocks on DataNodes is used for high performance. DataNodes cache the blocks in an off-heap cache.
APIs	HDFS provides a native Java API, Pipes API for C++, and Streaming API for scripting languages such as Python, Perl, and others. FileSystem Shell and web browsers can be used to access data as well. Also, WebHDFS and HttpFs can be used to access data over HTTP.
Data encryption	HDFS will encrypt the data at rest once enabled. Data encryption and decryption happens automatically without any changes to application code.
Kerberos authentication	When Kerberos is enabled, every service in the Hadoop cluster being accessed will have to be authenticated using the Kerberos principle. This provides tight security to Hadoop clusters.
NFS access	Using this feature, HDFS can be mounted as part of the local filesystem, and users can browse, download, upload, and append data to it.

Feature	Description
Metrics	Hadoop exposes many metrics that are useful in troubleshooting. **Java Management Extensions (JMX)** metrics can be viewed from a web UI or the command line.
Rack awareness	Hadoop clusters can be enabled with rack awareness. Once enabled, HDFS block placement will be done as per the rack awareness script, which provides better fault tolerance.
Storage policies	Storage policies are introduced in order to allow files to be stored in different storage types according to the storage policy (**Hot**, **Cold**, **Warm**, **All_SSD**, **One_SSD**, or **Lazy_Persist**).
WORM	**Write Once and Read Many (WORM)** times is a feature of HDFS that does not allow updating or deleting records in place. However, records can be appended to the files.

MapReduce

MapReduce (MR) is a framework to write analytical applications in batch mode on terabytes or petabytes of data stored on HDFS. An MR job usually processes each block (excluding replicas) of input file(s) in HDFS with the mapper tasks in a parallel manner. The MR framework sorts and shuffles the outputs of the mappers to the reduce tasks in order to produce the output. The framework takes care of computing the number of tasks needed, scheduling tasks, monitoring them, and re-executing them if they fail. The developer needs to focus only on writing the business logic, and all the heavy lifting is done by the HDFS and MR frameworks.

For example, in *Figure 2.1*, if an MR job is submitted for **File1**, one map task will be created and run on any Node 1, 2, or 3 to achieve data locality. In the case of **File2**, two map tasks will be created with map task 1 running on Node 1, 3, or 4, and map task 2 running on Node 1, 2, or 3, depending on resource availability. The output of the mappers will be sorted and shuffled to reducer tasks. By default, the number of reducers is one. However, the number of reducer tasks can be increased to provide parallelism at the reducer level.

MapReduce features

MR provides you with excellent features to build Big Data applications. The following table describes MR's key features and techniques used, such as sorting and joining:

Feature/techniques	Description
Data locality	MR moves the computation to the data. It ships the programs to the nodes where HDFS blocks reside. This reduces the network I/O significantly.

Feature/techniques	Description
APIs	Native Java API.
	Pipes: C++ API.
	Streaming: Any shell scripting such as Python and Perl.
Distributed cache	A distributed cache is used to cache files such as archives, jars, or any files that are needed by applications at runtime.
Combiner	The combiner feature is used to reduce the network traffic, or, in other words, reduce the amount of data sent from mappers to reducers over the network.
Custom partitioner	This controls which reducer each intermediate key and its associated values go to. A custom partitioner can be used to override the default hash partitioner.
Sorting	Sorting is done in the sort and shuffle phase, but there are different ways to achieve and control sorting—total sort, partial sort, and secondary sort.
Joining	Joining two massive datasets with the joining process is easy. If the join is performed by the mapper tasks, it is called a map-side join. If the join is performed by the reducer task, it is called a reduce-side join. Map-side joins are always preferred because it avoids sending a lot of data over the network for reducers to join.
Counters	The MR framework provides built-in counters that give an insight in to how the MR job is performing. It allows the user to define a set of counters in the code, which are then incremented as desired in the mapper or reducer.

MapReduce v1 versus MapReduce v2

Apache Hadoop's MapReduce has been a core processing engine that supports the distributed processing of large-scale data workloads. MR has undergone a complete refurbishment in the Hadoop 0.23 version and now it's called MapReduce 2.0 (MR v2) or YARN.

MapReduce v1, which is also called *Classic MapReduce*, has three main components:

- An API to develop MR-based applications
- A framework to execute mappers, shuffle the data, and execute reducers
- A resource management framework to schedule and monitor resources

MapReduce v2, which is also called *NextGen*, moves resource management to YARN, as shown in *Figure 2.2*:

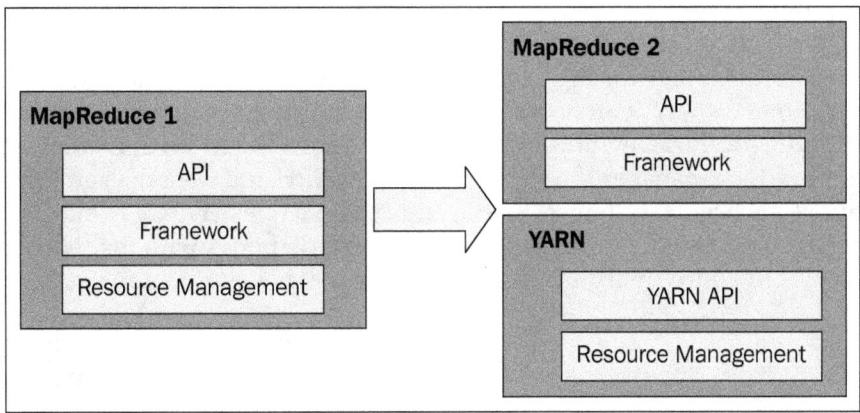

Figure 2.2: MapReduce v1 to MapReduce v2

MapReduce v1 challenges

MapReduce v1 had three challenges:

- Inflexible CPU slots configured on a cluster for Map and Reduce led to the underutilization of the cluster
- Resources could not be shared with non-MR applications (for example, Impala or Spark)
- Limited scalability, only up to 4,000 nodes

The following table shows you the differences between v1 and v2:

	MR v1	MR v2
Components used	Job tracker as master and task tracker as slave	Resource manager as master and node manager as slave
Resource allocation	DataNodes are configured to run a fixed number of map tasks and reduce tasks	Containers are allocated as needed for any type of task
Resource management	One job tracker per cluster, which supports up to 4,000 nodes	One resource manager per cluster, which supports up to tens of thousands of nodes
Types of jobs	MR jobs only	Supports MR and other frameworks such as Spark, Impala, and Giraph

YARN

YARN is the resource management framework that enables an enterprise to process data in multiple ways simultaneously for batch processing, interactive analytics, or real-time analytics on shared datasets. While HDFS provides scalable, fault-tolerant, and cost-efficient storage for Big Data, YARN provides resource management to clusters. *Figure 2.3* shows you how multiple frameworks are typically run on top of HDFS and YARN frameworks in Hadoop 2.0. YARN is like an operating system for Hadoop, which manages the cluster resources (CPU and Memory) efficiently. Applications such as MapReduce, Spark, and others request YARN to allocate resources for their tasks. YARN allocates containers on nodes with the requested amount of RAM and virtual CPU from the total available on that node:

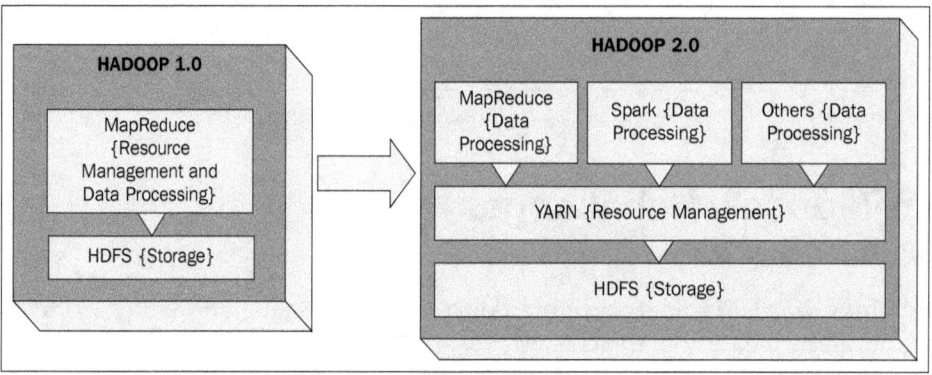

Figure 2.3: Hadoop 1.0 and 2.0 frameworks

YARN's original purpose was to split up the two major responsibilities of the JobTracker/TaskTracker (which are part of MapReduce v1) into separate entities:

- ResourceManager
- A per-application ApplicationMaster
- A per-node slave NodeManager
- A per-application container running on NodeManager

ResourceManager keeps track of the resource availability of the entire cluster and provides resources to applications when requested by ApplicationMaster.

ApplicationMaster negotiates the resources needed by the application to run their tasks. ApplicationMaster also tracks and monitors the progress of the application. Note that this monitoring functionality was handled by TaskTrackers and JobTrackers in MR v1, which led to overloading the JobTracker.

NodeManager is responsible for launching containers provided by ResourceManager, monitoring the resource usage on the slave nodes, and reporting to ResourceManager.

The application container is responsible for running the tasks of the application. YARN also has pluggable schedulers (Fair Scheduler and Capacity Scheduler) to control the resource assignments to different applications. Detailed steps of the YARN application life cycle are shown in *Figure 2.4* with two resource requests by an application:

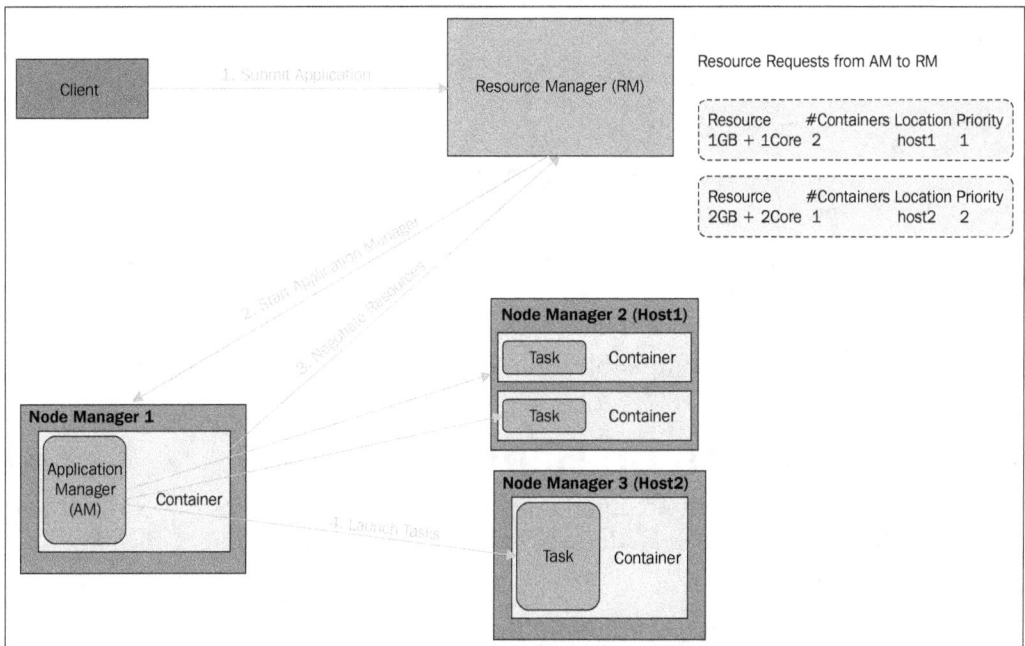

Figure 2.4: The YARN application life cycle

The following is our interpretation of the preceding figure:

- The client submits the MR or Spark job
- The YARN ResourceManager creates an ApplicationMaster on one NodeManager
- The ApplicationMaster negotiates the resources with the ResourceManager
- The ResourceManager provides resources, the NodeManager creates the containers, and the ApplicationMaster launches tasks (Map, Reduce, or Spark tasks) in the containers
- Once the tasks are finished, the containers and the ApplicationMaster will be terminated

Let's summarize the preceding points concerning YARN:

- MapReduce v2 is based on YARN:
    ◦ YARN replaced the JobTracker/TaskTracker architecture of MR v1 with the ResourceManager and NodeManager
    ◦ The ResourceManager takes care of scheduling and resource allocation
    ◦ The ApplicationMaster schedules tasks in containers and monitors the tasks

- Why YARN?
    ◦ Better scalability
    ◦ Efficient resource management
    ◦ Flexibility to run multiple frameworks

- Views from the user's perspective:
    ◦ No significant changes — the same API, CLI, and web UIs.
    ◦ Backward-compatible with MR v1 without any changes

Storage options on Hadoop

XML and JSON files are well-accepted industry standard formats. So, why can't we just use XML or JSON files on Hadoop? There are many disadvantages of XML and JSON, including the following:

- Larger size of the data because of storing schema along with the data
- Does not support schema evolution
- Files cannot be split on Hadoop when compressed
- Not efficient when transferring the data over network

When storing data and building applications on Hadoop, some fundamental questions arises: What storage format is useful for my application? What compression codec is optimum for my application?

Hadoop provides you with a variety of file formats built for different use cases. Choosing the right file format and compression codec provides optimum performance for the use case that you are working on. Let's go through the file formats and understand when to use them.

File formats

File formats are divided into two categories. Hadoop can store all the data regardless of what format the data is stored in. Data can be stored in its raw form using the standard file format or the special Hadoop container file format that offers benefits in specific use case scenarios, which can be split even when data is compressed. Broadly, there are two types of file formats: Standard file formats and Hadoop file formats:

- Standard file formats:
    - **Structured text data**: CSV, TSV, XML, and JSON files
    - **Unstructured text data**: Log files and documents
    - **Unstructured binary data**: Images, videos, and audio files

- Hadoop file formats:

    Provides splittable compression

    - File-based structures:

        Sequence file

    - Serialization format:

        Thrift

        Protocol buffers

        Avro

    - Columnar formats:

        RCFile

        ORCFile

        Parquet

Let's go through the Hadoop file format features and use cases in which they can be used.

Sequence file

Sequence files store data as binary key-value pairs. It supports the Java language only and does not support schema evolution. It supports the splitting of files even when the data is compressed.

Let's see a use case for the sequence file:

- **Small files problem**: On an average, each file occupies 600 bytes of space in memory. One million files of 100 KB need 572 MB of main memory on the NameNode. Additionally, the MR job will create one million mappers.

- **Solution**: Create a sequence file with the key as the filename and value as the content of the file, as shown in the following table. Only 600 bytes of memory space is needed in NameNode and an MR job will create 762 mappers with 128 MB block size:

Key	Value	Key	Value	Key	Value
File1.txt	File.txt content	File2.txt	File2.txt content	FileN.txt	FileN.txt content

Protocol buffers and thrift

Protocol buffers were developed by Google and open sourced in 2008. Thrift was developed at Facebook and offers more features and language support than protocol buffers. Both of these are serialization frameworks that offer high performance while sending over the network. Avro is a specialized serialization format that is designed for Hadoop.

A generic usage pattern for protocol buffers and thrift is as follows:

- Use Avro on Hadoop-specific formats and use protocol buffers and thrift for non-Hadoop projects.

Avro

Avro is a row-based data serialization system used for storage and sends data over the network efficiently. Avro provides the following benefits:

- Rich data structures
- Compact and fast binary data format
- Simple integration with any language
- Support for evolving schemas
- Great interoperability between Hive, Tez, Impala, Pig, and Spark

A use case for Avro is as follows:

- **Data warehouse offloading to Hadoop**: Data is offloaded to Hadoop where **Extract, Transform, and Load (ETL)** tasks are performed. The schema changes frequently.
- **Solution**: Sqoop imports data as Avro files that supports schema evolution, less storage space, and faster ETL tasks.

Parquet

Parquet is a columnar format that skips I/O and decompression (if applicable) on columns that are not part of the query. It is generally very efficient in terms of compression on columns because column data is similar within the same column than it is in a block of rows.

A use case for Parquet is as follows:

- **BI access on Hadoop**: Data marts created on Hadoop are accessed by users using **Business Intelligence** (**BI**) tools such as Tableau. User queries always need a few columns only. Query performance is poor.

- **Solution**: Store data in Parquet, which is a columnar format and provides high performance for BI queries.

RCFile and ORCFile

Record Columnar File (**RCFile**) was the first columnar format for Hive that provided efficient query processing. **Optimized Row Columnar** (**ORC**) format was introduced in Hive 0.11 and offered better compressions and efficiency than the RCFile format. ORCFile has lightweight indexing that enables the skipping of irrelevant columns.

A use case for ORC and Parquet files is as follows:

- Both ORC files and Parquet files are columnar formats and skip columns and rows (predicate pushdown) while reading data. Choose ORC or Parquet, depending on the application and integration requirements with other components of the project. A common use case for ORC will be same as the Parquet use case described earlier, exposing data to end users with BI tools.

Compression formats

A variety of compression formats are available for Hadoop storage. However, if Hadoop storage is cheap, then why do I need to compress my data? The following list answers your question:

- Compressed data can speed up I/O operations
- Compressed data saves storage space
- Compressed data speeds up data transfer over the network

Compression and decompression increases CPU time. Understanding these trade-offs is very important in providing optimum performance of jobs running on Hadoop.

Standard compression formats

The following table shows you the standard compression formats available on the Hadoop platform:

Compression format	Tool	Algorithm	File extension	Splittable?
gzip	Gzip	DEFLATE	`.gz`	No
bzip2	bizp2	bzip2	`.bz2`	Yes
LZO	Lzop	LZO	`.lzo`	Yes, if indexed
Snappy	N/A	Snappy	`.snappy`	No

Recommended usage patterns for compression are as follows:

- **For storage only**: Use gzip (high compression ratio)
- **For ETL tasks**: Use Snappy (optimum compression ratio and speed)

 In general, always compress data on Hadoop for better performance. Choosing the right compression codec depends on the trade-off between the compression ratio versus speed.

Introducing Apache Spark

Hadoop and **MR** have been around for 10 years and have proven to be the best solution to process massive data with high performance. However, MR lacked performance in iterative computing where the output between multiple MR jobs had to be written to HDFS. In a single MR job, it lacked performance because of the drawbacks of the MR framework.

Let's take a look at the history of computing trends to understand how computing paradigms have changed over the last two decades.

The trend has been to **Reference** the URI when the network was cheaper (in 1990), **Replicate** when storage became cheaper (in 2000), and **Recompute** when memory became cheaper (in 2010), as shown in *Figure 2.5*:

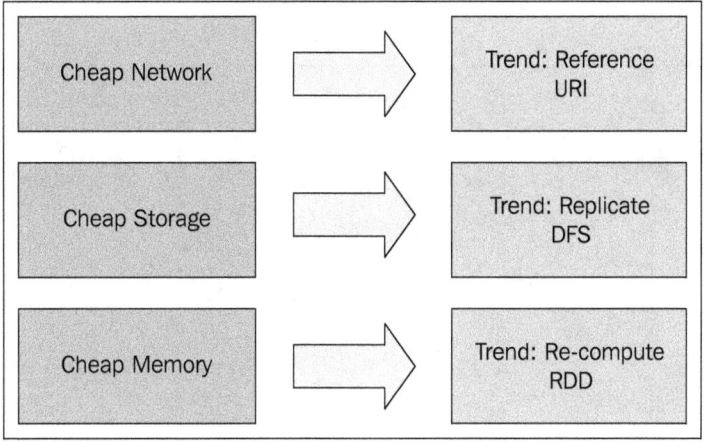

Figure 2.5: Trends of computing

 So, what really changed over a period of time?

Tape is dead, disk has become tape, and SSD has almost become the disk. Now, caching data in RAM is the current trend.

Let's understand why memory-based computing is important and how it provides significant performance benefits.

Figure 2.6 indicates the data transfer rates from various mediums to the CPU. Disk to CPU is **100 MB/s**, SSD to CPU is **600 MB/s**, and over the network to CPU is **1 MB to 1 GB/s**. However, RAM to CPU transfer speed is astonishingly fast, which is **10 GB/s**. So, the idea is to cache all or partial data in-memory so that higher performance can be achieved:

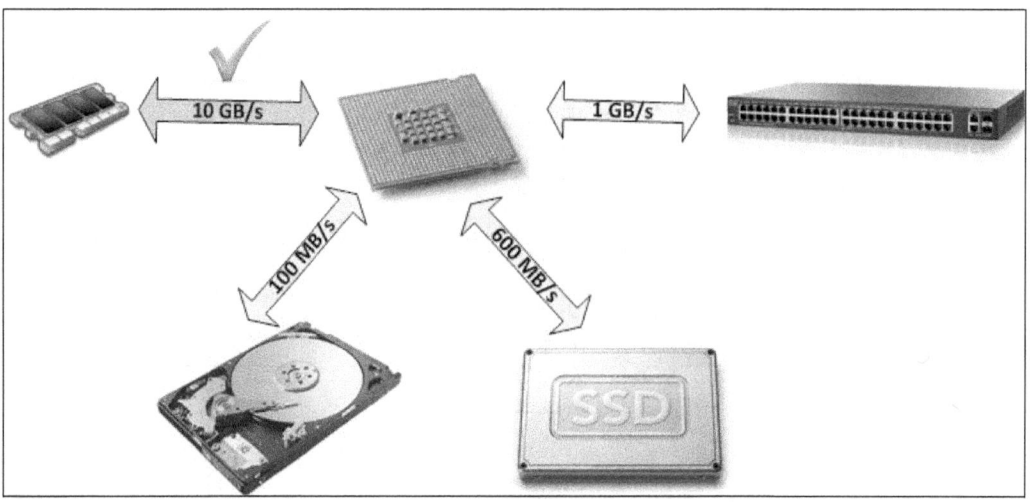

Figure 2.6: Why memory?

Spark history

Spark started in 2009 as a research project in the UC Berkeley RAD Lab, which later became the AMPLab. The researchers in the lab had previously been working on Hadoop MapReduce and observed that MR was inefficient for iterative and interactive computing jobs. Thus, from the beginning, Spark was designed to be fast for interactive queries and iterative algorithms, bringing in ideas such as support for in-memory storage and efficient fault recovery.

In 2011, the AMPLab started to develop higher-level components on Spark such as Shark and Spark Streaming. These components are sometimes referred to as the **Berkeley Data Analytics Stack (BDAS)**.

Spark was first open sourced in March 2010 and transferred to the Apache Software Foundation in June 2013.

In February 2014, it became a top-level project at the Apache Software Foundation. Spark has since become one of the largest open source communities in Big Data. Now, over 250 contributors in over 50 organizations are contributing to Spark development. The user base has increased tremendously from small companies to Fortune 500 companies. *Figure 2.7* shows you the history of Apache Spark:

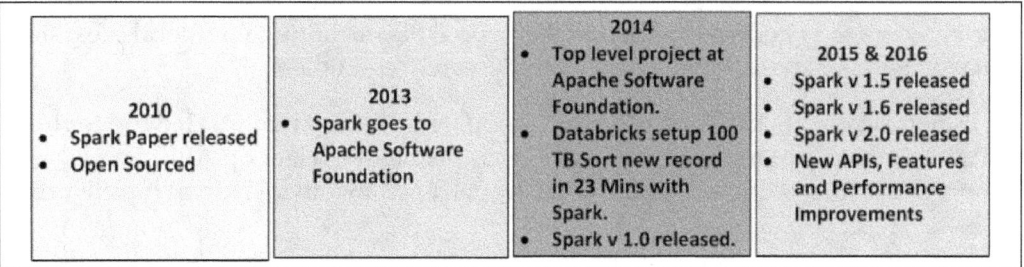

Figure 2.7: The history of Apache Spark

What is Apache Spark?

Let's understand what Apache Spark is and what makes it a force to reckon with in Big Data analytics:

- Apache Spark is a fast enterprise-grade large-scale data processing engine, which is interoperable with Apache Hadoop.

- It is written in Scala, which is both an object-oriented and functional programming language that runs in a JVM.

- Spark enables applications to distribute data reliably in-memory during processing. This is the key to Spark's performance as it allows applications to avoid expensive disk access and performs computations at memory speeds.

- It is suitable for iterative algorithms by having every iteration access data through memory.

- Spark programs perform 100 times faster than MR in-memory or 10 times faster on disk (http://spark.apache.org/).

- It provides native support for Java, Scala, Python, and R languages with interactive shells for Scala, Python, and R. Applications can be developed easily, and often 2 to 10 times less code is needed.

- Spark powers a stack of libraries, including Spark SQL and DataFrames for interactive analytics, MLlib for machine learning, GraphX for graph processing, and Spark Streaming for real-time analytics. You can combine these features seamlessly in the same application.

- Spark runs on Hadoop, Mesos, standalone cluster managers, on-premise hardware, or in the cloud.

What Apache Spark is not

Hadoop provides HDFS for storage and MR for compute. However, Spark does not provide any specific storage medium. Spark is mainly a compute engine, but you can store data in-memory or on Tachyon to process it.

Spark has the ability to create distributed datasets from any file stored in the HDFS or other storage systems supported by Hadoop APIs (including your local filesystem, Amazon S3, Cassandra, Hive, HBase, Elasticsearch, and others).

It's important to note that Spark is not Hadoop and does not require Hadoop to run it. It simply has support for storage systems implementing Hadoop APIs. Spark supports text files, sequence files, Avro, Parquet, and any other Hadoop InputFormat.

Does Spark replace Hadoop?

Spark is designed to interoperate with Hadoop. It's not a replacement for Hadoop, but it's a replacement for the MR framework on Hadoop. All Hadoop processing frameworks (Sqoop, Hive, Pig, Mahout, Cascading, and Crunch) using MR as an engine now use Spark as an additional processing engine.

MapReduce issues

MR developers faced challenges with respect to performance and converting every business problem to an MR problem. Let's understand the issues related to MR and how they are addressed in Apache Spark:

- MR creates separate JVMs for every Mapper and Reducer. Launching JVMs takes a considerable amount of time.

- MR code requires a significant amount of boilerplate coding. The programmer needs to think and design every business problem in terms of Map and Reduce, which makes it a very difficult program. One MR job can rarely do a full computation. You need multiple MR jobs to finish the complete task, and need to design and keep track of optimizations at all levels. Hive and Pig solve this problem. However, they are not suitable for all use cases.

- An MR job writes the data to disk between each job and hence is not suitable for iterative processing.

- A higher level of abstraction, such as Cascading and Scalding, provides better programming of MR jobs. However, it does not provide any additional performance benefits.

- MR does not provide great APIs either.

MR is slow because every job in an MR job flow stores the data on disk. Multiple queries on the same dataset will read data separately and create high disk I/O, as shown in *Figure 2.8*:

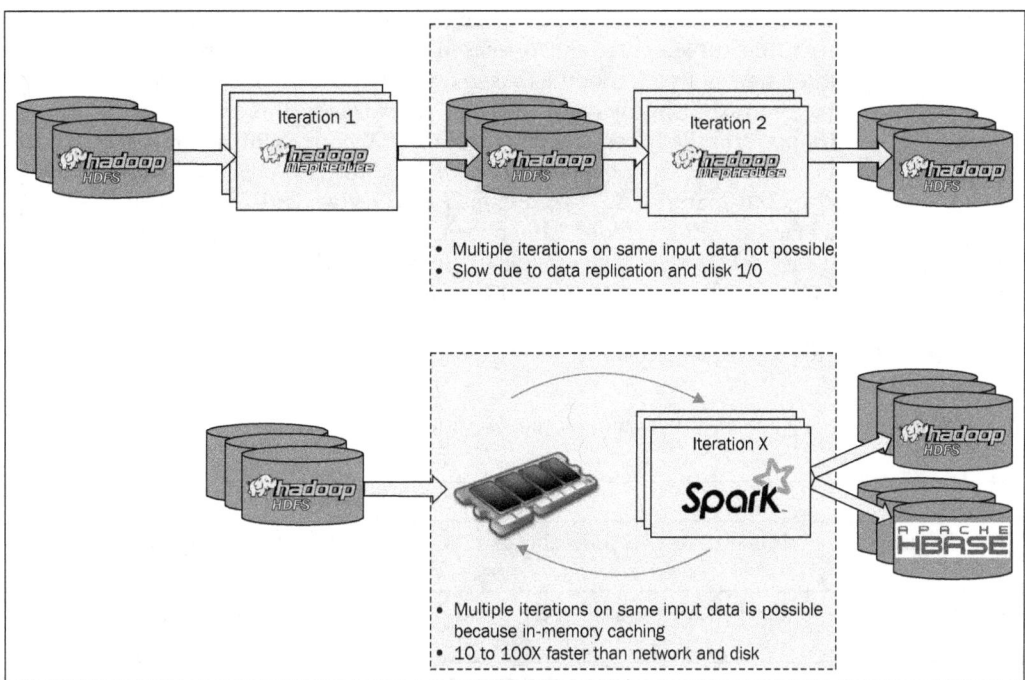

Figure 2.8: MapReduce versus Apache Spark

Spark takes the concept of MR to the next level to store intermediate data in-memory and reuses it, as needed, multiple times. This provides high performance at memory speeds, as shown in *Figure 2.8*.

If I have only one MR job, does it perform the same as Spark?

No, the performance of the Spark job is superior to the MR job because of in-memory computations and its shuffle improvements. The performance of Spark is superior to MR even when the memory cache is disabled. A new shuffle implementation (sort-based shuffle instead of hash-based shuffle), new network module (based on netty instead of using block manager to send shuffle data), and new external shuffle service make Spark perform the fastest petabyte sort (on 190 nodes with 46 TB RAM) and terabyte sort. Spark sorted 100 TB of data using 206 EC2 i2.8xlarge machines in 23 minutes. The previous world record was 72 minutes, set by a Hadoop MR cluster of 2,100 nodes. This means that Spark sorted the same data 3 times faster using 10 times fewer machines. All the sorting took place on disk (HDFS) without using Spark's in-memory cache (`https://databricks.com/blog/2014/10/10/spark-petabyte-sort.html`).

To summarize, here are the differences between MR and Spark:

	MR	Spark
Ease of use	It is not easy to code and use	Spark provides a good API, which is easy to code and use
Performance	Performance is relatively poor when compared with Spark	In-memory performance
Iterative processing	Every MR job writes the data to disk and the next iteration reads from the disk	Spark caches the data in-memory
Fault tolerance	It's achieved by replicating the data in HDFS	Spark achieves fault tolerance by **Resilient Distributed Dataset (RDD)** Lineage, which is explained in *Chapter 3, Deep Dive into Apache Spark*
Runtime architecture	Every Mapper and Reducer runs in a separate JVM	Tasks are run in a preallocated executor JVM, which is explained in *Chapter 3, Deep Dive into Apache Spark*
Shuffle	Stores data on disk	It stores data in-memory and on disk
Operations	Map and Reduce	Map, Reduce, Join, Cogroup, and many more
Execution model	Batch only	Batch, Interactive, and Streaming

	MR	Spark
Natively supported programming languages	Java only	Java, Scala, Python, and R

Spark's stack

Spark's stack components are Spark Core, Spark SQL, Datasets and DataFrames, Spark Streaming, Structured Streaming, MLlib, GraphX, and SparkR as shown in *Figure 2.9*:

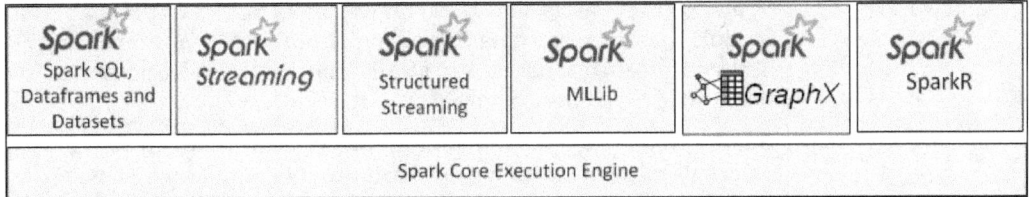

Figure 2.9: The Apache Spark ecosystem

Here is a comparison of Spark components with Hadoop Ecosystem components:

Spark	Hadoop Ecosystem
Spark Core	MapReduce
	Apache Tez
Spark SQL, Datasets and DataFrames	Apache Hive
	Apache Impala
	Apache Tez
	Apache Drill
Spark Streaming Structured Streaming	Apache Storm
	Apache Storm Trident
	Apache Flink
	Apache Apex
	Apache Samza
Spark MLlib	Apache Mahout
Spark GraphX	Apache Giraph
SparkR	RMR2
	RHive

To understand the Spark framework at a higher level, let's take a look at these core components of Spark and their integrations:

Feature	Details
Programming languages	Java, Scala, Python, and R. Scala, Python, and R shell for quick development.
Core execution engine	**Spark Core**: Spark Core is the underlying general execution engine for the Spark platform that all other functionality is built on top of. It provides Java, Scala, Python, and R APIs for the ease of development. **Tungsten**: It provides Memory Management and Binary Processing, Cache-aware Computation, and Code generation.
Frameworks	**Spark SQL, Datasets, and DataFrames**: Spark SQL is a Spark module for structured data processing. It provides a programming abstraction called Datasets and DataFrames and can also act as a distributed SQL query engine. **Spark Streaming**: Spark Streaming enables us to build scalable and fault-tolerant streaming applications. It integrates with a wide variety of data sources, including File Systems, HDFS, Flume, Kafka, and Twitter. **Structured Streaming**: Structured Streaming is a new paradigm shift in streaming computing that enables building *continuous applications* with end-to-end exactly once guarantee and data consistency, even in case of node delays and failures. **MLlib**: MLlib is a machine learning library used to create data products or extract deep meaning from the data. MLlib provides high performance because of in-memory caching of data. **GraphX**: GraphX is a graph computation engine with graph algorithms to build graph applications. **SparkR**: SparkR overcomes the R's single-threaded process issues and memory limitations with Spark's distributed in-memory processing engine. SparkR provides a distributed DataFrame based on DataFrame API and Distributed Machine Learning using MLlib.
Off-heap storage	**Tachyon**: Reliable data sharing at memory-speed within and across cluster frameworks/jobs. Spark's default `OFF_HEAP` (experimental) storage is Tachyon.

Feature	Details
Cluster resource managers	**Standalone**: By default, applications are submitted to the standalone mode cluster and each application will try to use all the available nodes and resources.
	YARN: YARN controls the resource allocation and provides dynamic resource allocation capabilities.
	Mesos: Mesos has two modes—coarse-grained and fine-grained. The coarse-grained approach has a static number of resources just like the standalone resource manager. The fine-grained approach has dynamic resource allocation just like YARN.
Storage	HDFS, S3, and other filesystems with the support of Hadoop InputFormat.
Database integrations	HBase, Cassandra, Mongo DB, Neo4J, and RDBMS databases.
Integrations with streaming sources	Flume, Kafka and Kinesis, Twitter, Zero MQ, and File Streams.
Packages	`http://spark-packages.org/` provides a list of third-party data source APIs and packages.
Distributions	Distributions from Cloudera, Hortonworks, MapR, and DataStax.
Notebooks	Jupyter and Apache Zeppelin.
Dataflows	Apache NiFi, Apache Beam, and StreamSets.

The Spark ecosystem is a unified stack that provides you with the power of combining SQL, streaming, and machine learning in one program. The advantages of unification are as follows:

- No need of copying or ETL of data between systems
- Combines processing types in one program
- Code reuse
- One system to learn
- One system to maintain

An example of unification is shown in *Figure 2.10*:

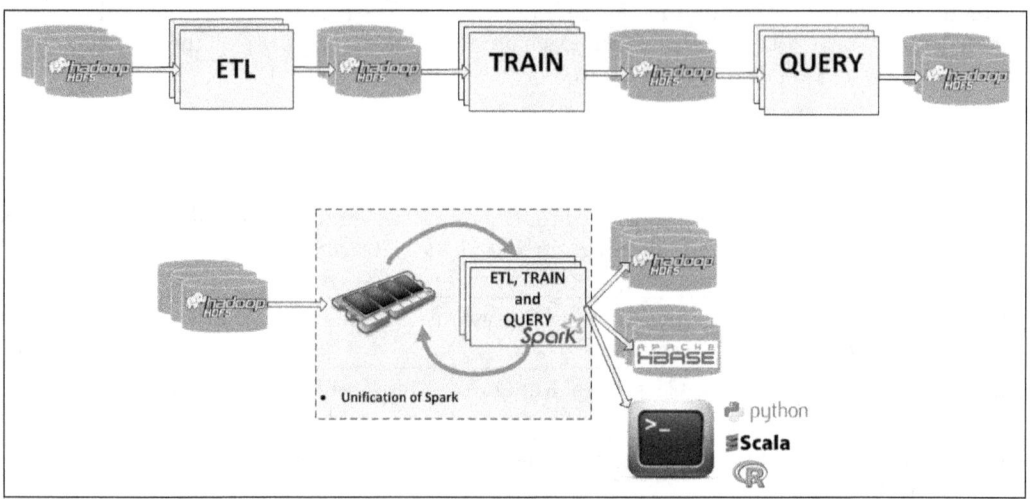

Figure 2.10: The unification of the Apache Spark ecosystem

Why Hadoop plus Spark?

Apache Spark shines better when it is combined with Hadoop. To understand this, let's take a look at Hadoop and Spark features.

Hadoop features

Feature	Details
Unlimited scalability	Stores unlimited data by scaling out HDFS
	Effectively manages cluster resources with YARN
	Runs multiple applications along with Spark
	Thousands of simultaneous users
Enterprise grade	Provides security with Kerberos authentication and ACLs authorization
	Data encryption
	High reliability and integrity
	Multi-tenancy

Feature	Details
Wide range of applications	**Files**: Structured, semi-structured, and unstructured
	Streaming sources: Flume and Kafka
	Databases: Any RDBMS and NoSQL database

Spark features

Feature	Details
Easy development	No boilerplate coding
	Multiple native APIs such as Java, Scala, Python, and R
	REPL for Scala, Python, and R
Optimized performance	Caching
	Optimized shuffle
	Catalyst Optimizer
Unification	Batch, SQL, machine learning, streaming, and graph processing
High level APIs	DataFrames, Data sets and Data Sources APIs

When both frameworks are combined, we get the power of enterprise-grade applications with in-memory performance, as shown in *Figure 2.11*:

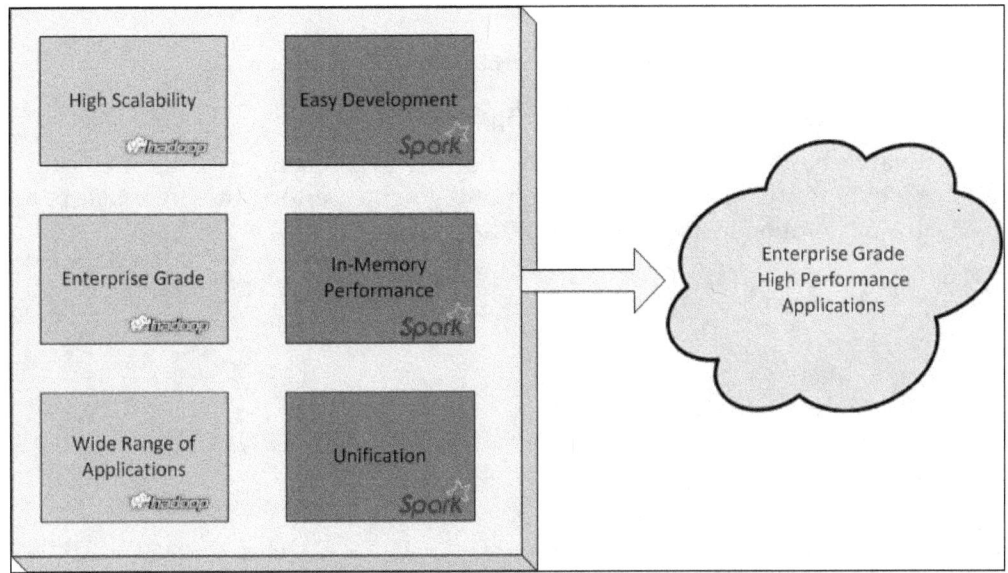

Figure 2.11: Spark applications on the Hadoop platform

Frequently asked questions about Spark

The following are frequent questions that practitioners raise about Spark:

- My dataset does not fit in-memory. How can I use Spark?

  Spark's operators spill the data to disk if it does not fit in-memory, allowing it to run on data of any size. Likewise, cached datasets that do not fit in-memory are either spilled to disk or recomputed on the fly when needed, as determined by the RDD's storage level. By default, Spark will recompute the partitions that don't fit in-memory. The storage level can be changed as MEMORY_AND_DISK to spill partitions to disk.

  Figure 2.12 shows you the performance difference between fully cached and on disk:

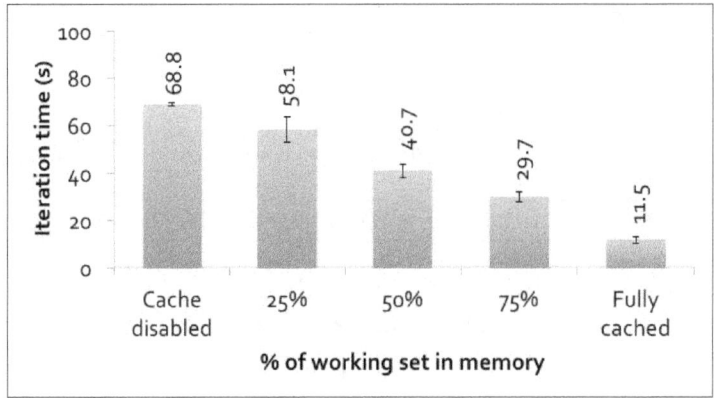

Figure 2.12: Spark performance: Fully cached versus disk

- How does fault recovery work in Spark?

  Spark's built-in fault tolerance based on the RDD lineage will automatically recover from failures. *Figure 2.13* shows you the performance over failure in the 6th iteration in a k-means algorithm:

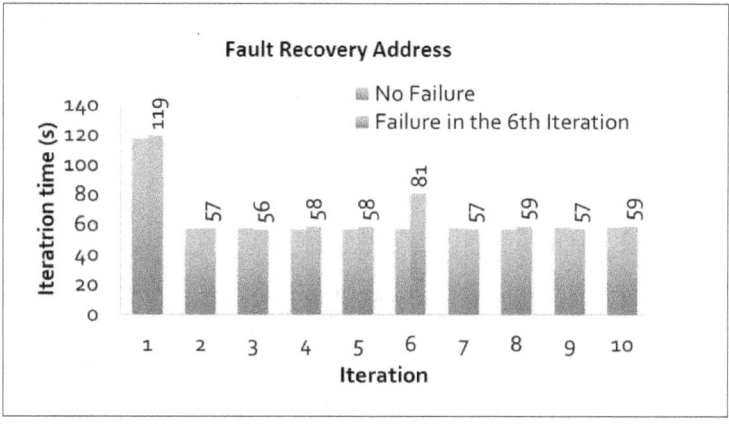

Figure 2.13: Fault recovery performance

Installing Hadoop plus Spark clusters

Before installing Hadoop and Spark, let's understand the versions of Hadoop and Spark. Spark is offered as a service in all three popular Hadoop distributions from Cloudera, Hortonworks, and MapR. The current Hadoop and Spark versions are 2.7.2 and 2.0 respectively as of writing this book. However, Hadoop distributions might have a lower version of Spark as Hadoop and Spark release cycles do not coincide.

For the upcoming chapters' practical exercises, let's use one of the free **virtual machines** (**VM**) from Cloudera, Hortonworks, and MapR, or use an open source version of Apache Spark. These VMs makes it easy to get started with Spark and Hadoop. The same exercises can be run on bigger clusters as well.

The prerequisites to use virtual machines on your laptop are as follows:

- RAM of 8 GB and above
- At least two virtual CPUs
- The latest VMWare Player or Oracle VirtualBox must be installed for Windows or Linux OS
- The latest Oracle VirtualBox or VMWare Fusion for Mac
- Virtualization is enabled in BIOS
- Chrome 25+, IE 9+, Safari 6+, or Firefox 18+ is recommended (HDP Sandbox will not run on IE 10)
- Putty
- WinSCP

The instructions to download and run **Cloudera Distribution for Hadoop** (CDH) are as follows:

1. Download the latest quickstart CDH VM from `http://www.cloudera.com/content/www/en-us/downloads.html`. Download the appropriate version based on the virtualization software (VirtualBox or VMWare) installed on the laptop.

2. Extract it to a directory (use 7-Zip or WinZip).

3. In case of VMWare Player, click on **Open a Virtual Machine**, and point to the directory where you have extracted the VM. Select the `cloudera-quickstart-vm-5.x.x-x-vmware.vmx` file and click on **Open**.

4. Click on **Edit virtual machine settings** and then increase memory to 7 GB (if your laptop has 8 GB RAM) or 8 GB (if your laptop has more than 8 GB RAM). Increase the number of processors to four. Click on **OK**.

5. Click on **Play virtual machine**.

6. Select **I copied it** and click on **OK**.

7. This should get your VM up and running.

8. Cloudera Manager is installed on the VM but is turned off by default. If you would like to use Cloudera Manager, double-click and run **Launch Cloudera Manager Express** to set up Cloudera Manager. This will be helpful in the starting / stopping / restarting of services on the cluster.

9. Credentials for the VM are username (`cloudera`) and password (`cloudera`).

If you would like to use the Cloudera Quickstart Docker image, follow the instructions on `http://blog.cloudera.com/blog/2015/12/docker-is-the-new-quickstart-option-for-apache-hadoop-and-cloudera`.

The instructions to download and run **Hortonworks Data Platform** (HDP) Sandbox are as follows:

1. Download the latest HDP Sandbox from `http://hortonworks.com/products/hortonworks-sandbox/#install`. Download the appropriate version based on the virtualization software (VirtualBox or VMWare) installed on the laptop.

2. Follow the instructions from install guides on the same downloads page.

3. Open the browser and enter the address as shown in sandbox, for example, `http://192.168.139.158/`. Click on **View Advanced Options** to see all the links.

4. Access the sandbox with `putty` as the root user and `hadoop` as the initial password. You need to change the password on the first login. Also, run the `ambari-admin-password-reset` command to reset Ambari admin password.

5. To start using Ambari, open the browser and enter `ipaddressofsandbox:8080` with admin credentials created in the preceding step. Start the services needed in Ambari.

6. To map the hostname to the IP address in Windows, go to `C:\Windows\System32\drivers\etc\hosts` and enter the IP address and hostname with a space separator. You need admin rights to do this.

The instructions to download and run MapR Sandbox are as follows:

1. Download the latest sandbox from `https://www.mapr.com/products/mapr-sandbox-hadoop/download`. Download the appropriate version based on the virtualization software (VirtualBox or VMWare) installed on the laptop.

2. Follow the instructions to set up Sandbox at `http://doc.mapr.com/display/MapR/MapR+Sandbox+for+Hadoop`.

3. Use Putty to log in to the sandbox.

4. The root password is `mapr`.

5. To launch HUE or **MapR Control System (MCS)**, navigate to the URL provided by MapR Sandbox.

6. To map the hostname to the IP address in Windows, go to `C:\Windows\System32\drivers\etc\hosts` and enter the IP address and hostname with a space separator.

The instructions to download and run Apache Spark prebuilt binaries, in case you have a preinstalled Hadoop cluster, are given here. The following instructions can also be used to install the latest version of Spark and use it on the preceding VMs:

1. Download Spark prebuilt for Hadoop from the following location:

```
wget  http://apache.mirrors.tds.net/spark/spark-2.0.0/
    spark-2.0.0-bin-hadoop2.7.tgz

tar xzvf spark-2.0.0-bin-hadoop2.7.tgz

cd spark-2.0.0-bin-hadoop2.7
```

2. Add `SPARK_HOME` and `PATH` variables to the profile script as shown in the following commands so that these environment variables will be set every time you log in:

    ```
    [cloudera@quickstart ~]$ cat /etc/profile.d/spark2.sh

    export SPARK_HOME=/home/cloudera/spark-2.0.0-bin-hadoop2.7

    export PATH=$PATH:/home/cloudera/spark-2.0.0-bin-hadoop2.7/bin
    ```

3. Let Spark know about the Hadoop configuration directory and Java home by adding the following environment variables to `spark-env.sh`. Copy the template files in the `conf` directory:

    ```
    cp conf/spark-env.sh.template conf/spark-env.sh

    cp conf/spark-defaults.conf.template conf/spark-defaults.conf

    vi conf/spark-env.sh

    export HADOOP_CONF_DIR=/etc/hadoop/conf

    export JAVA_HOME=/usr/java/jdk1.7.0_67-cloudera
    ```

4. Copy `hive-site.xml` to the `conf` directory of Spark.

    ```
    cp /etc/hive/conf/hive-site.xml conf/
    ```

5. Change the log level to `ERROR` in the `spark-2.0.0-bin-hadoop2.7/conf/log4j.properties` file after copying the template file.

Programming languages version requirements to run Spark:

Java: 7+

Python: 2.6+/3.1+

R: 3.1+

Scala: Spark 1.6 and below 2.10, and Spark 2.0 and above 2.11

Note that the preceding virtual machines are single node clusters. If you are planning to set up multi-node clusters, follow the guidelines as per the distribution, such as CDH, HDP, or MapR. If you are planning to use a standalone cluster manager, the setup is described in the following chapter.

Summary

Apache Hadoop provides you with a reliable and scalable framework (HDFS) for Big Data storage and a powerful cluster resource management framework (YARN) to run and manage multiple Big Data applications. Apache Spark provides in-memory performance in Big Data processing and libraries and APIs for interactive exploratory analytics, real-time analytics, machine learning, and graph analytics. While MR was the primary processing engine on top of Hadoop, it had multiple drawbacks, such as poor performance and inflexibility in designing applications. Apache Spark is a replacement for MR. All MR-based tools, such as Hive, Pig, Mahout, and Crunch, have already started offering Apache Spark as an additional execution engine apart from MR.

Nowadays, Big Data projects are being implemented in many businesses, from large Fortune 500 companies to small start-ups. Organizations gain an edge if they can go from raw data to decisions quickly with easy-to-use tools to develop applications and explore data. Apache Spark will bring this speed and sophistication to Hadoop clusters.

In the next chapter, let's dive deep into Spark and learn Spark.

3
Deep Dive into Apache Spark

Apache Spark is growing at a fast pace in terms of technology, community, and user base. Two new APIs were introduced in 2015: the DataFrame API and DataSet API. These two APIs are built on top of the core API, which is based on RDDs. It is essential to understand the deeper concepts of RDDs including runtime architecture and behavior on various resource managers of Spark.

This chapter is divided into the following sub topics:

- Starting Spark daemons
- Spark core concepts
- Pairing RDDs
- The lifecycle of a Spark program
- Spark applications
- Persistence and caching
- Spark resource managers—Standalone, Yarn, and Mesos

Starting Spark daemons

If you are planning to use a standalone cluster manager, you need to start the Spark master and worker daemons which are the core components in Spark's architecture. Starting/stopping daemons varies slightly from distribution to distribution. Hadoop distributions such as Cloudera, Hortonworks, and MapR provide Spark as a service with YARN as the default resource manager. This means that all Spark applications will run on the YARN framework by default. But, we need to start spark master and worker roles to use Spark's standalone resource manager. If you are planning to use the YARN resource manager, you don't need to start these daemons. Please follow the following procedure depending on the type of distribution you are using. Downloading and installation instructions can be found in *Chapter 2, Getting Started with Apache Hadoop and Apache Spark*, for all these distributions.

Working with CDH

Cloudera Distribution for Hadoop (CDH) is an open source distribution including Hadoop, Spark, and many other projects needed for Big Data Analytics. Cloudera Manager is used for installing and managing the CDH platform. If you are planning to use the YARN resource manager, start the Spark service in Cloudera Manager. To start Spark daemons for Spark's standalone resource manager, use the following procedure:

1. Spark on the CDH platform is configured to work with YARN. Moreover, spark 2.0 is not available on CDH yet. So, download the latest pre-built spark 2.0 package for Hadoop as explained in *Chapter 2, Getting Started with Apache Hadoop and Apache Spark*. If you would like to use Spark 1.6 version, run the `/usr/lib/spark/start-all.sh` command.

2. Start the service with following commands.

   ```
   cd /home/cloudera/spark-2.0.0-bin-hadoop2.7/sbin
   sudo ./start-all.sh
   ```

3. Check the Spark UI at `http://quickstart.cloudera:8080/`.

Working with HDP, MapR, and Spark pre-built packages

Hortonworks Data Platform (HDP) and MapR Converged Data Platform distributions also include Hadoop, Spark, and many other projects needed for Big Data Analytics. While HDP uses Apache Ambari for deploying and managing the cluster, MapR uses the **MapR Control System** (MCS). Spark's pre-built package has no specific manager component for managing Spark. If you are planning to use the YARN resource manager, start the Spark service in Ambari or MCS. To Start Spark daemons for using Spark's standalone resource manager, use the following procedure.

1. Start services with the following commands:
   - HDP: `/usr/hdp/current/spark-client/sbin/start-all.sh`
   - MapR: `/opt/mapr/spark/spark-*/sbin/start-all.sh`
   - Spark Package pre-built for Hadoop: `./sbin/start-all.sh`

   For a multi node cluster, start spark worker roles on all machines with the following command:

   ```
   ./sbin/start-slave.sh spark://masterhostname:7077
   ```

Another option is to provide a list of the hostnames of the workers in the /conf/slaves file and then use the ./start-all.sh command to start worker roles on all machines automatically.

2. Check logs located in the logs directory. Look at the master web UI at http://masterhostname:8080. If this port is already taken by another service, the next available port will be used. For example, in HDP, port 8080 is taken by Ambari, so the standalone master will bind to 8081. To find the correct port number, check the logs.

 All programs in this chapter are executed on CDH 5.8 VM. For other environments, the file paths might change but the concepts are the same in any environment.

Learning Spark core concepts

Let's understand the core concepts of Spark in this section. The main abstraction Spark provides is a **Resilient Distributed Dataset (RDD)**. So, let's understand what an RDD is and operations in RDDs that provide in-memory performance and fault tolerance. But, let's learn the ways to work with Spark first.

Ways to work with Spark

There are a couple of ways to work with Spark—Spark Shell and Spark Applications.

Spark Shell

Interactive **REPL (read-eval-print loop)** for data exploration using Scala, Python, or R:

```
// Entering to Scala Shell . :q to exit the shell.
[cloudera@quickstart spark-2.0.0-bin-hadoop2.7]$ bin/spark-shell


# Entering to Python Shell. ctrl+d to exit the shell.
[cloudera@quickstart spark-2.0.0-bin-hadoop2.7]$ bin/pyspark


// Entering to R Shell. Need to install R first. ctrl+d to exit shell
[cloudera@quickstart spark-2.0.0-bin-hadoop2.7]$ bin/sparkR
```

For a complete list of spark-shell options, use the following command.

```
[cloudera@quickstart spark-2.0.0-bin-hadoop2.7]$ bin/spark-shell help
Usage: ./bin/spark-shell [options]
```

Exploring the Spark Scala shell

The Scala shell provides lots of utilities and tab completion for ease of use. Some of these useful utilities are shown in the following examples.

Executing system commands and checking return code:

```
import sys.process._
val res = "ls /tmp" ! // notice the "!" operator
println("result = "+res) // result can be zero or non-zero
```

Executing system commands and checking output:

```
import sys.process._
val output = "hadoop fs -ls" !! // notice the "!!" operator
println("result = "+output)
```

Pasting spark code lines in the shell:

```
:paste
// Entering paste mode (ctrl-D to finish)
```

To exit from the Scala shell use the :q command.

Entering the Scala shell by passing a set of commands to run:

```
[root@myhost ~]# spark-shell -i spark_commands.txt
```

Enter the Scala shell, execute commands, and exit:

```
[root@myhost ~]# cat spark_commands.txt | spark-shell
```

The Python shell does not provide tab completion but iPython notebook provides tab completion.

Spark applications

While the Spark shell is used for development and testing, Spark applications are used for creating and scheduling large scale data processing applications in production. Applications can be created in natively-supported languages such as Python, Scala, Java, SQL, R, or external programs using the pipe method. Spark-submit is used for submitting a spark application as shown in the following Scala-based application example:

```
[root@myhost ~]# spark-submit \
  --class com.example.loganalytics.MyApp \
  --master yarn \
  --name "Log Analytics Application" \
  --executor-memory 2G \
  --num-executors 50 \
  --conf spark.shuffle.spill=false \
  myApp.jar \
  /data/input \
  /data/output


Spark-submit for Python based application.


[root@myhost ~]# spark-submit --master yarn-client myapp.py
```

Connecting to the Kerberos Security Enabled Spark Cluster

The user can acquire a Kerberos ticket with the kinit command to work with shells or applications. For applications submitting spark jobs, use the klist command to display the principals of the spark keytab as shown in the following:

```
klist -ket /path/to/spark.keytab
```

Use the kinit command with keytab and principal to get a ticket as shown in the following:

```
kinit -kt /path/to/spark.keytab principal_name
```

Once the ticket is acquired, the application should be able to connect to the Spark cluster using a shell or application.

You can also pass the `--keytab` and `--principal` options with spark-submit when using YARN as the resource manager.

Resilient Distributed Dataset

RDDs are a fundamental unit of data in Spark and Spark programming revolves around creating and performing operations on RDDs. They are immutable collections partitioned across clusters that can be rebuilt (re-computed) if a partition is lost. They are created by transforming data in a stable storage using data flow operators (map, filter, group-by) and can be cached in memory across parallel operations:

- **Resilient**: If data in memory is lost, it can be recreated (or recomputed)
- **Distributed**: Distributed across clusters
- **Dataset**: Initial data can come from a file or created programmatically

There are a couple of ways to create an RDD: parallelize, or read from a file:

Method 1 – parallelizing a collection

Take an existing in-memory collection of data and pass it to SparkContext's parallelize method. This is not generally used in production systems but used for prototyping and testing since it requires an entire dataset in memory on one machine.

Examples of creating an RDD using the parallelize method:

```
// Parallelize a list in Java
JavaRDD<String> myRDD = sc.parallelize(Arrays.asList("hdfs", "spark",
"rdd"));

# Parallelize a list in Python
myRDD = sc.parallelize(["hdfs", "spark", "rdd"])

// Parallelize a list in Scala
val myRDD= sc.parallelize(List("hdfs", "spark", "rdd"))
```

Method 2 – reading from a file

The second method is to read data from HDFS, S3, HBase, Avro, a Parquet file, and other Hadoop-supported formats. Input can be a file or a directory. Wildcards are supported as well.

Example of creating a RDD called as `inputRDD` by reading an input file:

```
// Read a file in Java
JavaRDD<String> inputRDD = sc.textFile("/path/to/input");

# Read a file in Python
inputRDD = sc.textFile("/path/to/input")

// Read a file in Scala
val inputRDD = sc.textFile("/path/to/input")
```

Reading files from HDFS

There are a couple of ways for reading files from HDFS.

The first method is to specify the HDFS URI with namenode hostname and RPC port number:

```
// Read a HDFS file in Scala
val inputRDD = sc.textFile("hdfs://namenodehostname:8020/data/input")
```

The second method is to set and specify the `HADOOP_CONF_DIR` environment variable in `spark-env.sh` and specify the path directly:

```
// Read a HDFS file in Scala
val inputRDD = sc.textFile("/data/input")
```

`HADOOP_CONF_DIR` can be set in `/etc/spark/conf/spark-env.sh` or you can add Hadoop configuration files to the spark configuration directory.

`SparkContext.textFile` calls `org.apache.hadoop.mapred.FileInputFormat.getSplits` which in turn uses `org.apache.hadoop.fs.getDefaultUri`. This method reads the `fs.defaultFS` parameter of Hadoop conf (`core-site.xml`).

Reading files from HDFS with HA enabled

When namenode **High Availability (HA)** is enabled, do not use the active namenode hostname in URI, because HA will switch the active namenode to standby namenode in the case of any failures. So, use the value of the property name `fs.defaultFS` from `core-site.xml`. Example: `hdfs://Nameservice1:8020/`.

Spark context

Every Spark application requires a Spark context, which is the main entry point to the Spark RDD API. The Spark shell provides a pre-configured Spark context called "sc" and a pre-configured Spark session called "spark" as shown in the following screenshot (*Figure 3.1*):

```
[cloudera@quickstart spark-2.0.0-bin-hadoop2.7]$ bin/spark-shell
Spark context Web UI available at http://192.168.139.175:4040
Spark context available as 'sc' (master = local[*], app id = local-147052
7900398).
Spark session available as 'spark'
Welcome to
      ____              __
     / __/__  ___ _____/ /__
    _\ \/ _ \/ _ `/ __/  '_/
   /___/ .__/\_,_/_/ /_/\_\   version 2.0.0
      /_/

Using Scala version 2.11.8 (Java HotSpot(TM) 64-Bit Server VM, Java 1.7.0
_67)
Type in expressions to have them evaluated.
Type :help for more information.

scala> ▮
```

Figure 3.1: Spark context "sc" in Spark shell.

In Spark applications, `SparkContext` must be created first as shown in the following Scala code. To create a `SparkContext` object, build a `SparkConf` object that has the information about the application. Only one `SparkContext` is created per application:

```
val conf = new SparkConf().setAppName("App1").setMaster("yarn")
val mysc = new SparkContext(conf)
val an = mysc.appName
println("App Name = "+an)
Output of this application:  App Name = App1
```

Transformations and actions

There are two types of RDD operations—transformations and actions. Transformations define new RDDs based on the current RDD. Actions return values from RDDs.

Let's go through some examples of transformations and actions with visualizations to understand them better.

Figure 3.2 shows how a sample text file is read (using the Python code) to create a base RDD called `fileRDD`, transformed with the 'map' transformation to create `upperRDD`. Finally, `upperRDD` is filtered with the 'filter' transformation and output is generated with the 'collect' action. Transformations do not cause any execution until they see an action. So, Transformations are lazily evaluated and actions kick off the job to execute all transformations. In this example, the actual job execution starts from line number 3 because of the 'collect' action.

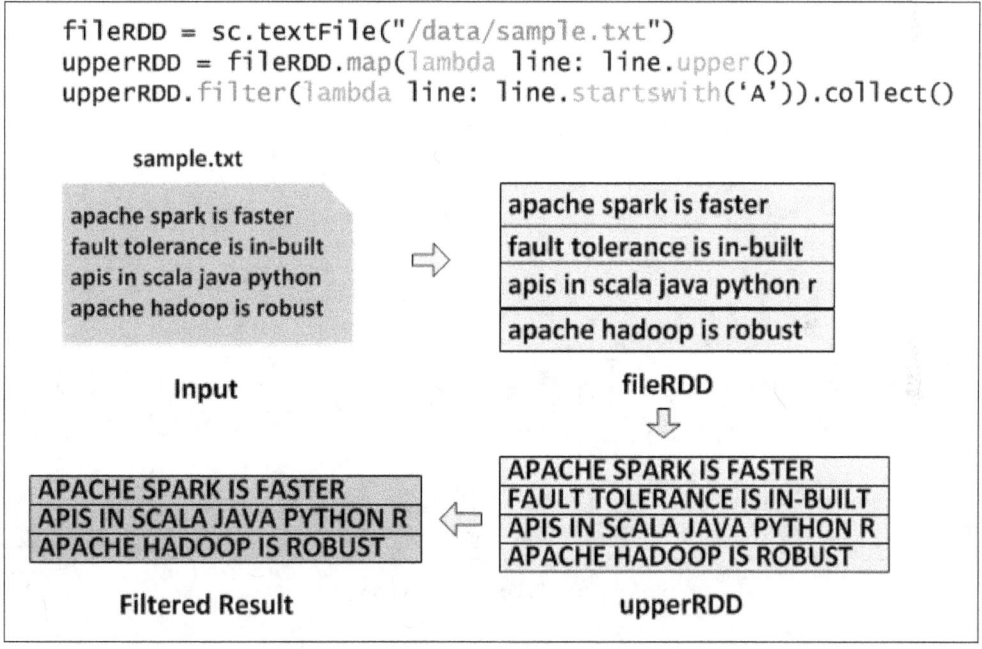

Figure 3.2: Map and Filter Transformation using Python.

In the preceding example, we have seen how the data is transformed and the action produced the result. Let's deep dive to understand what exactly is happening internally with a Log Analytics example using the Python language:

```
access_log = sc.textFile("hdfs://...")
#Filter Lines with ERROR only
error_log = access_log.filter(lambda x: "ERROR" in x)
# Cache error log in memory
cached_log = error_log.cache()
# Now perform an action -  count
print "Total number of error records are %s" % (cached_log.count())
# Now find the number of lines with
print "Number of product pages visited that have Errors is %s" %
(cached_log.filter(lambda x: "product" in x).count())
```

Figure 3.3 explains the log analytics example.

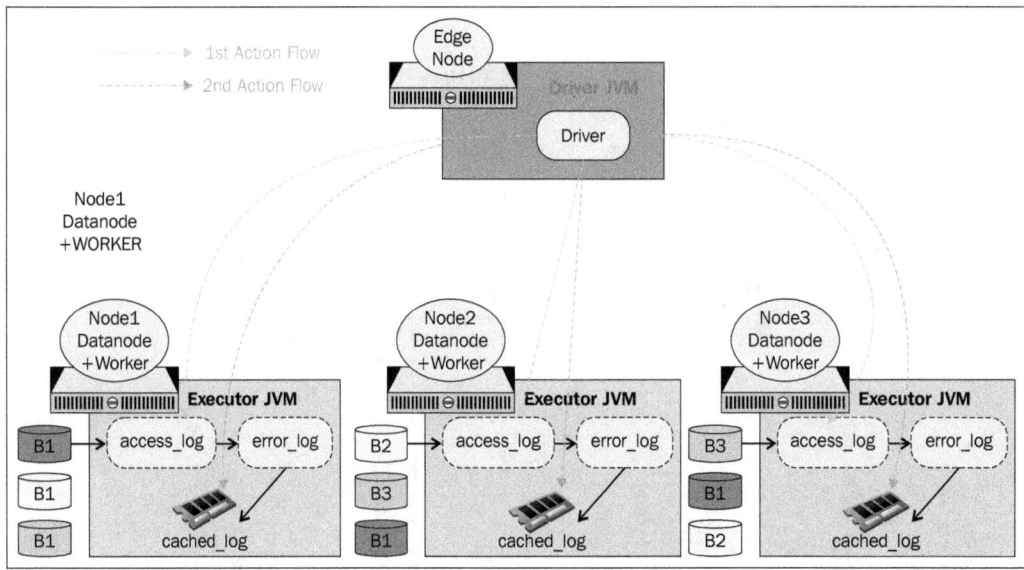

Figure 3.3: Log analytics flow

The log analytics example is reading files from a HDFS directory with three blocks (**B1**, **B2**, and **B3**) and creating a base RDD called `access_log`. The base RDD is then filtered to create `error_log` RDD that contains records with ERROR. `Error_log` RDD is cached in memory with the RDD name `cached_log`. A couple of actions are performed on `cached_log` RDD. As actions cause transformations to be executed, the first action will create `access_log`, `error_log` and `cached_log` and then the result is sent to the client. The second action will not create the `access_log`, `error_log`, and `cached_log`. It will directly read data from `cached_log`. So, the performance of the second action will be much faster than the first action. It is always recommended to cache data if more than one action is to be performed on the same RDD. Caching can be done at any point in the program. For example, caching can be done directly after creating the base RDD `access_log`. But, in this case, you will be storing a huge amount of data in the cache. So, it's always recommended to filter out data that is not needed and then cache it. RDDs that are not cached are garbage collected. So, in the log analytics example, `access_log` and `error_log` RDDs are garbage collected.

> A list of available RDD transformations and actions can be found in the following links:
> - Python: https://spark.apache.org/docs/latest/api/python/pyspark.html#pyspark.RDD
> - Scala: https://spark.apache.org/docs/latest/api/scala/index.html#org.apache.spark.rdd.RDD
> - Java: http://spark.apache.org/docs/latest/api/java/org/apache/spark/api/java/JavaRDD.html

Parallelism in RDDs

Parallelism in RDDs is controlled by a `spark.default.parallelism` parameter. This defaults to the total number of cores on executors or 2, whichever is larger. Let's understand this by looking at the following example.

Enter the python shell using the `pyspark` command and then check the default parallelism as shown in the following. Assuming that that the default number of cores available on your cluster is eight:

```
[cloudera@quickstart spark-2.0.0-bin-hadoop2.7]$ bin/pyspark --master spark://quickstart.cloudera:7077

>>> sc.defaultParallelism
8
```

But, if you enter the spark shell using the following command, the default parallelism will be the same as the number of cores allocated:

```
[cloudera@quickstart spark-2.0.0-bin-hadoop2.7]$ bin/pyspark --master
spark://quickstart.cloudera:7077 --total-executor-cores 4
```

```
For local mode:
```

```
[cloudera@quickstart spark-2.0.0-bin-hadoop2.7]$ bin/pyspark --master
local[4]
```

```
>>> sc.defaultParallelism
4
```

Let's create a list, parallelize it, and check the number of partitions:

```
>>> myList = ["big", "data", "analytics", "hadoop" , "spark"]
>>> myRDD = sc.parallelize(myList)
>>> myRDD.getNumPartitions()
```

This defaults to the same value as `sc.defaultParallelism`

To override the default parallelism, provide the specific number of partitions needed while creating the RDD. In this case, let's create the RDD with six partitions:

```
>>> myRDDWithMorePartitions = sc.parallelize(myList,6)
>>> myRDDWithMorePartitions.getNumPartitions()
6
```

Let's issue an action to count the number of elements in the list:

```
>>> myRDD.count()
5
```

The `getNumPartitions()` method shows that myRDD has four partitions in it. So, any action on this RDD would need four tasks. This means that in order to compute a .count() action, the Driver JVM shipped out the 'counting code' to four tasks (threads) running on different machines. Each task/thread reads and counts the data from only one partition and sends the results back to the Driver JVM. The driver then aggregates all four counts into a final answer. This can be visualized by looking at Spark's UI:

Spark's UI address: `http://masterhostname:8080`

Click on the application ID under **Running Applications** and then **Application Detail UI** which will take you to the UI `http://masterhostname:4040/jobs/`. You can see that four tasks are created for this action as shown in *Figure 3.4*. We can see the other details by clicking on the **Environment** and **Executors** tabs. The **Storage** tab will show the cached RDDs with the percentage cached and size of the data cached.

Figure 3.4: UI showing four tasks for four partitions.

If you click on the completed job, you can see the task duration, executor ID, hostname, and other details as shown in *Figure 3.5*.

Summary Metrics for 4 Completed Tasks

Metric	Min	25th percentile	Median	75th percentile	Max
Duration	0.4 s	0.4 s	0.4 s	0.4 s	0.4 s
GC Time	0.3 s	0.3 s	0.3 s	0.3 s	0.3 s

Aggregated Metrics by Executor

Executor ID ▲	Address	Task Time	Total Tasks	Failed Tasks	Succeeded Tasks
0	192.168.139.175:43785	5 s	4	0	4

Tasks

Index ▲	ID	Attempt	Status	Locality Level	Executor ID / Host	Launch Time	Duration	GC Time	Errors
0	0	0	SUCCESS	PROCESS_LOCAL	0 / 192.168.139.175	2016/08/06 18:06:19	0.4 s	0.3 s	
1	1	0	SUCCESS	PROCESS_LOCAL	0 / 192.168.139.175	2016/08/06 18:06:19	0.4 s	0.3 s	
2	2	0	SUCCESS	PROCESS_LOCAL	0 / 192.168.139.175	2016/08/06 18:06:19	0.4 s	0.3 s	
3	3	0	SUCCESS	PROCESS_LOCAL	0 / 192.168.139.175	2016/08/06 18:06:19	0.4 s	0.3 s	

Figure 3.5: UI showing task duration.

Now, the `mapPartitionsWithIndex()` transformation uses a lambda function that takes in a partition index (like the partition number) and an iterator (to the items in that specific partition). For every partition index + iterator pair that goes in, the lambda function returns a tuple of the same partition index number and also a list of the actual items in that partition:

```
>>> myRDD.mapPartitionsWithIndex(lambda index,iterator: ((index,
list(iterator)),)).collect()
```

```
[(0, ['big']), (1, ['data']), (2, ['analytics']), (3, ['hadoop',
'spark'])]
```

The preceding result explains how the list is distributed across the partitions of the RDD. Let's increase the number of partitions now and see how data is re-distributed to partitions of the new RDD.

```
>>> mySixPartitionsRDD = myRDD.repartition(6)
```

```
>>> mySixPartitionsRDD.mapPartitionsWithIndex(lambda index,iterator:
((index, list(iterator)),)).collect()
```

```
[(0, []), (1, ['big']), (2, []), (3, ['hadoop']), (4, ['data', 'spark']),
(5, ['analytics'])]
```

Now, it's interesting to see that Partition 0 and 2 are empty and other partitions have data. Any action performed on this RDD will have six tasks and task number 0 and task 2 have no data to work on. So, this will lead to scheduling overhead for tasks 0 and 2.

Now, Let's try to decrease the number of partitions using the `coalesce()` function:

```
>>> myTwoPartitionsRDD = mySixPartitionsRDD.coalesce(2)
```

```
>>> myTwoPartitionsRDD.mapPartitionsWithIndex(lambda index,iterator:
((index, list(iterator)),)).collect()
```

```
[(0, ['big']), (1, ['hadoop', 'data', 'spark', 'analytics'])]
```

The `coalesce` function is really useful in decreasing the number of partitions since it does not cause shuffle. Repartition causes data to be physically shuffled across a cluster. Notice that data from other partitions moved the data to partition 0 and partition 1 instead of shuffling all partitions. This is not a good representation of avoiding shuffling, but data with multiple partitions and more data elements will clearly show that data shuffling is limited.

> A higher number of partitions or smaller size partitions provide better parallelism but they have scheduling and distribution overhead. A lower number of partitions or bigger size partitions provide low scheduling and distribution overhead but they provide low parallelism and longer job execution time for skewed partitions. A reasonable range for a good partition size is 100 MB – 1 GB.

When reading a file from HDFS, Spark creates one partition per each block of HDFS. So, if an HDFS file has eight blocks, the RDD created will have eight partitions as shown in the following. However, the number of partitions can be increased by mentioning the number of partitions needed. Note that the number of partitions cannot be decreased:

```
>>> myRDD = sc.textFile('/path/to/hdfs/file')
>>> myRDD.getNumPartitions()
8
```

Lazy evaluation

As we have seen in the log analytics example, transformations on RDDs are lazily evaluated to optimize disk and memory usage in Spark.

- RDDs are empty when they are created, only the type and ID are determined
- Spark will not begin to execute the job until it sees an action.
- Lazy evaluation is used to reduce the number of passes it has to take over the data by grouping operations together
- In MapReduce, developers have to spend a lot of time thinking about how to group together operations to minimize the number of MR passes
- A task and all its dependencies are largely omitted if the partition it generates is already cached.

Lineage Graph

RDDs are never replicated in memory. In case of machine failures, RDDs are automatically rebuilt using a Lineage Graph. When RDD is created, it remembers how it was built, by reading an input file or by transforming other RDDs and using them to rebuild itself. It is a **DAG** (**Directed Acyclic Graph**) based representation that contains all its dependencies. In the log analytics example, using the toDebugString function, we can find out the lineage graph of the RDD.

```
>>> print myTwoPartitionsRDD.toDebugString()
(2) CoalescedRDD[5] at coalesce at NativeMethodAccessorImpl.java:-2 []
 |  MapPartitionsRDD[4] at repartition at NativeMethodAccessorImpl.java:-2
[]
 |  CoalescedRDD[3] at repartition at NativeMethodAccessorImpl.java:-2 []
 |  ShuffledRDD[2] at repartition at NativeMethodAccessorImpl.java:-2 []
 +-(4) MapPartitionsRDD[1] at repartition at NativeMethodAccessorImpl.
java:-2 []
 |  ParallelCollectionRDD[0] at parallelize at PythonRDD.scala:423 []
```

This result shows how the RDD was built from its parents. Spark's internal scheduler may truncate the lineage of the RDD graph if an RDD has already been cached in memory or on disk. Spark can "short-circuit" in this case and just begin computing based on the persisted RDD.

A second case when this truncation can happen is when an RDD is already materialized as a side-effect of an earlier shuffle, even if it was not explicitly cached. This is an under-the-hood optimization that takes advantage of the fact that spark shuffle outputs are written to disk, and many times portions of the RDD graph are re-computed. This behavior of spilling data to disk can be avoided by setting the spark.shuffle.spill parameter to false.

RDD is an interface that has the following information:

For lineage:

- Set of partitions (similar to splits in Hadoop)
- List of dependencies on parent RDDs (Lineage Graph)
- Function to compute a partition given its parent(s)

For optimized execution:

- Optional preferred locations
- Optional partitioning info (Partitioner)

Dependencies in point number 2 can be narrow or wide. In narrow dependencies, each partition of the parent RDD is used by, at most, one partition of the child RDD. In wide dependencies, multiple child partitions may depend on the parent RDD partition. *Figure 3.6* shows the narrow and wide dependencies.

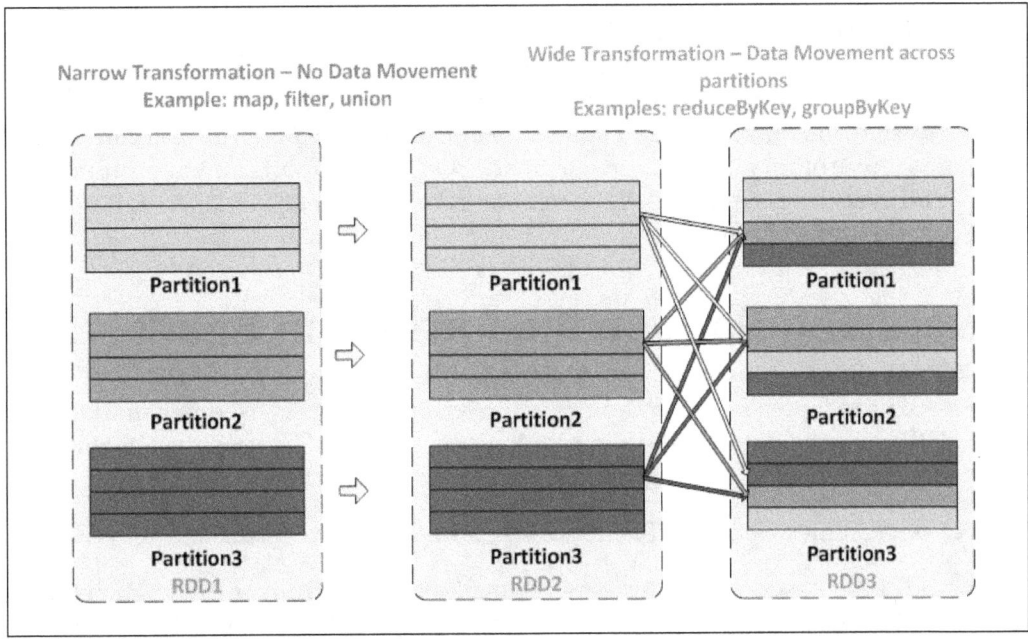

Figure 3.6: Narrow vs Wide Transformations.

Serialization

Every task sent from driver to executor and data sent across executors gets serialized. It is very important to use the right serialization framework to get optimum performance for the applications. Spark provides two serialization libraries: Java serialization and Kryo serialization.

While Java serialization is flexible, it is slow and leads to large serialized objects. Kryo serialization is most widely used for higher performance and better compactness.

Kryo serialization can be set in the scala application as:

```
conf.set("spark.serializer", "org.apache.spark.serializer.
KryoSerializer")
```

From the command line, it can be specified as:

```
--conf spark.serializer=org.apache.spark.serializer.KryoSerializer
```

Kryo serialization in PySpark will not be useful because PySpark stores data as byte objects. If the data is serialized with a Hadoop serialization format sequence file, AVRO, PARQUET, or Protocol Buffers, Spark provides in-built mechanisms to read and write data in these serialized formats. Using the `hadoopRDD` and `newAPIHadoopRDD` methods, any Hadoop-supported `Inputformat` can be read. Using `saveAsHadoopDataset` and `saveAsNewAPIHadoopDataset`, output can be written in any arbitrary `Outputformat`. Spark SQL also supports all Hive-supported storage formats (SerDes) to directly read data from a sequence file, Avro, ORC, Parquet, and Protocol Buffers.

Leveraging Hadoop file formats in Spark

Spark was built using the standard Hadoop libraries of `InputFormat` and `OutputFormat`. `InputFormat` and `OutputFormat` are Java APIs used to read data from HDFS or write data to HDFS in MapReduce programs. Spark supports this out-of-the-box even if Spark is not running on a Hadoop cluster.

Apart from text files, Spark's API supports several other data formats:

- `sc.wholeTextFiles`: This reads a small set of files from an HDFS directory as key value pairs, the filename as key, and the value as content.

- `sc.sequenceFile`: This reads a Hadoop sequence file. An example of creating a sequence file in Python:

  ```
  >>> mylist = [("Spark", 1), ("Sequence", 2), ("File", 3)]
  >>> seq = sc.parallelize(mylist)

  >>> seq.saveAsSequenceFile('out.seq')
  ```

Now you can check the content in Hadoop by the following:

```
[cloudera@quickstart ~]$ hadoop fs -text out.seq/part-0000*
Spark    1
Sequence    2
File    3
```

Examples of reading a sequence file in Python:

```
>>> seq = sc.sequenceFile('out.seq')
>>> seq = sc.sequenceFile('out.seq', "org.apache.hadoop.io.Text", "org.
apache.hadoop.io.IntWritable")
```

Other Hadoop Formats:

- `hadoopFile`: This reads an 'old' Hadoop `InputFormat` with an arbitrary key and value class from HDFS:

  ```
  rdd = sc.hadoopFile('/data/input/*',
                  org.apache.hadoop.mapred.TextInputFormat',
                  'org.apache.hadoop.io.Text',
                  'org.apache.hadoop.io.LongWritable',
                  conf={'mapreduce.input.fileinputformat
                  .input.dir.recursive':'true'})
  ```

- `newAPIHadoopFile`: This reads a 'new API' Hadoop `InputFormat` with an arbitrary key and value class from HDFS:

  ```
  fileLines = sc.newAPIHadoopFile('/data/input/*',
  'org.apache.hadoop.mapreduce.lib.input.TextInputFormat',
  'org.apache.hadoop.io.LongWritable',
  'org.apache.hadoop.io.Text',
  conf={'mapreduce.input.fileinputformat.input.dir.
  recursive':'true'})
  ```

Another way to set Hadoop configuration properties in a Spark Program:

- Scala:

  ```
  sc.hadoopConfiguration.set("custom.mapreduce.setting","someValue")
  ```

- Python:

  ```
  sc._jsc.hadoopConfiguration().set('custom.mapreduce.
  setting','someValue')
  ```

For writing data out using an arbitrary Hadoop `outputformat`, you can use the `saveAsHadoopFile` and `saveAsNewAPIHadoopFile` classes.

In addition to the `hadoopFile` and `newAPIHadoopFile`, you can use `hadoopDataset` and `newAPIHadoopDataset` for reading (and `saveAsHadoopDataset` and `saveAsNewAPIHadoopDataset` for writing) data in specialized Hadoop-supported data formats. The `hadoopDataset` family of functions just takes a configuration object on which you set the Hadoop properties needed to access your data source. The configuration is done in the same way as one would do for configuring a Hadoop MapReduce job, so you can follow the instructions for accessing one of these data sources in MapReduce and then pass the object to Spark:

- `RDD.saveAsObjectFile` and `sc.objectFile`: These are used for saving RDD as serialized Java objects in Java or Scala. In Python, the `saveAsPickleFile` and `pickleFile` methods are used with the pickle serialization library.

Data locality

Just like in MapReduce, data locality plays a crucial role in gaining performance while running a Spark job. Data locality determines how close data is stored to the code processing it. It is faster to ship serialized code rather than data from one place to another, because the size of the code is much smaller than the data. There are several levels of locality based on the data's current location. In order, from closest to farthest:

Storage Level	Description
PROCESS_LOCAL	Task is running in the same JVM where data is stored. This provides high performance.
NODE_LOCAL	Data is not the same JVM, but it is on the same node.
NO_PREF	Data is accessed quickly from anywhere with no preference.
RACK_LOCAL	Data is not in the same node, but in the same rack.
ANY	Data is not in the same rack, but outside the cluster.

The wait timeout for fallback between each level can be configured with the `spark.locality.wait` parameter, which is 3 seconds by default.

Data locality can be checked from the UI easily as shown in *Figure 3.7*. This indicates all tasks in this job are processed locally:

Tasks					
Index ▲	ID	Attempt	Status	Locality Level	Executor ID / Host
0	0	0	SUCCESS	PROCESS_LOCAL	0 / 192.168.139.164
1	1	0	SUCCESS	PROCESS_LOCAL	0 / 192.168.139.164
2	2	0	SUCCESS	PROCESS_LOCAL	0 / 192.168.139.164
3	3	0	SUCCESS	PROCESS_LOCAL	0 / 192.168.139.164

Figure 3.7: Data Locality Level.

When reading files from HDFS, Spark will get block locations from HDFS and try to assign tasks on nodes where blocks are stored. But it is to be noted that Spark creates executors first and then runs tasks. If executors are running on all nodes, Spark will be able to assign tasks on the nodes where HDFS blocks are stored. If only a few executors are assigned, it is difficult to achieve data locality. This is the behavior when using Spark's standalone resource manager. When using the YARN resource manager, executors will be placed on nodes where HDFS blocks are stored. This is achieved by the getPreferredLocations function in the code block. See the following link: https://github.com/apache/spark/blob/master/core/src/main/scala/org/apache/spark/rdd/HadoopRDD.scala.

Shared variables

When the Spark driver passes functions to executors, a separate copy of the variables is used for every function. So, for four tasks, four separate variables are created and they are never sent from the executor JVM to the driver JVM. While this is convenient, it can also be inefficient because the default task launching mechanism is optimized for small task sizes, and we might use the same variable in multiple parallel tasks. When the driver JVM ships a large object, such as a lookup table, to the executor JVM, performance issues are observed. Spark supports two types of shared variables:

Broadcast variables: Allows a read-only variable cached on every worker machine instead of sending it with every task. So, in a 20-node cluster with 200 tasks, only 20 broadcast variables are created instead of 200. In MapReduce terminology, this is equivalent to a distributed cache. Here is an example of using a broadcast variable in a PySpark shell:

```
>>> broadcastVar = sc.broadcast(list(range(1, 100)))
>>> broadcastVar.value
```

Accumulators: Allows tasks to write data to a shared variable instead of having a separate variable for each task. A driver can access the value of an accumulator. In MapReduce terminology, this is equivalent to counters. Here is an example of using a broadcast variable in the PySpark shell:

```
>>> myaccum = sc.accumulator(0)
>>> myrdd = sc.parallelize(range(1,100))
>>> myrdd.foreach(lambda value: myaccum.add(value))
>>> print myaccum.value
```

Pair RDDs

Spark provides special transformations and actions on RDDs containing key-value pairs. These RDDs are called Pair RDDs. Pair RDDs are useful in many spark programs, as they expose transformations and actions that allow you to act on each key in parallel or regroup data across the network. For example, Pair RDDs have a reduceByKey transformation that can aggregate data separately for each key, and a join transformation that can merge two RDDs together by grouping elements with the same key.

An example of creating a pair RDD in Python with word as the key, and length as the value:

```
>>> mylist = ["my", "pair", "rdd"]
>>> myRDD = sc.parallelize(mylist)
>>> myPairRDD = myRDD.map(lambda s: (s, len(s)))
>>> myPairRDD.collect()
[('my', 2), ('pair', 4), ('rdd', 3)]
>>> myPairRDD.keys().collect()
['my', 'pair', 'rdd']
>>> myPairRDD.values().collect()
[2, 4, 3]
```

Lifecycle of Spark program

The following steps explain the lifecycle of a Spark application with standalone resource manager, and *Figure 3.8* shows the scheduling process of a spark program:

1. The user submits a spark application using the spark-submit command.
2. Spark-submit launches the driver program on the same node in (client mode) or on the cluster (cluster mode) and invokes the main method specified by the user.

3.   The driver program contacts the cluster manager to ask for resources to launch executor JVMs based on the configuration parameters supplied.

4.   The cluster manager launches executor JVMs on worker nodes.

5.   The driver process scans through the user application. Based on the RDD actions and transformations in the program, Spark creates an operator graph.

6.   When an action (such as collect) is called, the graph is submitted to a DAG scheduler. The DAG scheduler divides the operator graph into stages.

7.   A stage comprises tasks based on partitions of the input data. The DAG scheduler pipelines operators together to optimize the graph. For instance, many map operators can be scheduled in a single stage. This optimization is the key to Spark's performance. The final result of a DAG scheduler is a set of stages.

8.   The stages are passed on to the task scheduler. The task scheduler launches tasks via cluster manager. (Spark Standalone/Yarn/Mesos). The task scheduler doesn't know about dependencies among stages.

9.   Tasks are run on executor processes to compute and save results.

10. If the driver's main method exits or it calls SparkContext.stop(), it will terminate the executors and release resources from the cluster manager.

Figure 3.8 illustrates the scheduling process of a Spark program:

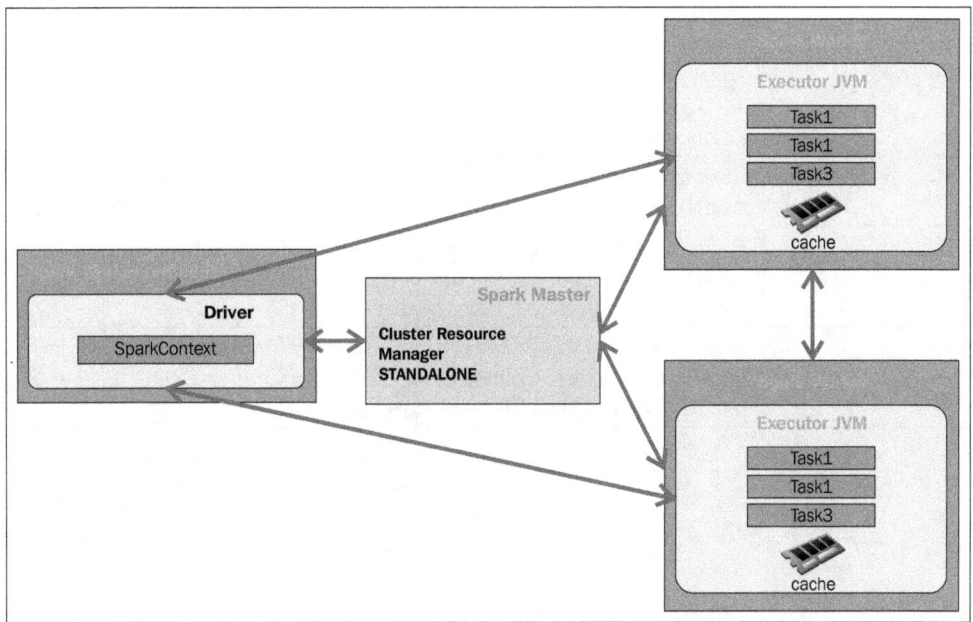

Figure 3.8: Spark scheduling process

Each task performs the same steps internally:

- Fetches its input: either from data storage (for input RDDs) or an existing RDD, or shuffle outputs
- Performs the operation or transformation to compute the RDD it represents
- Writes output to a shuffle, external storage, or back to the driver

Let's understand the terminology used in Spark before we drill down further to the lifecycle of a Spark program:

Term	Meaning
Application	It is a program started by `spark-shell` or `spark-submit`.
Driver program	A driver program runs on the driver and is responsible for creating the SparkContext.
Cluster manager	Responsible for allocating and managing the resources such as CPU and memory. Cluster resource managers are the standalone manager, Mesos, and YARN.
Worker node	Any node that can run application code in the cluster. It is a worker JVM and you can have multiple workers running on the same machine in a standalone cluster manager.
Executor	Executor JVM is responsible for executing tasks sent by Driver JVM. Typically, every application will have multiple executors running on multiple workers.
DAG	DAG (Directed Acyclic Graph) enables cyclic data flow. For every Spark job, a DAG of multiple stages is created and executed. For a MapReduce application, only two stages (Map and Reduce) are always created.
Job	Each action such as collect, count, or saveas in an application is created as a job, which consists of multiple stages and multiple tasks.
Stage	Each job can be performed in a single stage or multiple stages depending on the complexity of operations such as necessary data shuffling. A stage will have multiple tasks.
Task	A unit of work that is sent from the driver to executors. A task is performed on every partition of the RDD. So, If the RDD has 10 partitions, 10 tasks will be performed.

Pipelining

In some cases, the physical set of stages will not be an exact 1:1 correspondence to the logical RDD graph. Pipelining occurs when RDDs can be computed from its parents without data movement. For example, when a user calls both map and filter sequentially, those can be collapsed into a single transformation, which first maps, then filters each element. But, complex RDD graphs are split into multiple stages by the DAG scheduler.

Spark's event timeline and DAG visualizations are made easy through the Spark UI from Version 1.4 onwards. Let's execute the following code to view DAG visualizations of a job and stages:

```python
from operator import add
lines = sc.textFile("file:///home/cloudera/spark-2.0.0-bin-hadoop2.7/
README.md")
counts = lines.flatMap(lambda x: x.split(' ')) \
                .map(lambda x: (x, 1)) \
                .reduceByKey(add)
output = counts.collect()
for (word, count) in output:
    print("%s: %i" % (word, count))
```

Figure 3.9 shows the visual DAG for the job and stages for the word count code above. It shows that the job is split into two stages because of the data shuffling happening in this case.

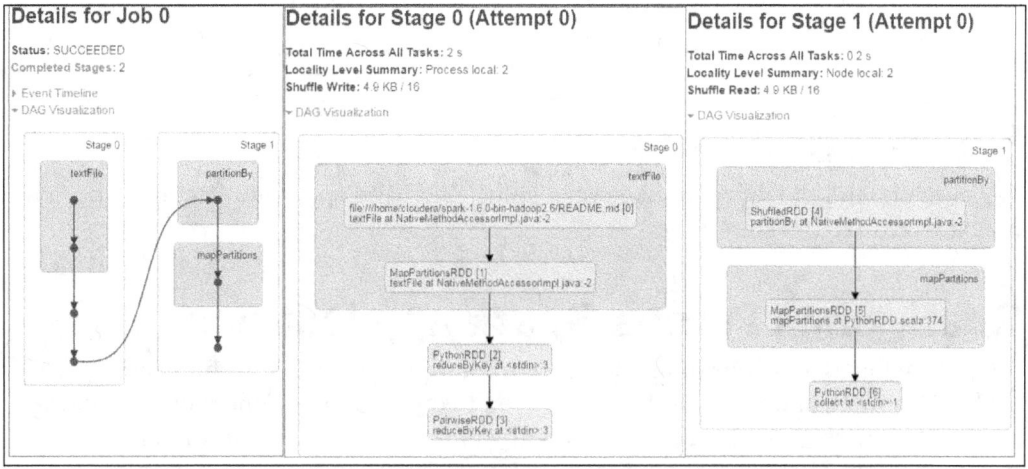

Figure 3.9: Spark Job's DAG visualization.

Figure 3.10 shows the event timeline for Stage 0, which indicates the time taken for each of the tasks.

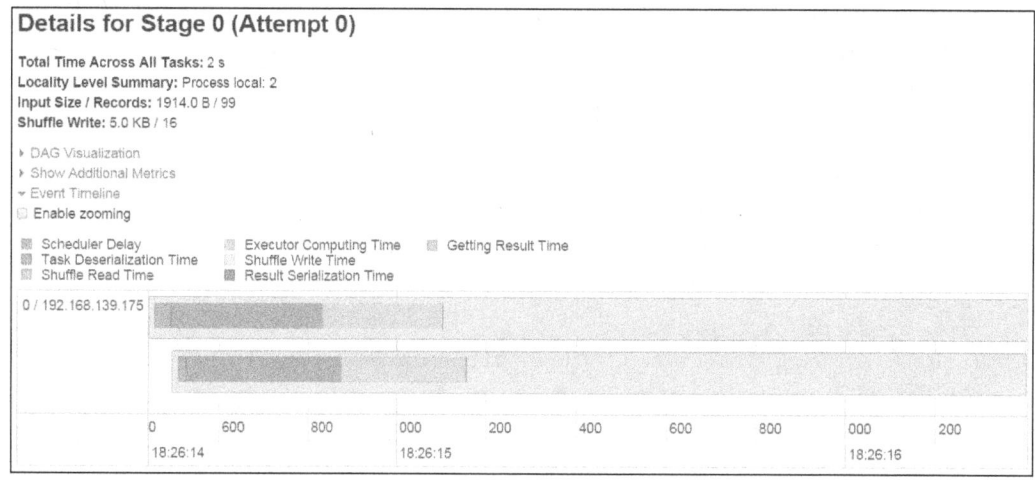

Figure 3.10: Spark Job Event Timeline within stage 0.

Spark execution summary

Spark execution summary in a nutshell is explained in the following:

- User code defines a DAG (Direct Acyclic Graph) of RDDs
- Actions force translation of the DAG to an execution plan
- Tasks are scheduled and executed on a cluster

Spark applications

Let's understand the difference between spark Shell and spark applications and how they are created and submitted.

Spark Shell versus Spark applications

Spark lets you access your datasets through a simple, yet specialized, Spark shell for Scala, Python, R, and SQL. Users do not need to create a full application to explore the data. They can start exploring data with commands that can be converted to programs later. This provides higher developer productivity. A Spark application is a complete program with SparkContext that is submitted with the `spark-submit` command.

Scala programs are generally written using Scala IDE or IntelliJ IDEA and SBT is used to compile the programs. Java programs are generally written in Eclipse and compiled with Maven. Python and R programs can be written in any text editor and also using IDEs such as Eclipse. Once the Scala and Java programs are written, they are compiled and executed with the spark-submit command as shown in the following. Since Python and R are interpreter languages, they are directly executed using the spark-submit command. Spark 2.0 is built with scala 2.11, so scala 2.11 is needed to build spark applications using Scala.

Creating a Spark context

The first step in any Spark program is to create a Spark context that provides an entry point to the Spark API. Set configuration properties by passing a SparkConf object to SparkContext, as shown in the following, in Python code:

```
from pyspark import SparkConf, SparkContext
conf = (SparkConf()
  .setMaster("spark://masterhostname:7077")
  .setAppName("My Analytical Application")
  .set("spark.executor.memory", "2g"))
sc = SparkContext(conf = conf)
```

SparkConf

SparkConf is the primary configuration mechanism in spark and an instance is required when creating a new SparkContext. A SparkConf instance contains string key/value pairs of configuration options that the user wants to override the defaults. SparkConf settings are hardcoded into the application code, passed from the command line, or passed from configuration files, as shown in the following code:

```
# Construct a conf
conf = new SparkConf()
conf.set("spark.app.name", "My Spark App")
conf.set("spark.master", "local[4]")
conf.set("spark.ui.port", "36000") # Override the default port
# Create a SparkContext with this configuration
sc = SparkContext(conf)
```

The SparkConf associated with a given application is immutable once it is passed to the SparkContext constructor. That means that all configuration decisions must be made before a SparkContext is instantiated.

SparkSubmit

The `spark-submit` script is used to launch spark applications on a cluster with any cluster resource manager.

`SparkSubmit` allows setting configurations dynamically and then injecting into the environment when the app is launched (when a new `SparkConf` is constructed). User apps can simply construct an 'empty' `SparkConf` and pass it directly to the `SparkContext` constructor if using `SparkSubmit`. The `SparkSubmit` tool provides built-in flags for the most common Spark configuration parameters and a generic `--conf` flag, which accepts any Spark config value as shown :

```
[cloudera@quickstart ~]$ spark-submit \
  --class com.example.loganalytics.MyApp \
  --master yarn \
  --name "Log Analytics Application" \
  --executor-memory 2G \
  --num-executors 50 \
  --conf spark.shuffle.spill=false \
  myApp.jar \
  /data/input \
  /data/output
```

In case of multiple configuration parameters, put all of them in a file and pass it to the application using `--properties-file`:

```
[cloudera@quickstart ~]$ spark-submit \
  --class com.example.MyApp \
  --properties-file my-config-file.conf \
  myApp.jar


## Contents of my-config-file.conf ##
spark.master spark://5.6.7.8:7077
spark.app.name "My Spark App"
spark.ui.port 36000
spark.executor.memory 2g
spark.serializer org.apache.spark.serializer.KryoSerializer
```

Application dependency JARs included with the --jars option will be automatically shipped to the worker nodes. For Python, the equivalent --py-files option can be used to distribute .egg, .zip, and .py libraries to executors. Note that JARs and files are copied to the working directory for each SparkContext on the executor nodes. It's always better to add all code dependencies within a JAR while creating the JAR. This can be easily done in Maven or SBT.

For getting a complete list of options for spark-submit, use the following command:

```
[cloudera@quickstart ~]$ spark-submit --help
Usage: spark-submit [options] <app jar | python file> [app arguments]
Usage: spark-submit --kill [submission ID] --master [spark://...]
Usage: spark-submit --status [submission ID] --master [spark://...]
```

Spark Conf precedence order

Spark configuration precedence, from higher to lower, is as follows:

1. Configurations declared explicitly in the user's code using the set() function on a SparkConf object.
2. Flags passed to spark-submit or spark-shell.
3. Values in the spark-defaults.conf properties file.
4. Default values of Spark.

Important application configurations

Some of the important configuration parameters for submitting applications are listed in below table:

Command Line Parameter	Equivalent Configuration Property	Default	Meaning
--master	spark.master	None. If this parameter is not mentioned, it will choose local mode.	Spark's master URL. Options are local, local(*), local(n), spark://masterhostname:7077, yarn-client, yarn-cluster, and mesos://host:port.
--class	None	None	Application class.

Command Line Parameter	Equivalent Configuration Property	Default	Meaning
`--deploy-mode`	None	Client Mode	Deploying application in client or cluster mode.
`--conf`	None	None	Pass arbitrary configuration in key value format.
`--py-files`	None	None	Add Python dependencies.
`--supervise`	None	None	Restart driver if it fails.
`--driver-memory`	`spark.driver.memory`	1G	Memory for Driver.
`--executor-memory`	`spark.executor.memory`	1G	Memory for executors.
`--total-executor-cores`	`spark.cores.max`	None. default will be `spark.deploy.defaultCores` on Spark's standalone cluster manager.	Used in Spark Standalone mode or Mesos coarse grained mode only.
`--num-executors`	`spark.executor.instances`	2	Number of executors in YARN mode.
`--executor-cores`	`spark.executor.cores`	1 in YARN mode, all the available cores on the worker in standalone mode.	Number of cores on each executor.

Persistence and caching

One of the unique features of Spark is persisting RDDs in memory. You can persist an RDD with persist or cache transformations as shown in the following:

```
>>> myRDD.cache()
>>> myRDD.persist()
```

Both the preceding statements are the same and cache data at the MEMORY_ONLY storage level. The difference is cache refers to the MEMORY_ONLY storage level, whereas persist can choose different storage levels as needed, as shown in the following table. The first time it is computed with an action, it will be kept in memory on the nodes. The easiest way to know the percentage of the cached RDD and its size is to check the **Storage** tab in the UI as shown in *Figure 3.11*:

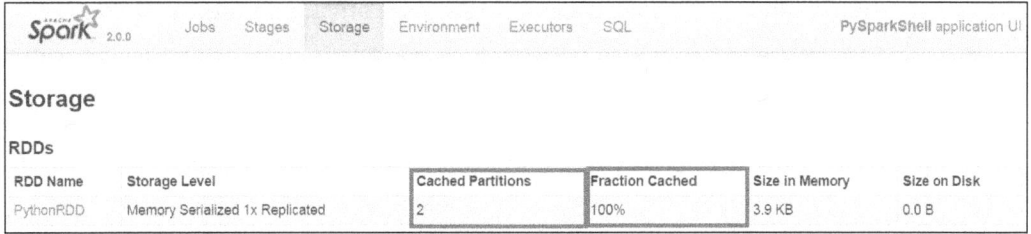

Figure 3.11: Cached RDD – percentage and size cached.

Storage levels

RDDs can be stored using different storage levels as needed by application requirements. The following table shows the storage levels of Spark and their meaning.

Storage Level	Meaning
MEMORY_ONLY	Store RDDs in memory only. A partition that does not fit in memory will be re-computed.
MEMORY_AND_DISK	Store RDDs in memory and a partition that does not fit in memory will be stored on disk.
MEMORY_ONLY_SER	Store RDDs in memory only but as serialized Java objects.
MEMORY_AND_DISK_SER	Store RDDs in memory and disk as serialized Java objects.
DISK_ONLY	Store the RDDs on disk only.
MEMORY_ONLY_2 MEMORY_AND_DISK_2	Same as MEMORY_ONLY and MEMORY_AND_DISK, but replicate every partition for faster fault recovery.
OFF_HEAP (experimental)	Store RDDs in eTachyon, which provides less GC overhead.

What level to choose?

Spark's storage levels provide different trade-offs between memory usage and CPU efficiency. Follow the process to select one:

- If the entire RDD fits in memory, choose MEMORY_ONLY.

- Use MEMORY_ONLY_SER for better compactness and better performance. This does not matter for Python because objects are always serialized with the pickle library.

- Use MEMORY_AND_DISK if re-computing is more expensive than reading from disk.

- Do not replicate the RDD storage until fast fault recovery is needed.

Spark resource managers – Standalone, YARN, and Mesos

We have already executed spark applications in the Spark standalone resource manager in other sections of this chapter (within the PySpark shell and applications). Let's try to understand how these cluster resource managers are different from each other and when they should be used.

Local versus cluster mode

Before moving on to cluster resource managers, let's understand how cluster mode is different from local mode.

It is important to understand the scope and life cycle of variables and methods when executing code across a cluster. Let's look at an example with the foreach action:

```
counter = 0
rdd = sc.parallelize(data)
rdd.foreach(lambda x: counter += x)
print("Counter value: " + counter)
```

In local mode, the preceding code works fine because the counter variable and RDD are in the same memory space (single JVM).

In cluster mode, the counter value will never change and always remains at 0. In cluster mode, spark computes the closure with variables and methods and ships them to executors. When executors perform the `foreach` function it refers to the new copy of the counter on the executor. The counter on the driver is not accessible to the executor. Hence, every time you execute this, a local counter is incremented and never returned to the driver. To address this challenge in cluster mode, create a separate copy of the variable for every closure or use an accumulator.

Cluster resource managers

You can run a Spark application in four different modes:

- **Local mode**: In local mode, all the processes run in a single JVM and with no data shuffle, as in cluster mode.

If the `spark.master` (or `--master`) configuration property is specified, the application will run on one of the cluster resource managers in client or cluster mode depending on the `--deploy-mode` specified.

- **Standalone mode**: Submit Spark application to Spark's in-built cluster manager
- **YARN mode**: Submit the Spark application to the YARN resource manager.
- **Mesos mode**: Submit the spark application to the Mesos cluster manager

Standalone

By default, an application submitted in standalone mode will acquire all cores (in the `spark.deploy.defaultCores` property) of the cluster with 1G memory for every executor. In multiple application environments, it is important to cap the resource usage for every application. Cap the usage with the `--total-executor-cores` argument to spark-submit or use `spark.cores.max` in the spark configuration file. Use the `--executor-memory` argument to spark-submit or use `spark.executor.memory` in the spark configuration file to cap the amount of memory needed.

In this example, we use a 20-node cluster with four CPU cores in every node:

- With no parameters specified, an application will launch 20 executors with four cores and 1 GB memory
- `--executor-memory 1G` and `--total-executor-cores 8`: Spark will launch eight executors, each with 1 GB of RAM
- `spark.deploy.spreadOut` to `false` in `spark conf`: Spark will launch two executors, each with 1 GB RAM and four cores

YARN

Applications are submitted with `--master yarn-client` for client mode and `--master yarn-cluster` for cluster mode. In Yarn mode, you can specify the number of executors needed with the number of cores, as opposed to `-total-executor-cores` in spark standalone master.

- `--num-executors` controls how many executors will be allocated (the default is 2). This property is set within the configuration using `spark.executor.instances`.

- `--executor-memory` is the RAM for each executor.

- `--executor-cores` is the number of CPU cores for each executor.

In this example, we use a 20-node cluster with four CPU cores in every node:

- With no parameters specified, an application will launch two executors with 1 core and 1 GB memory

- `--num-executors 8 --executor-memory 2G --executor-cores 4` : Spark will launch eight executors, each with 2 GB of memory and four cores

Downloading the example code

Detailed steps to download the code bundle are mentioned in the Preface of this book. Please have a look.

The code bundle for the book is also hosted on GitHub at `https://github.com/PacktPublishing/big-data-analytics`. We also have other code bundles from our rich catalog of books and videos available at `https://github.com/PacktPublishing/`. Check them out!

Dynamic resource allocation

The dynamic resource allocation feature was introduced in Spark 1.2. An application may give resources back to the cluster if they are no longer used and request them again later when there is demand. Dynamic resource allocation of resources will efficiently control the resource usage on the cluster. As shown in *Figure 3.12*, there is a big variation in allocated and used resources in all spark applications due to stragglers, scheduling, waiting, idling, and so on.

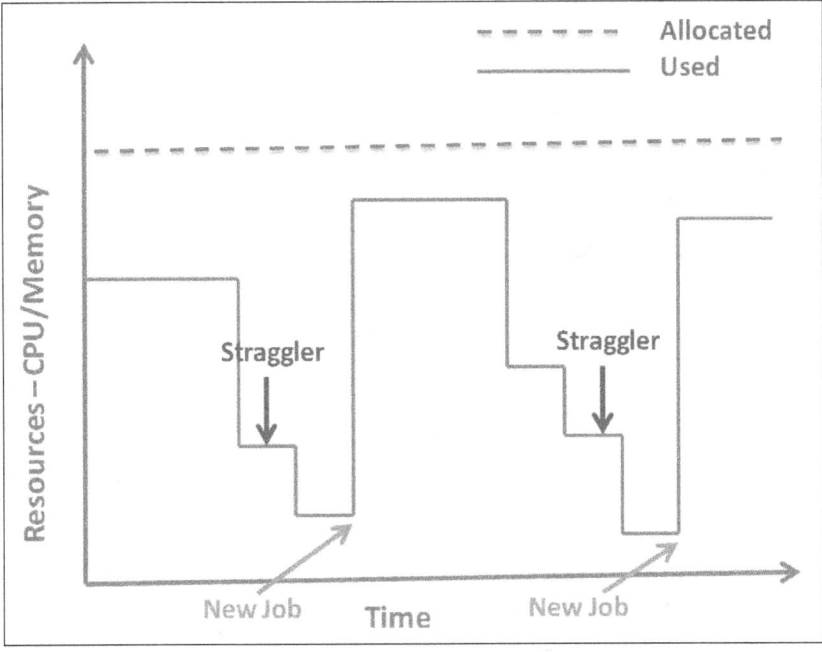

Figure 3.12: Resource allocation versus resources used

To enable this feature, the following configuration properties are to be set in an application:

- `spark.dynamicAllocation.enabled`
- `spark.dynamicAllocation.minExecutors`
- `spark.dynamicAllocation.maxExecutors`
- `spark.dynamicAllocation.initialExecutors`
- `spark.shuffle.service.enabled`

 Note that `spark.executor.instances` (or `--num-executors`) should not be used when dynamic allocation is enabled. If both are used, dynamic allocation will be disabled and `--num-executors` will be used.

Client mode versus cluster mode

When running Spark in YARN client mode, the driver runs on the client machine and application master and executors run on the cluster. Each Spark executor runs as a YARN container in client or cluster mode.

In yarn-cluster mode, the driver runs within the application master. So, the application master is responsible for both running drivers and requesting resources from the YARN resource manager. The client that starts the application doesn't need to stick around for its entire lifetime.

Yarn-cluster is to be used for production jobs, while yarn-client mode is to be used in interactive mode where you want to see your application's output immediately.

Yarn client mode and cluster modes are illustrated in *Figure 3.13*:

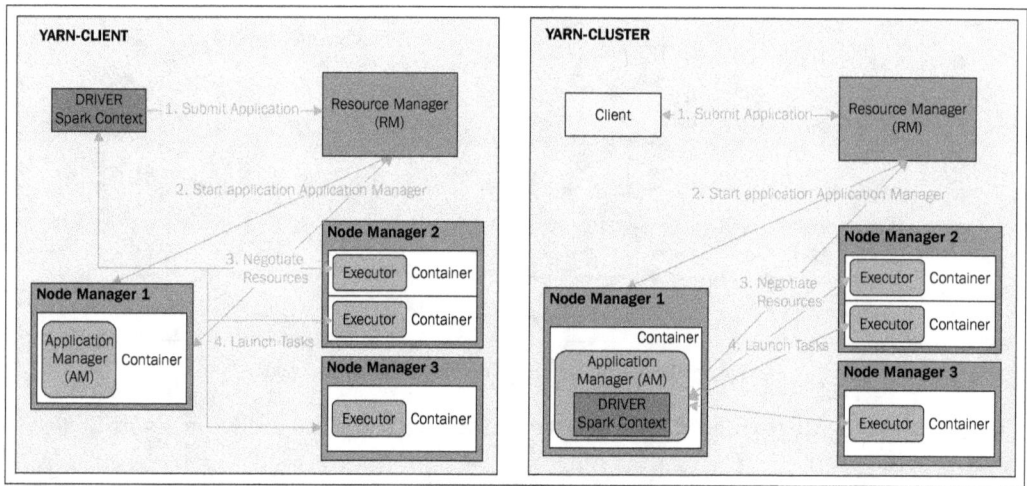

Figure 3.13: YARN client vs. YARN cluster mode.

 More YARN settings are available at: `http://spark.apache.org/docs/latest/running-on-yarn.html`

Mesos

Apache Mesos is a general-purpose cluster manager that can run both analytic workloads and long-running services (for example, Web applications or key-value stores) on a cluster. See the following example usage:

```
spark-submit --master mesos://masternode:5050
```

Two types of scheduling modes are available in Mesos:

- **Fine-grained**: Fine-grained mode behavior is similar to Yarn. Executors scale the number of CPUs they claim from Mesos up and down as they execute tasks, and so a machine running multiple executors can dynamically share CPU resources between them. This is the default mode.

- **Coarse-grained**: Coarse-grained mode behavior is similar to standalone. Spark allocates a fixed number of CPUs to each executor in advance and never releases them until the application ends, even if the executor is not currently running tasks. You can enable coarse-grained mode by passing the following:

```
--conf spark.mesos.coarse=true
```

Which resource manager to use?

When using Spark along with other applications on Hadoop clusters, it is better to use YARN for better sharing of resources. Where better performance and sharing resources are not a constraint, the standalone manager can be used. Mesos and Yarn offer similar resource sharing capabilities. On Hadoop clusters, it makes sense to use YARN because all other frameworks of Hadoop are integrated with Yarn. For clusters other than Hadoop, it makes sense to use Mesos.

Summary

RDDs are a fundamental unit of data in Spark and Spark programming revolves around creating and performing operations on RDDs such as transformations and actions. Apache Spark programs can be interactively executed in a shell or by submitting applications. Parallelism is defined by the number of partitions in an RDD. The number of partitions is decided by the number of blocks in the HDFS file, or type of resource manager and configuration properties used for non-HDFS files.

Caching RDDs in memory is useful for performing multiple actions on the same RDD as it provides higher performance. When an RDD is cached with the MEMORY_ONLY option, partitions that do not fit in memory will be re-computed as and when needed. If re-compute is expensive, it is better to choose MEMORY_AND_DISK as the persistence level.

Spark's application can be submitted in client or cluster mode. While client mode is used for development and testing, cluster mode is used for production deployment. Spark has three different resource managers to choose from: standalone, Yarn, and Mesos. Choosing a cluster resource manager depends on the sharing of resources and the expected performance level. In all cases, Spark's default standalone resource manager provides higher performance because of low scheduling cost.

The next chapter introduces big data analytics with Spark SQL, DataFrames, and Datasets.

4
Big Data Analytics with Spark SQL, DataFrames, and Datasets

As per the Spark Summit presentation by Matei Zaharia, creator of Apache Spark (`http://www.slideshare.net/databricks/spark-summit-eu-2015-matei-zaharia-keynote`), Spark SQL and DataFrames are the most used components of an entire Spark ecosystem. This indicates Spark SQL is one of the key components used for Big Data Analytics by companies.

Users of Spark have three different APIs to interact with distributed collections of data:

- RDD API allows users to work with objects of their choice and express transformations as lambda functions

- DataFrames API provides high-level relational operations and an optimized runtime, at the expense of type-safety

- Dataset API that combines the worlds of RDD and DataFrames

We have learned how to use RDD API in *Chapter 3*, *Deep Dive into Apache Spark*. In this chapter, let's understand the in-depth concepts of Spark SQL including exploring the Data Sources API, the DataFrame API, the Dataset API, and how to perform big data analytics with most common sources, such as Json, Xml, Parquet, ORC, Avro, CSV, JDBC, and Hive. Also, let's understand how to use Spark SQL as a distributed SQL engine.

This chapter is divided into the following sub-topics:

- History of Spark SQL
- Architecture of Spark SQL
- Evolution of DataFrames and Datasets
- Why Datasets and DataFrames?
- Analytics with DataFrames
- Analytics with Dataset API
- Data Sources API with Xml, Parquet, ORC, Avro, CSV, JDBC, and Hive
- DataFrame based Spark-on-HBase connector
- Spark SQL as a distributed SQL engine
- Hive on Spark

History of Spark SQL

To address the challenges of performance issues of Hive queries, a new project called Shark was introduced into the Spark ecosystem in early versions of Spark. Shark used Spark as an execution engine instead of the MapReduce engine for executing hive queries. Shark was built on the hive codebase using the Hive query compiler to parse hive queries and generate an abstract syntax tree, which is converted to a logical plan with some basic optimizations. Shark applied additional optimizations and created a physical plan of RDD operations, then executed them in Spark. This provided in-memory performance to Hive queries. But, Shark had three major problems to deal with:

- Shark was suitable to query Hive tables only. Running relational queries on RDDs was not possible
- Running Hive QL as a string within spark programs was error-prone
- Hive optimizer was created for the MapReduce paradigm and it was difficult to extend Spark for new data sources and new processing models

Shark was discontinued from version 1.0 and Spark SQL was introduced in version 1.0 in May 2014. In Spark SQL, a new type of RDD called SchemaRDD was introduced that has an associated schema. SchemaRDD offered relational queries and spark functions to be executed on top of them.

Starting with Spark 1.3, SchemaRDD has been renamed DataFrames which is similar to DataFrames in Python or R Statistics language. DataFrame is similar to a relational table, which offers rich **Domain Specific Language (DSL)** functions, RDD functions, and SQL.

Starting with Spark 1.6, a new Dataset API has been introduced that provides the best features of RDDs and the DataFrame API together. RDDs are useful because of the static typing nature and easy to implement user-defined functions. The DataFrame API provided easy to use functionality and higher performance than RDDs, but it does not support static typing, which is error-prone.

Starting with Spark 2.0, the Dataset and DataFrame APIs are unified to provide a single abstraction of the Dataset API.

The Spark SQL history is depicted in *Figure 4.1*:

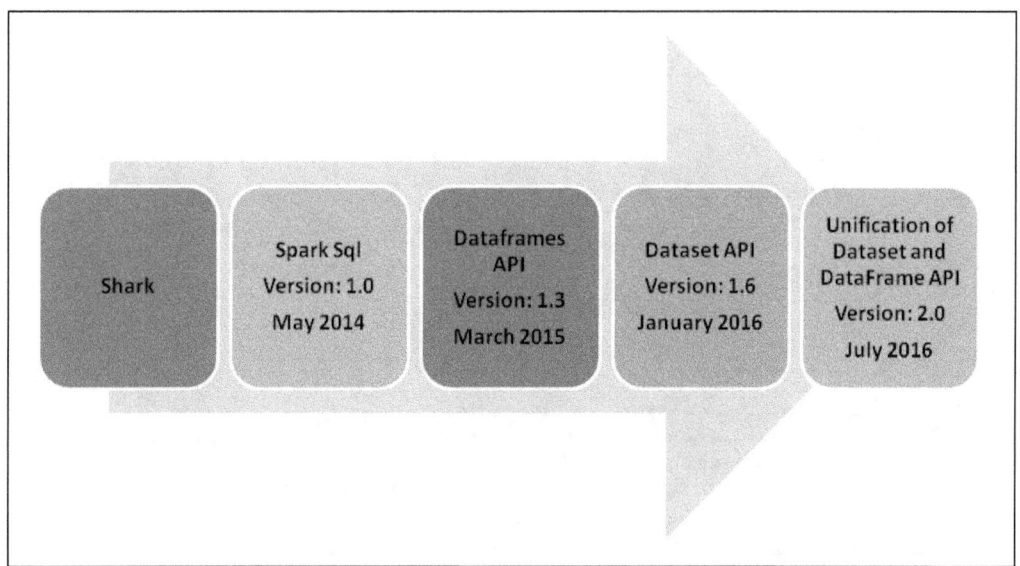

Figure 4.1: Spark SQL history

Architecture of Spark SQL

Spark SQL is a library on top of the Spark core execution engine, as shown in *Figure 4.2*. It exposes SQL interfaces using JDBC/ODBC for Data Warehousing applications or through a command-line console for interactively executing queries. So, any **Business Intelligence (BI)** tools can connect to Spark SQL to perform analytics at memory speeds. It also exposes a Dataset API and DataFrame API, which are supported in Java, Scala, Python, and R. Spark SQL users can use the Data Source API to read and write data from and to a variety of sources to create a DataFrame or a Dataset. *Figure 4.2* also indicates the traditional way of creating and operating on RDDs from programming languages to the Spark core engine.

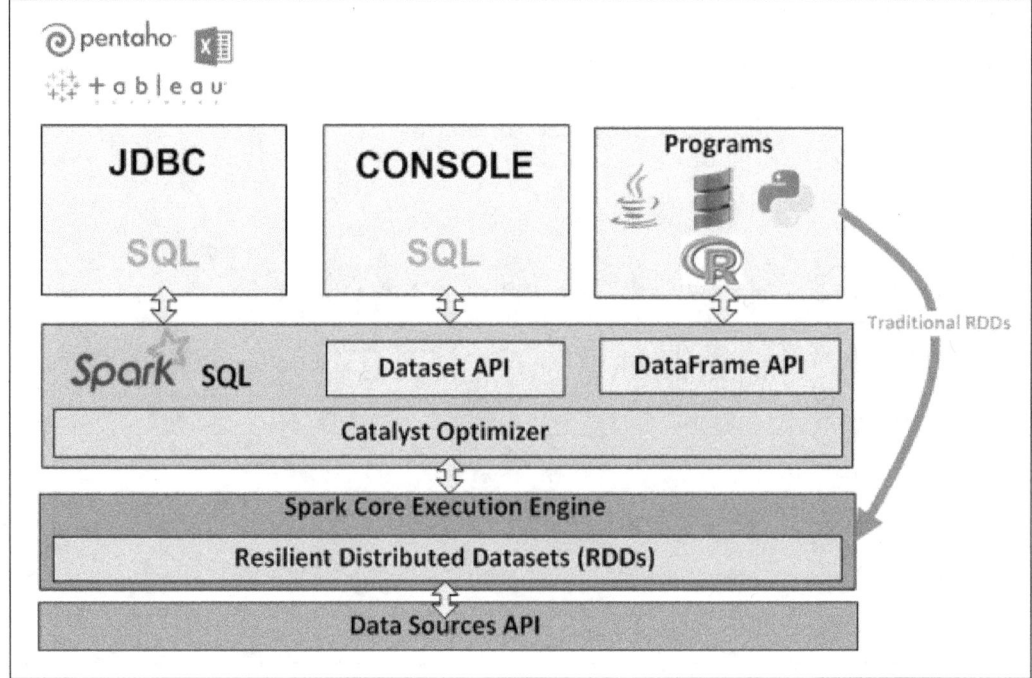

Figure 4.2: Spark SQL architecture

Spark SQL also extends the Dataset API, DataFrame API, and Data Sources API to be used across all other Spark libraries such as SparkR, Spark Streaming, Structured Streaming, Machine Learning Libraries, and GraphX as shown in *Figure 4.3*. Once the Dataset or DataFrame is created, it can be used in any library, and they are interoperable and can be converted to traditional RDDs.

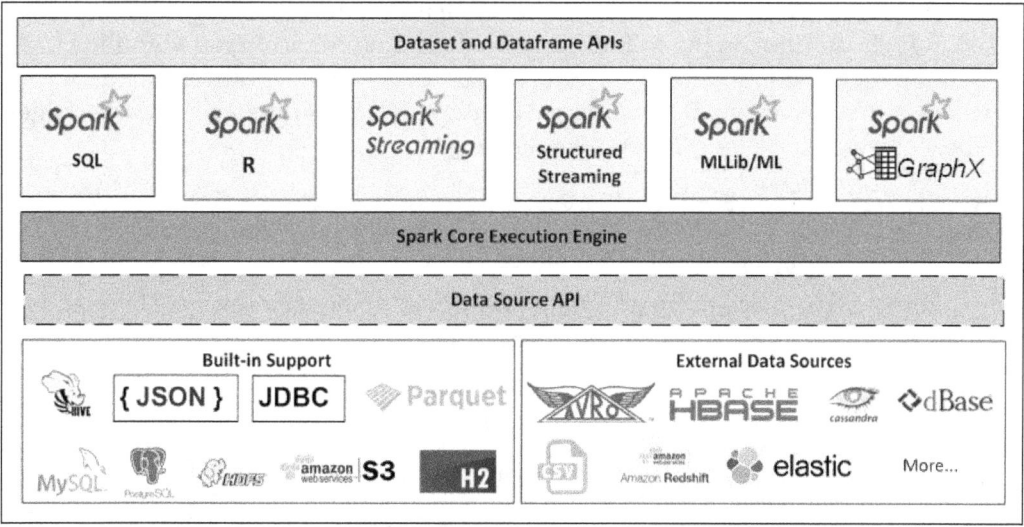

Figure 4.3: Spark ecosystem with Data Sources API and DataFrame API

Spark SQL introduced an extensible optimizer called **Catalyst** to support most common data sources and algorithms. Catalyst enables the adding of new data sources, optimization rules, and data types for domains such as machine learning. Catalyst uses the pattern matching feature of Scala to express rules. It offers a general framework for transforming trees, which are used to perform analysis, planning, and runtime code generation.

Introducing SQL, Datasources, DataFrame, and Dataset APIs

Let's understand four components in Spark SQL—SQL, the Data Sources API, the DataFrame API, and the Dataset API.

Spark SQL can write and read data to and from Hive tables using the SQL language. SQL can be used within Java, Scala, Python, R languages, over JDBC/ODBC, or using the command-line option. When SQL is used in programming languages, the results will be converted as DataFrames.

Advantages of SQL are:

- Can work with Hive tables easily
- Can connect BI tools to a distributed SQL engine using Thrift Server and submit SQL or Hive QL queries using JDBC or ODBC interfaces

The Data Sources API provides a single interface for reading and writing data using Spark SQL. In addition to the in-built sources that come prepackaged with the Apache Spark distribution, the Data Sources API provides integration for external developers to add custom data sources. All external data sources and other packages can be viewed at `http://spark-packages.org/`.

Advantages of the Data Source API are:

- Easy loading/saving of DataFrames.
- Efficient data access by predicate pushdown to the data source. This enables reading less data from data sources.
- Building libraries for any new data source.
- No need to include in Spark code.
- Easy to share a new Data Source with Spark packages.

The DataFrame API is designed to make big data analytics easier for a variety of users. This API is inspired by DataFrames in R and Python (Pandas), but designed for distributed processing of massive datasets to support modern big data analytics. DataFrame can be seen as an extension to the existing RDD API and are an abstraction over RDDs.

Advantages of the DataFrame API are:

- Easy to develop applications with **Domain Specific Language (DSL)**
- High performance over traditional RDDs and similar performance for Scala, Java, Python, or R
- Automatic schema discovery and partition discovery of sources
- Supports a wide array of data sources
- Optimization and code generation through the Catalyst optimizer
- Interoperability with RDDs, Datasets, Pandas and external sources like RDBMS databases, HBase, Cassandra, and so on

The Dataset API introduced in version 1.6 combined the best of RDDs and DataFrames. Datasets use encoders for converting JVM objects to a dataset table representation, which is stored using Spark's Tungsten binary format.

Advantages of the Dataset API are:

- Just like RDDs, Datasets are typesafe
- Just like DataFrame, Datasets are faster than RDDs
- Interoperability between DataFrames and RDDs
- Cached Datasets take less space than RDDs
- Serialization with encoders is faster than Java or Kryo serializers

The following table shows the differences between SQL, DataFrames, and Datasets in terms of compile time and runtime safety.

	SQL	DataFrames	Datasets
Syntax Errors	Runtime	Compile time	Compile time
Analysis Errors	Runtime	Runtime	Compile time

The Dataset API and its subset DataFrame APIs will become the mainstream API instead of the RDD API. If possible, always use Datasets or DataFrames only, instead of RDDs, because it provides much higher performance due to optimizations done in Catalyst.

Evolution of DataFrames and Datasets

A DataFrame is used for creating rows and columns of data just like a **Relational Database Management System (RDBMS)** table. DataFrames are a common data analytics abstraction that was introduced in the R statistical language and then introduced in Python with the proliferation of the Pandas library and the pydata ecosystem. DataFrames provide easy ways to develop applications and higher developer productivity.

Spark SQL DataFrame has richer optimizations under the hood than R or Python DataFrame. They can be created from files, pandas DataFrames, tables in Hive, external databases like MySQL, or RDDs. The DataFrame API is available in Scala, Java, Python, and R.

While DataFrames provided relational operations and higher performance, they lacked type-safety, which led to run-time errors. While it is possible to convert a DataFrame to a Dataset, it required a fair amount of boilerplate code and it was expensive. So, the Dataset API is introduced in version 1.6 and combined the best of both worlds; RDDs and DataFrames - static typing, easier implementation of the function features of RDDs, and the superior performance features of DataFrames.

However, Dataset and DataFrame were separate classes in version 1.6. In version 2.0, DataSet and DataFrame APIs are unified to provide a single API for developers. A DataFrame is a specific *Dataset[T]*, where *T=Row type*, so DataFrame shares the same methods as Dataset.

The Dataset API is offered in Scala and Java languages. It is not supported in Python and R languages. However, many benefits of the Dataset API are already available in Python and R languages naturally. DataFrame API is available in all four languages; Java, Scala, Python, and R.

What's wrong with RDDs?

Let's understand why RDDs were not enough and led to the creation of DataFrames and Datasets.

Spark computes the closure, serializes, and ships them to executors. This means your code is shipped in raw form without much optimization. There is no way of representing structured data in RDD and querying RDD. Working with RDDs is pretty easy but the code gets messy sometimes dealing with tuples. The following code illustration is for getting the average age of people by name using RDD and DataFrames. DataFrames are easier to use and yet provide superior performance than conventional RDDs because of optimizations done in Catalyst.

```
input = sc.textFile(hdfs://localhost:8020/data/input).split("\t")
input.map(lambda a: (a[0], [int(a[1], 1])) \
    .reduceByKey(lambda a,b: [a[0] + b[0], a[1] + b[1]) \
    .map(lambda a: [a[0], a[1][0] / a[1][1]) \
    .collect()

spark.table("emp_table")  \
    .groupBy("emp_name")  \
    .agg("emp_name", avg("emp_age"))  \
    .collect()
```

In comparison to the Hadoop world, a pure handwritten MapReduce job might be slower than a hive or pig job because of the optimizations done in hive and pig under the hood. DataFrames can be seen in a similar way.

RDD Transformations versus Dataset and DataFrames Transformations

Let's understand the differences between RDD transformations and DataFrame transformations in detail. The following table shows the differences:

RDD Transformations	Dataset and DataFrame Transformations
Transformations are lazily evaluated by a spark action.	Dataset and DataFrame transformations are lazy as well.
Operators in a spark job are used to construct a **Directed Acyclic Graph (DAG)** with optimizations such as combining or re-arranging operators.	Dataset or DataFrame creates an **Abstract Syntax Tree (AST)**, which is parsed by Catalyst to check and improve using both rules-based optimization and cost-based optimizations.
Spark computes the closure, serializes, and ships them to executors. Optimizations must be done by user.	Optimized code generated transformation is shipped to the executors.
Lowest API on Spark.	High-level API on Spark.
Schema is not needed for RDDs.	Schema is imposed while creating Datasets and DataFrames.
No optimizations for predicate pushdown. It uses Hadoop Input format for Hadoop sources with no built-in optimizations.	Makes use of smart sources using the Data Sources API, which enables predicate pushdown optimizations at sources.
Performance varies in different languages.	Same performance in Scala, Python, Java, or R.
Reading and combining multiple sources is difficult.	Reading and combining multiple sources is easy because of underlying Datasources API.

Why Datasets and DataFrames?

The simple answer is: speed and ease of use. DataFrames provide the benefits of optimization, speed, automatic schema discovery, working with multiple sources, and multiple languages support; they read less data, and provide inter-operability between RDDs. Let's delve into these concepts.

Optimization

Catalyst provides optimization for DataFrames. It provides two optimizations:

- Predicate push down to sources, to read only the data needed
- Creates a physical plan for execution and generates JVM bytecode that is better optimized than handwritten code

The DataFrame is not defining **Directed Acyclic Graph (DAG)** as in the case of RDDs. **Abstract Syntax Trees (AST)** are created, which the catalyst engine will parse, check, and improve using both rules-based optimization and cost-based optimization.

Figure 4.4 shows the phase of query planning in Spark Sql. So, any DataFrame, Dataset operation or SQL query will follow the same optimization path to create a physical plan and execute on the Spark Cluster.

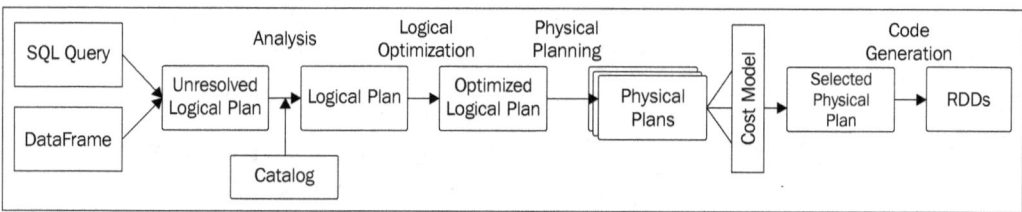

Figure 4.4: Phases in Spark SQL Catalyst optimizer. Rounded rectangles are catalyst trees.

Just like RDD, DataFrames and Datasets can be cached as well. When cached, they automatically store data in an efficient columnar format that is significantly more compact than Java/Python objects and provide optimizations.

Speed

Since the optimizer generates JVM bytecode for execution, Scala and Python programs provide similar performance as shown in *Figure 4.5*. The chart shows groupBy aggregation on 10 million integer pairs on a single machine. The Scala and Python DataFrame operations provide similar execution time since they are compiled into the same JVM bytecode for execution. Source: `https://databricks.com/blog/2015/02/17/introducing-DataFrames-in-spark-for-large-scale-data-science.html`.

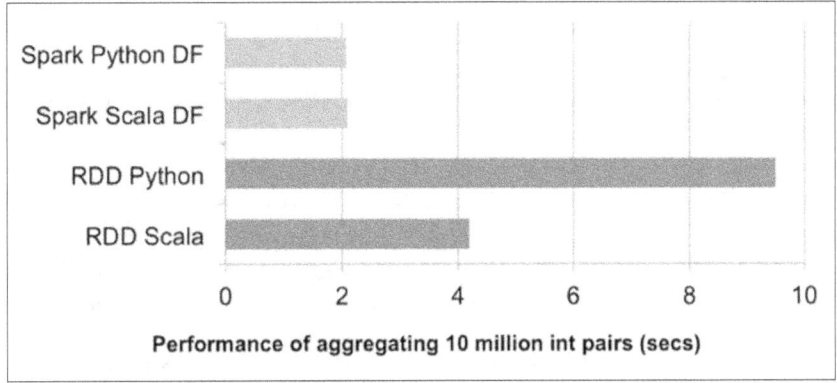

Figure 4.5: DataFrames performance in Scala and Python languages

Datasets use optimized encoders to serialize and deserialize objects for processing and transmitting over the network. Encoders provide significantly higher performance than Java or Kryo serialization as shown in *Figure 4.6*.

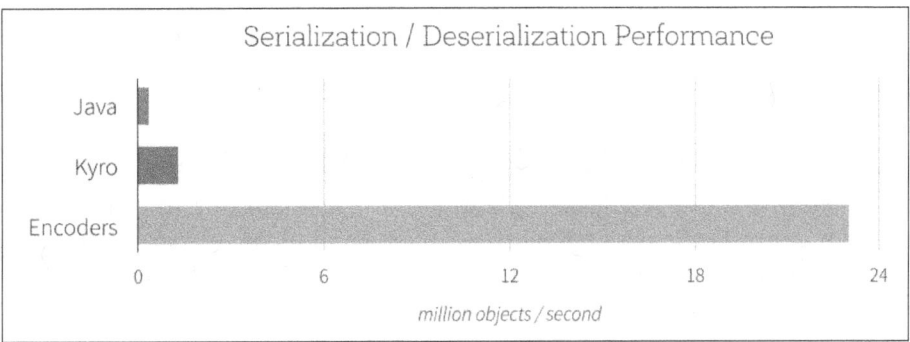

Figure 4.6: Encoder serialization/deserialization performance

Automatic Schema Discovery

To create a DataFrame from an RDD, a schema must be provided. When creating a DataFrame from JSON, Parquet, and ORC files, a schema is automatically discovered including the partitions discovery. This is possible because of the Data Sources API framework.

Multiple sources, multiple languages

Big Data Analytical applications need to collect and analyze data from a variety of data sources and formats. The DataFrame API enables reading and writing from most widely used formats including JSON files, Parquet files, ORC files, and Hive tables. It can read from local file systems, HDFS, S3, and external RDBMS databases using the JDBC protocol. Spark SQL's Data Sources API can be extended to support any third-party data formats or sources. Existing third-party extensions are available for Avro, CSV, XML, HBase, ElasticSearch, Cassandra, and so on. The URL `http://spark-packages.org/` provides a complete list of third-party packages.

Spark SQL can be implemented in the Java, Scala, Python, and R languages. Using the distributed SQL engine of Spark SQL, pure SQLs can also be written.

Interoperability between RDDs and others

Datasets and DataFrames can interoperate with RDDs easily. DataFrames can be converted to RDDs or Pandas DataFrames and vice versa using the `.rdd`, `.toDF`, and `.toPandas` `.toDS` methods. Also, DataFrames can be used with Spark Streaming and Machine learning libraries as well.

Select and read necessary data only

One of the good features of Datasets, DataFrames, and Datasources API is to provide richer optimizations by pushing the predicates to the source systems. Column pruning, predicate pushdown, and partition pruning is done automatically by the framework. So, only the data that is needed is read and processed.

When to use RDDs, Datasets, and DataFrames?

The following table describes the scenarios in which RDDs, Datasets, or DataFrames are to be used:

Scenario	What to use?
Use of the Python programming language	RDDs or DataFrames
Use of the R programming language	DataFrames
Use of the Java or Scala programming languages	RDDs, Datasets, or DataFrames
Unstructured data such as images and videos	RDDs

Scenario	What to use?
Use of low level transformations, actions, and controls data flow programmatically	RDDs
Use of high-level domain-specific APIs	Datasets and DataFrames
Use of functional programming constructs to process data	RDDs
Use of higher level expressions including SQLs	Datasets and DataFrames
Imposing structure is not needed and low-level optimizations are not needed	RDDs
High compile time safety and rich optimizations	Datasets
No compile time safety and rich optimizations are needed	DataFrames
Unification is needed across Spark libraries	Datasets or DataFrames

Analytics with DataFrames

Let's learn how to create and use DataFrames for Big Data Analytics. For easy understanding and a quick example, the `pyspark` shell is to be used for the code in this chapter. The data needed for exercises used in this chapter can be found at `https://github.com/apache/spark/tree/master/examples/src/main/resources`. You can always create multiple data formats by reading one type of data file. For example, once you read `.json` file, you can write data in parquet, ORC, or other formats.

 All programs in this chapter are executed on CDH 5.8 VM except the programs in the *DataFrame based Spark-on-HBase connector* section, which are executed on HDP2.5. For other environments, file paths might change, but the concepts are the same in any environment.

Creating SparkSession

In Spark versions 1.6 and below, the entry point into all relational functionality in Spark is the `SQLContext` class. To create `SQLContext` in an application, we need to create a `SparkContext` and wrap `SQLContext` around it. Also, when working with Hive, we need to create `HiveContext` as shown in the following code:

```
from pyspark.sql import SQLContext
sqlContext = SQLContext(sc)

from pyspark.sql import HiveContext
sqlContext = HiveContext(sc)
```

From Spark version 2.0 and above, SparkSession is the entry point for relational functionality. When working with Hive, SparkSession must be created with the enableHiveSupport method to get access to Hive Metastore, SerDes, and user-defined functions.

```
from pyspark.sql import SparkSession

spark = SparkSession \
    .builder \
    .appName("Log Analytics") \
    .config("configuration_key", "configuration_value") \
    .enableHiveSupport() \
    .getOrCreate()
```

In pyspark shell or spark-shell, a pre-configured SparkSession called spark will be created automatically.

Creating DataFrames

There are multiple ways to create a DataFrame. It can be created from structured data files such as .json, .avro, .parquet, or it can be created from RDDs, hive tables, external databases, or pandas DataFrames. Copy the input files located in Spark's /examples/src/main/resources/ directory to HDFS before executing the following code.

Creating DataFrames from structured data files

To create DataFrames from Parquet, Json, and ORC files, use the sqlContext.read API as shown in the following. Start a pyspark shell, which will provide a pre-built SparkSession called spark.

```
>>> df_parquet = spark.read.parquet("users.parquet")
```

```
>>> df_json = spark.read.json("people.json")
```

Creating DataFrames from RDDs

There are multiple ways to create a DataFrame from RDDs. RDDs have no schema, so schema must be assigned before creating the DataFrame. Let's use the following list and schema to create a DataFrame in multiple ways:

```
>>> mylist = [(50, "DataFrame"),(60, "pandas")]
```

```
>>> myschema = ['col1', 'col2']
```

1. Create a DataFrame with a list, schema, and default data types:

   ```
   >>> df = spark.createDataFrame(mylist, myschema)
   ```

2. Create a DataFrame by parallelizing a list and converting the RDD to a DataFrame. Print the schema and show the contents of the DataFrame as shown in *Figure 4.7*:

   ```
   >>> mylist = [(50, "DataFrame"),(60, "pandas")]
   >>> myschema = ['col1', 'col2']
   >>> df = sc.parallelize(mylist).toDF(myschema)
   >>> df.printSchema()
   >>> df.show()
   ```

```
>>> mylist = [(50, "DataFrame"),(60, "pandas")]
>>> myschema = ['col1', 'col2']
>>> df = sc.parallelize(mylist).toDF(myschema)
>>> df.printSchema()
root
 |-- col1: long (nullable = true)
 |-- col2: string (nullable = true)

>>> df.show()
+----+---------+
|col1|     col2|
+----+---------+
|  50|DataFrame|
|  60|   pandas|
+----+---------+
```

Figure 4.7: Creating a DataFrame using a list and displaying it

3. Read the data from a file, infer schema, and convert it to DataFrame:

   ```
   >>> from pyspark.sql import Row
   >>> peopleRDD = sc.textFile("people.txt")
   >>> people_sp = peopleRDD.map(lambda l: l.split(","))
   >>> people = people_sp.map(lambda p: Row(name=p[0],
   age=int(p[1])))
   >>> df_people = spark.createDataFrame(people)
   >>> df_people.createOrReplaceTempView("people")
   >>> spark.sql("SHOW TABLES").show()
   +---------+-----------+
   ```

```
|tableName|isTemporary|
+---------+-----------+
|   people|       true|
+---------+-----------+
```

```
>>> spark.sql("SELECT name,age FROM people where age > 19").show()
+-------+---+
|   name|age|
+-------+---+
|Michael| 29|
|   Andy| 30|
+-------+---+
```

4. Read the data from the file and assign schema programmatically:

```
>>> from pyspark.sql.types import *
>>> peopleRDD = sc.textFile("people.txt")
>>> people_sp = peopleRDD.map(lambda l: l.split(","))
>>> people = people_sp.map(lambda p: Row(name=p[0],
age=int(p[1])))
>>> df_people = people_sp.map(lambda p: (p[0], p[1].strip()))
>>> schemaStr = "name age"
>>> fields = [StructField(field_name, StringType(), True) \
for field_name in schemaStr.split()]
>>> schema = StructType(fields)
>>> df_people = spark.createDataFrame(people,schema)
>>> df_people.show()
>>> df_people.createOrReplaceTempView("people")
>>> spark.sql("select * from people").show()
```

Creating DataFrames from tables in Hive

To create DataFrames from Hive tables, create a SparkSession with the enableHiveSupport method. This is equivalent to creating HiveContext. Use the following code for working with the existing `sample_07` Hive table. If the `sample_07` table does not exist in Hive, install Hive examples from step 2 in the HUE quick start wizard:

```
>>> sample_07 = spark.table("sample_07")
>>> sample_07.show()


>>> spark.sql("select * from sample_07 limit 5").show()
```

Creating DataFrames from external databases

To create a DataFrame from external databases, use the `sqlContext.read` API with `jdbc` as the format and provide the connect string, table name, user ID, and password as options.

First, copy the `/usr/lib/hive/lib/mysql-connector-java.jar` to the JARs directory of Spark, or when starting pyspark shell provide the `--jars` dependency for `mysql-connector-java.jar`:

```
>>> df = spark.read.format('jdbc').options(url='jdbc:mysql://
localhost:3306/retail_db?user=root&password=cloudera',
dbtable='departments').load()


# This code can be re-written as follows.
>>> df = spark.read.format('jdbc').options(url='jdbc:mysql://
localhost:3306/retail_db', dbtable='departments', user='root',
password='cloudera').load()
>>> df.show()
```

Converting DataFrames to RDDs

Converting DataFrames to RDDs is very simple and you just need to use the .rdd method as shown in *Figure 4.8*. Let's display the content of the df DataFrame from the previous example, convert it to a .rdd, and collect the content of the .rdd. Notice that when you convert the DataFrame to an RDD, you get an RDD of the rows:

```
>>> df.show() // Print the content of DataFrame
```

```
>>> df2rdd.df.rdd
```

```
>>> df2rdd.take(2)
```

```
>>> df = spark.read.format('jdbc').options(url='jdbc:mysql://loc
alhost:3306/retail_db?user=root&password=cloudera', dbtable='dep
artments').load()
>>> df.show()
+-------------+---------------+
|department_id|department_name|
+-------------+---------------+
|            2|        Fitness|
|            3|       Footwear|
|            4|        Apparel|
|            5|           Golf|
|            6|       Outdoors|
|            7|       Fan Shop|
+-------------+---------------+

>>> df2rdd = df.rdd
>>> df2rdd.take(2)
[Row(department_id=2, department_name=u'Fitness'), Row(departmen
t_id=3, department_name=u'Footwear')]
```

Figure 4.8: DataFrame and RDD from MySQL database

Common Dataset/DataFrame operations

A Dataset/DataFrame has many functions for reading and writing data, transforming data with **Domain Specific Language** (DSL), and actions to kick off transformations. Let's go through some of the most commonly-used DataFrame functions.

Input and Output Operations

Input and Output operations are used for loading and saving data:

- read: Provides generic read functions for any data source
- write: Provides generic write functions for any data source

Basic Dataset/DataFrame functions

Basic Dataset/DataFrame functions are to create DataFrames and perform operations for debugging on console:

- `As[U]`: Returns new Dataset mapping records to specific types
- `toDF`: Returns a new DataFrame with columns renamed
- `explain`: Prints the (logical and physical) plans to the console for debugging purposes
- `printSchema`: Prints out the schema in the tree format
- `createTempView`: Registers this DataFrame as a temporary table using the given name
- `cache()` or `persist()`: Persists the Dataset with specified persistence level

DSL functions

Domain Specific Language (DSL) functions are used for analytics. These functions are lazy and do not kick off the execution.

- `agg`: Aggregates on the entire Dataset/DataFrame without groups
- `distinct`: Return a new Dataset/DataFrame with unique rows
- `drop`: Return a new Dataset/DataFrame with a column dropped
- `filter`: Filters rows using the given condition
- `join`: Join with another Dataset/DataFrame using the given join expression
- `limit`: Returns a new Dataset/DataFrame by taking the first n rows
- `sort`: Returns a new Dataset/DataFrame sorted in ascending order by the specified column
- `groupby`: Groups the Dataset/DataFrame using the specified columns
- `unionAll`: Returns a new Dataset/DataFrame containing a union of rows from two DataFrames
- `na`: For working with missing or null values

Built-in functions, aggregate functions, and window functions

Built-in functions or user-defined functions operate on single rows to calculate a single value. Examples of built-in functions are `substr` or `round`. Aggregate functions operate on a set of rows and calculate a single value. Examples of aggregate functions are `min`, `max`, `sum`, `mean`, `first`, `last`, `avg`, `count`, `countDistinct`, and `approxCountDistinct`. Window functions operate on a set of rows related to the current row. Examples of DataFrame window functions are `rank`, `denseRank`, `percentRank`, `ntile`, and `rowNumber`.

Actions

Actions begin execution. Some examples of actions are:

- `collect`: Returns an array that contains all rows in this DataFrame
- `count`: Counts the number of rows in the DataFrame
- `describe`: Computes statistics for numeric columns
- `show`: Prints the first n rows to the console
- `take`: Returns the first num rows as a list of rows

RDD operations

Regular RDD operations such as `map`, `flatMap`, `coalesce`, `repartition`, `foreach`, `toJson`, and `toJavaRDD` can be applied on DataFrames. These are really helpful because all kinds of functions are not available within DSL. For example, you can apply the `foreach` function to print `col2` of the DataFrame as shown in the following:

```
>>> def f(mydf):
...     print(mydf.department_name)
...
>>> df.foreach(f)
Fitness
Footwear
Apparel
Golf
Outdoors
Fan Shop
```

Caching data

Spark SQL tables can be cached in an in-memory columnar format by using the `df.persist()` method. Spark SQL will scan only the required columns from the columnar in-memory table. It also automatically tunes compression to minimize memory usage and garbage collection pressure. The DataFrame can be un-persisted using `df.unpersist()`.

Performance optimizations

Let's look at some of the important performance tuning parameters of Spark SQL:

- `spark.sql.inMemoryColumnarStorage.compressed` is enabled to true by default, which will compress the data.

- `spark.sql.inMemoryColumnarStorage.batchSize` is set to `10000`, which controls the batch size for columnar caching.

- `spark.sql.autoBroadcastJoinThreshold` is set to 10 MB by default. This configures the maximum size in bytes for a table that will be broadcast to all worker nodes when performing a join.

- `spark.sql.files.maxPartitionBytes` is set to 128 MB, which is the size to store in a single partition while reading data.

- `spark.sql.shuffle.partitions` is set to `200` by default. This configures the number of partitions when shuffling data.

- `spark.sql.planner.externalSort` is set to `true` by default. This performs sorts that spill to disk as needed; otherwise it sorts each partition in memory.

Analytics with the Dataset API

Datasets are similar to RDDs; however, instead of using Java or Kryo Serialization, they use a specialized Encoder to serialize the objects for processing or transmitting over the network. While both encoders and standard serialization are responsible for turning an object into bytes, encoders are generated dynamically and use a format that allows Spark to perform many operations such as filtering, sorting, and hashing without deserializing the bytes back into an object. Source: `https://spark.apache.org/docs/latest/sql-programming-guide.html#creating-datasets`.

Creating Datasets

The following Scala example creates a Dataset and DataFrame from an RDD. Enter the scala shell with the spark-shell command:

```
scala> case class Dept(dept_id: Int, dept_name: String)
defined class Dept


scala> val deptRDD = sc.makeRDD(Seq(Dept(1,"Sales"),Dept(2,"HR")))
deptRDD: org.apache.spark.rdd.RDD[Dept] = ParallelCollectionRDD[0] at
makeRDD at <console>:26


scala> val deptDS = spark.createDataset(deptRDD)
deptDS: org.apache.spark.sql.Dataset[Dept] = [dept_id: int, dept_name:
string]


scala> val deptDF = spark.createDataFrame(deptRDD)
deptDF: org.apache.spark.sql.DataFrame = [dept_id: int, dept_name:
string]


scala> deptDS.rdd
res12: org.apache.spark.rdd.RDD[Dept] = MapPartitionsRDD[5] at rdd at
<console>:31


scala> deptDF.rdd
res13: org.apache.spark.rdd.RDD[org.apache.spark.sql.Row] =
MapPartitionsRDD[8] at rdd at <console>:31
```

Notice that when you convert a Dataset to RDD, you get RDD[Dept]. But, when you convert a DataFrame to RDD, you get RDD[Row].

A compile-time safety check is done as shown in the following code. Since dept_location is not a member of the Dept case class, it will throw an error.

```
scala> deptDS.filter(x => x.dept_location > 1).show()
<console>:31: error: value dept_location is not a member of Dept
        deptDS.filter(x => x.dept_location > 1).show()
```

Converting a DataFrame to a Dataset

A DataFrame can be converted to a Dataset by providing a class with the as method as shown in the following example:

```scala
scala> val newDeptDS = deptDF.as[Dept]

newDeptDS: org.apache.spark.sql.Dataset[Dept] = [dept_id: int, dept_name:
string]

scala> newDeptDS.show()
+-------+---------+
|dept_id|dept_name|
+-------+---------+
|      1|    Sales|
|      2|       HR|
+-------+---------+
```

Converting a Dataset to a DataFrame

Use the toDF function to convert a Dataset to a DataFrame. Here is another Scala example for converting the Dataset created above to a DataFrame:

```scala
scala> newDeptDS.first()
res27: Dept = Dept(1,Sales)


scala> newDeptDS.toDF.first()
res28: org.apache.spark.sql.Row = [1,Sales]
```

Note that res27 is resulting in a Dept case class object and res28 is resulting in a Row object.

Accessing metadata using Catalog

Accessing metadata information about Hive tables and UDFs is made easy with the Catalog API. The following commands explain how to access metadata:

```scala
scala> spark.catalog.listDatabases().select("name").show()
+--------+
|    name|
+--------+
| default|
```

```
+-------+
```

```
scala> spark.catalog.listTables.show()
+---------+--------+-----------+---------+-----------+
|     name|database|description|tableType|isTemporary|
+---------+--------+-----------+---------+-----------+
|customers| default|       null| EXTERNAL|      false|
|sample_07| default|       null|  MANAGED|      false|
|sample_08| default|       null|  MANAGED|      false|
| web_logs| default|       null|  MANAGED|      false|
|jsontable|    null|       null|TEMPORARY|       true|
+---------+--------+-----------+---------+-----------+
```

```
scala> spark.catalog.isCached("sample_07")
res29: Boolean = false
```

The `createTempView` and `dropTempView` methods are used to create and drop temporary tables using the DataFrame API or the Dataset API.

`spark.catalog.listFunctions().show()` will list the functions available with a description.

Data Sources API

The Data Sources API provides a single interface for loading and storing data using Spark SQL. In addition to the built-in sources, this API provides an easy way for developers to add support for custom data sources. All available external packages are listed at `http://spark-packages.org/`. Let's learn how to use built-in sources and external sources in this section.

Read and write functions

The Data Sources API provides generic read and write functions that can used for any kind of data source. Generic read and write functions provide two functionalities as given in the following:

- Parses text records, JSON records, and other formats and deserializes data stored in binary
- Converts Java objects to rows of Avro, JSON, Parquet, and HBase records

The default data source is set to parquet with the `spark.sql.sources.default` configuration property. This can be changed as needed.

Built-in sources

Built-in sources are pre-packaged with Spark by default. Examples of built-in sources are Text, JSON, Parquet, ORC, JDBC, and CSV.

Working with text files

To load text files, we use the text method, which will return a single column with the column name set to value and type as string. Note that the Dataset API is not supported in Python language. So, in Python language, a DataFrame is returned while in Scala language Dataset it is returned, as shown in the following:

```
>>> df_txt = spark.read.text("people.txt")
>>> df_txt.show()
+-----------+
|      value|
+-----------+
|Michael, 29|
|   Andy, 30|
| Justin, 19|
+-----------+
>>> df_txt
DataFrame[value: string]
```

Working with JSON

Spark SQL can automatically infer the schema of a JSON dataset when loading to a DataFrame:

```
>>> df_json = spark.read.json("people.json")
>>> df_json.printSchema()
root
 |-- age: long (nullable = true)
 |-- name: string (nullable = true)
```

You can also use the load method to load files. The following command will throw an exception with the message **NOT A PARQUET FILE**. Because, the default data source is configured to parquet. So, to read a `.json` file, use format to specify the type of datasource:

```
>>> df_json = spark.read.load("people.json")
```

Manually specify the type of file with `format`:

```
>>> df_json = spark.read.load("people.json", format="json")
```

To write data to another JSON file, use one of the following commands:

```
>>> df_json.write.json("newjson_dir")
>>> df_json.write.format("json").save("newjson_dir2")
```

To write data to any other format, just mention the format you want to save. The following example saves the `df_json` DataFrame in Parquet format:

```
>>> df_json.write.parquet("parquet_dir")
>>> df_json.write.format("parquet").save("parquet_dir2")
```

Working with Parquet

Apache Parquet is a columnar storage format that provides superior performance and is available in any Hadoop project. File format documentation can be found at `https://parquet.apache.org/documentation/latest/`.

As mentioned earlier, whatever the type of data source, similar read and write functions of DataSources API are used. So, let's use read and write functions for parquet files in the parquet_dir directory as well.

To create a DataFrame from a Parquet file and issue SQL commands, use the following command:

```
>>> df_parquet = spark.read.load("parquet_dir")
```

Or use the following command:

```
>>> df_parquet = spark.read.parquet("parquet_dir")
```

Note that format is not needed when using the load method because parquet is the default data source. This reads all parquet files from the `parquet_dir` directory:

```
>>> df_parquet.createOrReplaceTempView("parquet_table");
>>> teenagers = spark.sql("SELECT name from parquet_table where age >= 13 AND age <= 19")
```

To write the data from a parquet DataFrame to `.json` format, use one of the write commands:

```
>>> df_parquet.write.json("myjson_dir")
>>> df_parquet.write.format("json").save("myjson_dir2")
```

There are multiple modes while writing data. By default, error mode is enabled, which will throw an error if output already exists. Other modes are `append`, `overwrite`, and `ignore` when the target data source already exists. The following example appends data to the `myjson_dir` and `parquet_dir` directory:

```
>>> df_parquet.write.mode("append").json("myjson_dir")
>>> df_parquet.write.mode("append").save("parquet_dir")
```

A DataFrame can be written to a Hive Table. The following example writes data to a hive managed table in the default Parquet format:

```
>>> df_parquet.write.saveAsTable("hive_parquet_table")
```

Parquet supports schema evolution such as ProtocolBuffer, Avro, and Thrift. Multiple schemas can be merged by setting the global option, `spark.sql.parquet.mergeSchema` to `true` or using the `mergeSchema` option as shown in the following:

```
>>> df_parquet = spark.read.option("mergeSchema", "true").
parquet("parquet_dir")
```

Table partitioning is a common optimization approach used in parquet hive tables as well. Partition discovery and partition pruning happen automatically for queries performed on Parquet tables. Also, while writing the parquet tables, data can be partitioned using the `partitionBy` method.

Since Parquet is a columnar format, column pruning is automatic and also predicate pushdown is automatic by default with the `spark.sql.parquet.filterPushdown` parameter set to `true`.

Working with ORC

The **Optimized Row Columnar (ORC)** file format provides an efficient way to store data. More details on file format and documentation can be found at `https://cwiki.apache.org/confluence/display/Hive/LanguageManual+ORC`.

1. Let's create an ORC file by writing data from a json DataFrame. Use one of the two commands listed:

```
>>> df_json.write.orc("myorc_dir")
>>> df_json.write.format("orc").save("myorc_dir")
```

2. Then, let's read the ORC files with a generic read function:

```
>>> df_orc = spark.read.orc("myorc_dir")
>>> df_orc = spark.read.load("myorc_dir", format="orc")
```

3. Write the DataFrame created in JSON format to a hive managed table in ORC format:

```
>>> df_json.write.saveAsTable("hive_orc_table","orc")
```

Column Pruning: Since ORC is a columnar format, columns needed by the query are read-only.

Predicate Push-down: ORC enables predicate pushdown with the following parameter (with the help of indexes within each file). Check the current configuration and then change the value:

```
>>> spark.conf.get("spark.sql.orc.filterPushdown")
u'false'
>>> spark.conf.set("spark.sql.orc.filterPushdown","true")
>>> spark.conf.get("spark.sql.orc.filterPushdown")
u'true'
```

Partition Pruning: Just like Parquet tables, partition discovery and partition pruning are automatic for ORC tables too. To create ORC files, partitioning data by a column, use the following syntax:

```
>>> df_json.write.format("orc").partitionBy("age").save("partitioned_
orc")
```

Working with JDBC

Spark SQL provides easy integration with external databases using JDBC. To use this functionality, you will need to include the JDBC driver for your particular database on the spark classpath. For example, in order to connect to a Postgres database from the Spark shell, you will use the following command or copy the jdbc jar to the jars directory of SPARK_HOME:

```
[cloudera@quickstart spark-2.0.0-bin-hadoop2.7 ]$  SPARK_
CLASSPATH=postgresql-9.3-1102-jdbc41.jar bin/pyspark
```

Tables from external databases can be loaded into Spark SQL as a DataFrame or as a temporary table. The following options are supported while creating a DataFrame using jdbc:

Parameter	Meaning
`url`	JDBC URL connection string
`Dbtable`	Name of the table
	This can be a SQL query as well
`Driver`	Class name of the JDBC driver
`partitionColumn`, `lowerBound`, `upperBound`, `numPartitions`	Partitioning info on the database
	All options must be used together

Let's create a DataFrame using one of the two commands given in the following:

```
>>> df = spark.read.format('jdbc').options(url='jdbc:mysql://
localhost:3306/retail_db?user=root&password=cloudera',
dbtable='departments').load()
```

```
>>> df = spark.read.format('jdbc').options(url='jdbc:mysql://
localhost:3306/retail_db', dbtable='departments', user='root',
password='cloudera').load()
```

```
>>> df.show()
```

Then, register it as a temporary table and query it:

```
>>> df.createTempView("dept")
```

```
>>> df_new = spark.sql("select * from dept where department_id> 5")
```

Let's write the DataFrame to another table in the MySQL database. This will create the table and write the data out:

```
>>> df_new.write.jdbc("jdbc:mysql://localhost:3306/retail_db?user=root&pa
ssword=cloudera","new_table")
```

To write the DataFrame to another table in the MySQL database (and also specify the overwrite option to overwrite the data if the table is already existing):

```
>>> df_new.write.jdbc("jdbc:mysql://localhost:3306/retail_db?user=root&pa
ssword=cloudera","new_table","overwrite")
```

Working with CSV

Download a `.csv` dataset as shown in the following and then copy it to HDFS. Start a pyspark shell to create a DataFrame from a `.csv` file:

```
[cloudera@quickstart spark-2.0.0-bin-hadoop2.7 ]$  wget https://raw.
githubusercontent.com/databricks/spark-csv/master/src/test/resources/
cars.csv --no-check-certificate
```

```
[cloudera@quickstart spark-2.0.0-bin-hadoop2.7 ]$ hadoop fs -put cars.csv
```

```
>>> csv_df = spark.read.options(header='true',inferSchema='true').
csv("cars.csv")
>>> csv_df.printSchema()
root
 |-- year: integer (nullable = true)
 |-- make: string (nullable = true)
 |-- model: string (nullable = true)
 |-- comment: string (nullable = true)
 |-- blank: string (nullable = true)
```

Let's select a few columns and write the DataFrame to another CSV file with a different compression codec.

```
>>> csv_df.select('year', 'model').write.options(codec="org.apache.
hadoop.io.compress.GzipCodec").csv('newcars.csv')
```

External sources

External data sources are not included in spark by default. External data sources are available in Spark Packages, which is an index of packages contributed by the Spark community.

Spark Packages offers packages for reading different file formats and data from NoSQL databases such as HBase, Cassandra, and so on. When you want to include a Spark package in your application you need to use the `--packages` command-line option with a comma-separated list of maven coordinates of JARs to include on the driver and executor classpaths. When specified, it will search the local maven repo, then maven central and any additional remote repositories given by the `--repositories` option. The format for the coordinates should be `groupId:artifactId:version`.

Working with AVRO

Let's start the pyspark shell by providing the `--packages` dependency:

```
[cloudera@quickstart spark-2.0.0-bin-hadoop2.7 ]~  bin/pyspark --packages
com.databricks:spark-avro_2.11:3.0.0
```

Let's read the JSON file, write it in AVRO format, and then read the same file:

```
>>> df_json = spark.read.json("people.json")
```

```
>>> df_json.write.format("com.databricks.spark.avro").save("avro_out")
```

```
>>> df_avro = spark.read.format("com.databricks.spark.avro").load("avro_
out")
```

You can specify the record name and namespace to use when writing out by passing `recordName` and `recordNamespace` as optional parameters to Spark:

```
>>> df_avro.write.format("com.databricks.spark.avro").
option("recordName","AvroTest").option("recordNamespace","com.cloudera.
spark").save("newavro")
```

Working with XML

Reading XML data will be same as AVRO where we include external `.xml` package with pyspark shell. Perform the following steps to download `.xml` file and work with it:

1. Let's download a sample `.xml` file from the following mentioned location and copy it to HDFS:

    ```
    [cloudera@quickstart ~]$ wget https://raw.githubusercontent.com/
    databricks/spark-xml/master/src/test/resources/books.xml --no-
    check-certificate
    ```

    ```
    [cloudera@quickstart ~]$ hadoop fs -put books.xml
    ```

2. Let's start the pyspark shell by providing `--packages` dependency. Spark compiled with Scala 2.11 use spark-xml_2.11:0.4.0 and Spark compiled with Scala 2.10 use spark-xml_2.10:0.4.0:

    ```
    [cloudera@quickstart spark-2.0.0-bin-hadoop2.7]$ bin/pyspark
    --master yarn --packages com.databricks:spark-xml_2.11:0.4.0
    ```

3. Then, let's read the `.xml` file and select data elements from DataFrame:

    ```
    >>> df_xml = spark.read.format('com.databricks.spark.xml').options
    (rowTag='book',attributePrefix='@').load('books.xml')
    ```

    ```
    >>> df_xml.select('@id','author','title').show(5,False)
    ```

```
+-----+-------------------+--------------------+
|@id  |author             |title               |
+-----+-------------------+--------------------+
|bk101|Gambardella, Matthew|XML Developer's Guide|
|bk102|Ralls, Kim         |Midnight Rain       |
|bk103|Corets, Eva        |Maeve Ascendant     |
|bk104|Corets, Eva        |Oberon's Legacy     |
|bk105|Corets, Eva        |The Sundered Grail  |
+-----+-------------------+--------------------+
>>> df_xml.where(df_xml.author == "Corets, Eva").select("@id",
"author", "title", "price").withColumn("new_price",df_xml.price *
10).drop("price").show()
+-----+-----------+------------------+---------+
| @id|     author|             title|new_price|
+-----+-----------+------------------+---------+
|bk103|Corets, Eva|   Maeve Ascendant|     59.5|
|bk104|Corets, Eva|   Oberon's Legacy|     59.5|
|bk105|Corets, Eva|The Sundered Grail|     59.5|
+-----+-----------+------------------+---------+
```

Working with Pandas

Pandas is a Python library for data manipulation. Use the following commands
to create a DataFrame in Pandas and convert it to Spark DataFrame and vice versa.
Install pandas using pip if it is not done already:

```
>>> import pandas
>>> data = [
('v1', 'v5', 'v9'),
('v2', 'v6', 'v10'),
('v3', 'v7', 'v11'),
('v4', 'v8', 'v12')]

>>> pandas_df = pandas.DataFrame(data, columns=['col1', 'col2', 'col3'])

>>> spark_df = spark.createDataFrame(pandas_df)

>>> spark_df.toPandas()
```

DataFrame based Spark-on-HBase connector

HBase does not offer SQL as a means to query the data. It exposes GET, SCAN, and FILTER APIs, which are difficult to implement in ad-hoc queries. So usually, for analyzing the data on HBase, it is common to write MapReduce programs using Java. Integration with Hive or Pig provides an easy way to write SQLs or scripts to analyze the data, but they are not efficient since they use TableInputFormat instead of the native HBase API. Apache Phoenix provides an easy way to integrate with HBase and write relational queries. Spark-on-HBase connector is a new connector based on the DataFrame framework and is created using the standard Datasource API so it can be simply used by specifying the packages option. It does not leverage TableInputFormat, but it creates a customized RDD that can implement partition and column pruning, predicate push down, and data locality. It also leverages the Spark Catalyst optimizer for optimizations. The following exercise was tried on HDP 2.5 sandbox version with Spark version 1.6.2.

Let's get started with Spark-on-HBase connector using the following steps:

1. Copy `hbase-site.xml` to the spark configuration directory:

    ```
    cp /etc/hbase/conf/hbase-site.xml /etc/spark/conf/
    ```

2. Create an HBase table and insert some data into it. Though there is a way to create a table and insert data using this connector, it is more common to analyze the data on an existing table:

    ```
    hbase(main):001:0> create 'IOTEvents', {NAME => 'e', VERSIONS =>
    100}

    hbase(main):002:0> put 'IOTEvents', '100', 'e:status', 'active'

    hbase(main):003:0> put 'IOTEvents', '100', 'e:e_time',
    '1470009600'

    hbase(main):004:0> put 'IOTEvents', '200', 'e:status', 'active'

    hbase(main):005:0> put 'IOTEvents', '200', 'e:e_time',
    '1470013200'

    hbase(main):006:0> put 'IOTEvents', '300', 'e:status', 'inactive'
    ```

3. Start spark shell with the packages option:

    ```
    [cloudera@quickstart spark-2.0.0-bin-hadoop2.7 ]$ spark-shell
    --packages zhzhan:shc:0.0.11-1.6.1-s_2.10
    ```

4. Define a catalog with HBase and DataFrame mapping and define a function
    to read data from HBase. Create a DataFrame using the `catalog` and
    `read` functions:

```
import org.apache.spark.sql.execution.datasources.hbase._


def iotCatalog = s"""{
  |"table":{"namespace":"default", "name":"IOTEvents"},
  |"rowkey":"key",
  |"columns":{
    |"Rowkey":{"cf":"rowkey", "col":"key", "type":"string"},
    |"Status":{"cf":"e", "col":"status", "type":"string"},
    |"Event_time":{"cf":"e", "col":"e_time", "type":"string"}
  |}
|}""".stripMargin


import org.apache.spark.sql._


def readHBase(cat: String): DataFrame = {
  sqlContext
  .read
  .options(Map(HBaseTableCatalog.tableCatalog->cat))
  .format("org.apache.spark.sql.execution.datasources.hbase")
  .load()
}


val iotEventsDF = readHBase(iotCatalog)
```

5. Once the DataFrame is created, all DataFrame operations can be applied on
    top of it:

```
iotEventsDF.show()


+------+----------+--------+
|Rowkey|Event_time|  Status|
+------+----------+--------+
|   100|1470009600|  active|
|   200|1470013200|  active|
```

```
|   300|      null|inactive|
+------+---------+--------+
```

```
iotEventsDF.filter($"Status" === "inactive").show()
```

```
+------+---------+--------+
|Rowkey|Event_time|  Status|
+------+---------+--------+
|   300|      null|inactive|
+------+---------+--------+
```

6. Register the DataFrame as a temporary table and query it:

```
iotEventsDF.registerTempTable("iotevents")
```

```
sqlContext.sql("select count(Rowkey) as count from iotevents").
show
```

```
+-----+
|count|
+-----+
|    3|
+-----+
```

```
sqlContext.sql("select Rowkey, Event_time, Status from iotevents
where Status = 'active'").show
+------+----------+------+
|Rowkey|Event_time|Status|
+------+----------+------+
|   100|1470009600|active|
|   200|1470013200|active|
+------+----------+------+
```

Spark SQL as a distributed SQL engine

Spark SQL is generally used in two different ways. The first way is to use it as a library to write SQL, Hive QL, DSL, or to write queries in languages such as Java, Scala, Python, or R. The second way is to use it as a distributed SQL engine in which clients connect to a Thrift server and submit SQL or Hive QL queries using JDBC or ODBC interfaces. It is really useful for data warehousing users to write and execute queries from **Business Intelligence (BI)** tools interactively. So, Spark SQL can be used for data warehousing solutions as well a distributed SQL query engine.

Spark SQL's Thrift server for JDBC/ODBC access

Spark SQL's thrift server provides JDBC access to Spark SQL.

The Thrift JDBC server corresponds to HiveServer2 in Hive. You can test the JDBC server with the beeline client or any SQL client. From Spark 1.6, by default, the Thrift server runs in multi-session mode.

For a complete list of options for starting `thriftserver`, use the following command. Note the similar options for `spark-submit`, `spark-shell`, or `pyspark` shell:

```
./start-thriftserver.sh --help
```

```
Usage: ./sbin/start-thriftserver [options] [thrift server options]
```

To start the JDBC/ODBC server, run the following command in Spark's `sbin` directory:

```
./start-thriftserver.sh --master yarn --hiveconf hive.server2.thrift.
bind.host=localhost --hiveconf hive.server2.thrift.port=10001
```

Check the `thriftserver` log in the logs directory, which shows that it is connecting to the Hive metastore and thrift server listening on port number 10001. You can check the JDBC/ODBC Server tab in Spark's UI to check the number of users connected, their details, and also SQL statistics. The easiest way to open this UI is to go to Yarn's resource manager UI and then click on the Application Master's tracking UI.

Apache Spark needs to be built with Hive support by adding the `-Phive` and `-Phive-thriftserver` profiles to the build options.

Querying data using beeline client

After starting the Thrift server, it can be tested using `beeline`:

```
bin/beeline -u "jdbc:hive2://localhost:10001/default;hive.server2.
transport.mode=http;hive.server2.thrift.http.path=cliservice"
```

`beeline` will ask you for a username and password. In non-secure mode, providing a blank user ID and password will work.

Once you are connected to the beeline client, issue Hive QL or SQL commands:

```
0: jdbc:hive2://localhost:10001/default> show tables;
+-------------+---------------+--+
| tableName   | isTemporary   |
+-------------+---------------+--+
| customers   | false         |
| log         | false         |
| sample_07   | false         |
| sample_08   | false         |
| web_logs    | false         |
+-------------+---------------+--+


CREATE TEMPORARY TABLE jsonTable
USING org.apache.spark.sql.json
OPTIONS (
path "/user/cloudera/people.json"
);

0: jdbc:hive2://localhost:10001/default> show tables;
+-------------+---------------+--+
| tableName   | isTemporary   |
+-------------+---------------+--+
| customers   | false         |
| log         | false         |
| sample_07   | false         |
| sample_08   | false         |
| web_logs    | false         |
| jsontable   | true          |
+-------------+---------------+--+

0: jdbc:hive2://localhost:10001/default> select * from jsontable;
+-------+----------+--+
|  age  |   name   |
+-------+----------+--+
```

```
| NULL  | Michael  |
| 30    | Andy     |
| 19    | Justin   |
+-------+----------+--+
3 rows selected (1.13 seconds)
0: jdbc:hive2://localhost:10001/default> select * from jsontable where
age > 19;
+------+-------+--+
| age  | name  |
+------+-------+--+
| 30   | Andy  |
+------+-------+--+
1 row selected (0.624 seconds)
0: jdbc:hive2://localhost:10001/default> REFRESH TABLE jsonTable

CREATE TEMPORARY TABLE jdbcTable
USING org.apache.spark.sql.jdbc
OPTIONS (
url "jdbc:postgresql:dbserver",
dbtable "schema.tablename"
)
```

The SQL tab on Spark's UI will show the all the jobs finished with the logical plan, physical plan, and visual DAG for the jobs. This is useful in debugging and performance tuning.

Querying data from Hive using spark-sql CLI

The Spark SQL CLI is a command line tool to run the Hive metastore service in local mode and execute queries from the command line. Spark SQL CLI cannot talk to the Thrift JDBC server.

To start the Spark SQL CLI, use the following command:

```
./bin/spark-sql
spark-sql> show tables;
spark-sql> select count(*) from tab1;
```

You may run `./bin/spark-sql --help` for a complete list of all available options.

Integration with BI tools

To integrate BI tools such as Tableau or Qlikview, install the ODBC drivers for Spark from: `http://databricks.com/spark-odbc-driver-download`.

Configure and start the thrift server as mentioned in the previous section. Start Tableau and select the option to connect to Spark SQL. Configure the hostname, port number 10001, and necessary authentication details and click **OK**. This will enable us to access tables from the Hive Metastore and execute queries on the Spark Execution engine.

Note that you can only query tables that registered with the Hive Metastore.

Hive on Spark

The Hive on Spark project was created to enable existing Hive users to run hive queries directly on the Spark execution engine instead of MapReduce.

Hive on Spark (`https://issues.apache.org/jira/browse/HIVE-7292`) is supported in the Cloudera distribution. To start using the service, change the execution to Spark in the Hive or beeline client:

```
hive> set hive.execution.engine=spark;

0: jdbc:hive2://localhost:10000/default> set hive.execution.engine=spark;
```

Summary

Users of Spark have three different APIs to interact with distributed collections of data: the RDD API, the DataFrames API, and the new Dataset API. Traditional RDD APIs provide type safety and powerful lambda functions but not optimized performance. The Dataset API and the DataFrame API provide easier ways to work with domain-specific language and provide superior performance over RDDs. The Dataset API combines both RDDs and DataFrames. Users have a choice to work with RDDs, DataFrames, or Datasets depending on their needs. But, in general, DataFrame or Dataset are preferred over conventional RDDs for better performance. Spark SQL uses a catalyst optimizer under the hood to provide optimization.

Dataset/DataFrame APIs provide optimization, speed, automatic schema discovery, multiple sources support, multiple language support, and predicate pushdown; moreover, they are interoperable with RDDs and Datasets. The Dataset API was introduced in version 1.6, which is available in Scala and Java languages. Spark 2.0 unified the Dataset and DataFrame APIs to provide a single abstraction for users. So, in Spark 2.0, DataFrame is equivalent to Dataset[Row].

The Data Sources API provides an easy way to read and save various sources including built-in sources such as Parquet, ORC, JSON, CSV, and JDBC, and external sources such as AVRO, XML, HBASE, Cassandra, and so on.

Spark SQL can be used as a distributed SQL query engine using Thrift server, which provides JDBC access to Spark SQL. Once the Thrift server is started, it can be accessed from any SQL client such as beeline, or any business intelligence tool such as Tableau or Qlikview.

Hive-on-Spark project was created for existing users to run Hive queries. So, existing HiveQL scripts can be run on the Spark execution engine instead of the MapReduce engine.

The next chapter introduces real-time analytics with Spark Streaming.

5
Real-Time Analytics with Spark Streaming and Structured Streaming

Spark Streaming supports real-time processing of fast moving, streaming data to gain insights for business and make business decisions in real-time or near real-time. It is an extension to Spark core to support stream processing. Spark Streaming is production-ready and is used in many organizations. This chapter helps you get started with writing real-time applications including Kafka and HBase. This chapter also helps you to get started with the new concept of Structured Streaming introduced in Spark 2.0.

This chapter is divided into the following sub-topics:

- Introducing real-time processing
- Architecture of Spark Streaming
- Stateless and stateful stream processing
- Transformations and actions
- Input sources and output stores
- Spark Streaming with Kafka and HBase
- Advanced Spark Streaming concepts
- Monitoring applications
- Introducing Structured Streaming

Introducing real-time processing

Big Data is generally ingested in real-time and the value of Big Data must be extracted on its arrival to make business decisions in real-time or near real-time, for example, fraud detection in financial transaction streams to accept or reject a transaction.

But, what is real-time and near real-time processing? The meaning of real-time or near real-time can vary from business to business and there is no standard definition for this. According to me, real-time means processing at the speed of a business. For a financial institution doing fraud detection, real-time means milliseconds for them. For a retail company doing click-stream analytics, real-time means seconds.

There are really only two paradigms for data processing: batch and real-time. Batch processing applications fundamentally provide high-latency, while real-time applications provide low latency. So, processing a few terabytes of data all at once will not be finished in a second. Real-time processing looks at smaller amounts of data as they arrive, to do intense computations as per the business requirements.

Real-time or near real-time systems allow you to respond to data as it arrives without necessarily persisting it to a database first. Stream processing is one kind of real-time processing that essentially processes a stream of events at high volume.

Every business wants to process the data in real-time to sustain their business. Real-time analytics are becoming a new standard way of data processing.

But, unlike batch processing, implementing real-time systems is more complex and requires a robust platform and framework for low latency response, high scalability, high reliability, and fault tolerance to keep applications running *24 x 7 x 365*. Failures can happen while receiving data from a streaming source, processing the data, and pushing the results to a database. So, the architecture should be robust enough to take care of failures at all levels, process a record exactly once, and not miss any records.

Spark Streaming provides near real-time processing responses with an approximate few hundred milliseconds latency and efficient fault tolerance. Many other frameworks such as Storm, Trident, Samza, and Apache Flink are available for real-time stream processing. The following table shows the differences between these frameworks:

	Spark Streaming	**Storm**	**Trident**	**Samza**	**Apache Flink**
Architecture	Micro-batch	Record-at-a-time	Micro-batch	Record-at-a-time	Continuous flow, operator-based
Language APIs	Java, Scala, Python	Java, Scala, Python, Ruby, Clojure	Java, Clojure, Scala	Java, Scala	Java, Scala
Resource Managers	Yarn, Mesos, Standalone	Yarn and Mesos	Yarn and Mesos	Yarn	Standalone, Yarn
Latency	~0.5 seconds	~100 Milliseconds	~0.5 seconds	~100 Milliseconds	~100 Milliseconds
Exactly once processing	Yes	No	Yes	No	Yes
Stateful Operations	Yes	No	Yes	Yes	Yes
Functions of sliding windows	Yes	No	Yes	No	Yes

Pros and cons of Spark Streaming

Let's take a look at some of the pros and cons of Spark Streaming.

Pros:

- Provides a simple programming model using Java, Scala, and Python APIs
- High throughput with fast fault recovery
- Integrates batch and streaming processing
- Easy to implement Spark SQL and **Machine Learning Library (MLlib)** operations within Spark Streaming

Cons:

- While micro-batch processing provides many benefits, latency is relatively higher than other record-at-time-based systems.

History of Spark Streaming

Spark Streaming was introduced to the Apache Spark project with its 0.7 release in February 2013. From the alpha testing phase, a stable version, 0.9, was released in February 2014. The Python API was added in Spark 1.2 with some limitations. All new releases introduced many new features and performance improvements such as Streaming UI, **write-ahead logs (WAL)**, exactly once write ahead log, direct Kafka support, and back pressure support.

Architecture of Spark Streaming

Spark Streaming processes a continuous stream of data by dividing the stream into micro-batches called a **Discretized Stream** or **DStream**. DStream is an API provided by Spark Streaming that creates and processes micro-batches. DStream is nothing but a sequence of RDDs processed on Spark's core execution engine like any other RDD. DStream can be created from any streaming source such as Flume or Kafka.

As shown in the following *Figure 5.1*, input data from streaming sources are received by the Spark Streaming application to create sub-second DStreams, which are then processed by the Spark core engine. Batches of each output are then sent to various output sinks. The input data is received by receivers and distributed across the cluster to form the micro-batch. Once the time interval completes, the micro-batch is processed through parallel operations such as join, transform, window operations, or output operations.

From deployment and execution perspective, Spark Streaming is just like a regular Spark job. But each executor will run a receiver to receive streaming data from input sources. Spark Streaming receivers chunk data into blocks before storing in the cluster. A new block is generated every `spark.streaming.blockInterval` milliseconds which is set to 200 milliseconds by default, and each block is turned into a partition of the RDD that Spark will work with.

Typically, one RDD is created in a batch by all receivers using the `getOrCompute` method of DStream. The number of partitions in the RDD created by DStream is determined by dividing `batchInterval` by `spark.streaming.blockInterval` and then multiplying it by the number of receivers. For example, if the batch interval is `1` second, the block interval is `200` miliseconds (default), and has a single receiver, your RDD will contain 10 partitions.

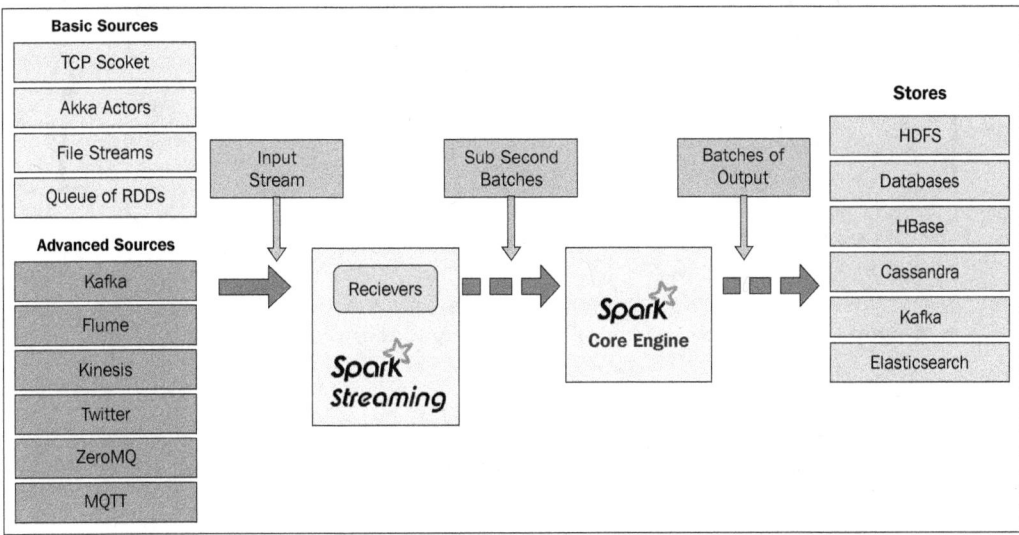

Figure 5.1: Spark Streaming architecture

Dividing input stream into micro-batches allows multiple advantages. Let's understand the benefits of DStream processing:

- **Dynamic load balancing**: Traditional record-at-a-time stream processing frameworks tend to partition streams unevenly to different nodes. Spark Streaming schedules tasks based on the availability of resources.

- **Fast failure recovery**: If any node fails, the tasks handled by the node will fail. Failed tasks are re-launched on other nodes to provide quick fault recovery.

- **Unification of batch and streaming**: Batch and Streaming workloads can be combined in the same program instead of separate processing.

- **Machine learning and SQL**: Machine learning models can be applied in real-time on DStreams. Also, DataFrames can be created from RDDs generated by DStreams and DataFrame operations can be applied with SQL or DSL.

- **Performance**: Spark Streaming provides higher throughput than other streaming frameworks, but the latency can be more than a few hundred milliseconds.

For reference visit `https://databricks.com/blog/2015/07/30/diving-into-spark-streamings-execution-model.html`.

Spark Streaming application flow

Let's understand the Spark Streaming application flow with a simple network word count example provided along with Spark installation, which can be found at `/spark/examples/lib/streaming/network_wordcount.py`:

 All programs in this chapter are executed on CDH 5.8 VM. For other environments, the file paths might change, but the concepts are the same in any environment.

```python
from __future__ import print_function
import sys
from pyspark import SparkContext
from pyspark.streaming import StreamingContext

if __name__ == "__main__":
    if len(sys.argv) != 3:
        print("Usage: network_wordcount.py <hostname> <port>",
file=sys.stderr)
        exit(-1)
    sc = SparkContext(appName="PythonStreamingNetworkWordCount")
    ssc = StreamingContext(sc, 1)

    lines = ssc.socketTextStream(sys.argv[1], int(sys.argv[2]))
    counts = lines.flatMap(lambda line: line.split(" "))\
                  .map(lambda word: (word, 1))\
                  .reduceByKey(lambda a, b: a+b)
    counts.pprint()
    ssc.start()
    ssc.awaitTermination()
```

The previous program creates a StreamingContext called ssc in local mode with the available number of execution threads and with a batch interval of 1 second. Using the ssc context, you can create a DStream called lines from a TCP source. Regular wordcount operations such as flatmap, map, and reduceByKey are applied to create a new DStream and the results are printed on screen. The ssc context then starts and waits for termination. The procedure to execute this program is shown in the next section.

Stateless and stateful stream processing

A stateless transformation applies a function on every batch of the DStream and produces the output. They do not depend on previous batches to create new batches. A stateful transformation creates a state for DStream and it will be updated with incoming batches of DStreams. There are two types of stateful transformations, window operations, which act on sliding windows, and updateStateByKey, which is used to track the state across all events. To understand stateless and stateful transformations, let's go through the examples provided along with Spark installation.

Let's start two terminals with the following commands:

- **Terminal 1**: Execute the Linux netcat command against port number 9999 as shown here:

  ```
  [cloudera@quickstart ~]$ nc -lk 9999
  ```

- **Terminal 2**: Submit network_wordcount.py shown in the previous section:

  ```
  [cloudera@quickstart ~]$ cd /usr/lib/spark/examples/lib/streaming/
  [cloudera@quickstart ~]$ sudo tar xvzf python.tar.gz
  [cloudera@quickstart lib]$ spark-submit --master local[*] network_
  wordcount.py localhost 9999
  ```

Enter some data in the `netcat` terminal as shown in the following *Figure 5.2*. You can see that `hadoop` and `spark` words are processed in the first batch to provide the count of 3 and then the next batch is processed to provide a count of 3 again. Notice that the counts are displayed every second because our streaming context is created with a batch of 1 second. You can increase this to see the difference:

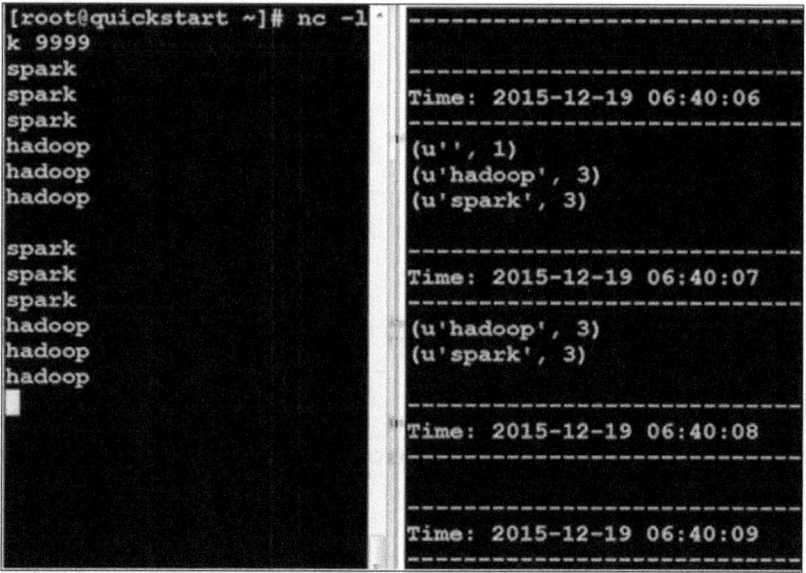

Figure 5.2: Stateless transformation example

Now let's take a look at a stateful transformation example:

- Terminal 1:

  ```
  [cloudera@quickstart ~]$ nc -lk 9999
  ```

- Terminal 2:

  ```
  [cloudera@quickstart streaming]$ spark-submit --master local[*]
  stateful_network_wordcount.py localhost 9999
  ```

```
[root@quickstart ~]# nc -l  Time: 2015-12-19 06:44:54
k 9999                      --------------------------
spark
spark                       (u'hadoop', 3)
spark                       (u'spark', 3)
hadoop
hadoop                      --------------------------
hadoop                      Time: 2015-12-19 06:44:55
spark                       --------------------------
spark
spark                       (u'hadoop', 5)
hadoop                      (u'spark', 6)
hadoop
hadoop                      --------------------------
                            Time: 2015-12-19 06:44:56
                            --------------------------

                            (u'hadoop', 6)
                            (u'spark', 6)

                            --------------------------
                            Time: 2015-12-19 06:44:57
                            --------------------------

                            (u'hadoop', 6)
                            (u'spark', 6)
```

Figure 5.3: Stateful transformation example

The `stateful_network_wordcount.py` program creates a DStream called `running_counts` and it is updated by the `updateStateByKey()` function with the incoming batches. Note that the second set of `hadoop` and `spark` words are added to the first set count to result in 6 as shown in *Figure 5.3*.

Fault tolerance in stateless transformation is achieved by replicating the DStreams in memory, but it is not fully recoverable in case of machine failures. The stateful transformation example writes the data to the checkpoint directory on HDFS for better recovery during failures. You can check the checkpoint directory with the following command. Checkpointing is explained in more detail in the *Advanced concepts of Spark Streaming* section:

```
[cloudera@quickstart streaming]$ hadoop fs -ls checkpoint
```

Also, check the number of jobs, tasks, and their DAG visualization on the UI at `http://localhost:4040/jobs`. The streaming application provides a **streaming** tab in the UI, which provides complete information about the streaming application. This is explained in detail in the *Monitoring applications* section at the end of this chapter.

Spark Streaming transformations and actions

Transformations and actions on DStream boils down to transformations and actions on RDDs. The DStream API has many of the transformations available on normal RDD API with special functions applicable for streaming applications. Let's go through some of the important transformations.

Union

Two DStreams can be combined to create one DStream. For example, data received from multiple receivers of Kafka or Flume can be combined to create a new DStream. This is a common approach in Spark Streaming to increase scalability:

```
stream1 = ...
stream2 = ...
MultiDStream = stream1.union(stream2)
```

Join

Joins two DStreams of *(K, V)* and *(K, W)* pairs and returns a new DStream of *(K, (V, W))* pairs with all pairs of elements for each key:

```
stream1 = ...
stream2 = ...
joinedDStream = stream1.join(stream2)
```

Transform operation

The `transform` operation can be used to apply any RDD operation that is not available in the DStream API. For example, joining a DStream with a dataset is not directly exposed. So, use the `transform` operation to join them as shown in the following:

```
cleanRDD = sc.textFile("hdfs://hostname:8020/input/cleandata.txt")
# join existing DStream with CleanRDD and filter out.
myCleanedDStream = myDStream.transform(lambda rdd:
  rdd.join(cleanRDD).filter(...))
```

This is nothing but combining both batch and streaming processing.

updateStateByKey

As we have seen in the stateful transformation example, the
`updateStateByKey(func)` function returns a new DStream where the state for each
key and value is updated by applying a function. Checkpointing is mandatory for
the `updateStateByKey` operation.

mapWithState

`mapWithState` is a stateful transformation introduced in version 1.6. This makes
it easier to implement user logic and also provides better performance than
`updateStateByKey`.

Window operations

Spark Streaming also provides powerful window computations which allow
applying transformations over a sliding window of data. Let's consider the following
Twitter example:

```
val countsDStream = hashTagsDStream.window(Minutes(10),Seconds(1))
  .countByValue()
```

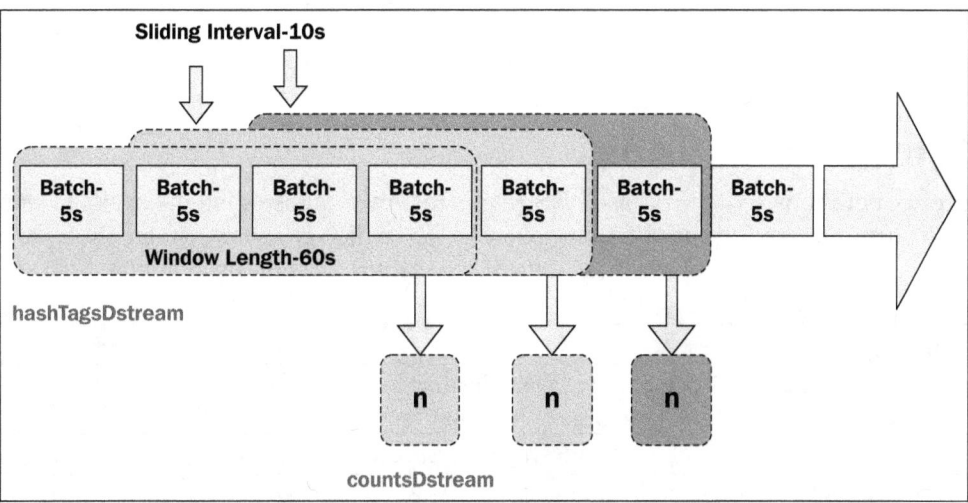

Figure 5.4: Spark Streaming window operation

As shown in *Figure 5.4*, it has a window length of 60 seconds, a sliding interval of 10 seconds, and a batch interval of 5 seconds. It is counting the number of hashtags from Twitter in a sliding window of 60 seconds. When the window slides every 10 seconds, a count of hashtags is computed in the 60 seconds window. This means most of the records are counted again in the next window. This is normal because the goal of this exercise is to find out the number of specific hashtags from Twitter over 60 seconds. If double counting is not needed, Spark Streaming provides smart window operations such as `countByValueAndWindow`, which will subtract the counts from the previous batch window and add the count from the current window.

The following table shows the common window operations used in Spark Streaming:

Window transformation	Description
`window`	Returns a new DStream with window of batches
`countByWindow`	Returns a new DStream with sliding window count of elements in stream
`reduceByWindow`	Returns a new DStream by aggregating elements using a function
`reduceByKeyAndWindow`	Returns a new DStream by aggregating values for each key using a function
`countByValueAndWindow`	Returns a new DStream with key and value pairs where the value of each key is its frequency within a sliding window only

Output operations

Output operations write processed DStreams to any database systems or file systems. These output operations are like actions in RDDs, which cause transformations to trigger. The following table shows some of the output operations available:

Output operation	Meaning
`print()` or `pprint()` in Python	Prints the first 10 elements of every batch of the DStream in the console
`saveAsTextFiles`	Saves the DStream to a text file
`saveAsObjectFiles`	Saves the DStream as a sequence file
`saveAsHadoopFile` or `saveAsNewAPIHadoopDataset`	Saves the DStream to any Hadoop file format such as Avro, Parquet, HBase, and so on
`saveToCassandra`	Saves the DStream to Cassandra. Requires Cassandra connector

Output operation	Meaning
foreachRDD(func)	Applies a function for every RDD in the stream. An example of foreachRDD is shown below. It creates a connection object and writes data to an external database

A typical use of a `foreachRDD` operation to create a connection and send records is as follows:

```
def sendPartition(iter):
    conn = ConnectionPool.getConnection()
    for record in iter:
        conn.send(record)
    ConnectionPool.returnConnection(conn)

dstream.foreachRDD(lambda x: x.foreachPartition(sendPartition))
```

Input sources and output stores

Spark Streaming supports three kinds of input sources:

- **Basic sources**: Sources directly available in the StreamingContext API. Examples: file systems, socket connections, and Akka actors.

- **Advanced sources**: Sources like Kafka, Flume, Kinesis, Twitter, and so on, which are available through extra utility classes.

- **Custom sources**: Requires implementing a user-defined receiver.

Multiple receivers can be created in the same application to receive data from different sources. It is important to allocate enough resources (cores and memory) for enabling receivers and tasks to execute simultaneously. For example, if you start your application with one core, it will be taken by the receiver and no tasks will be executed because of a lack of available cores.

Basic sources

There are four basic sources available in Spark StreamingContext as shown in the following table:

Source	Description
TCP stream	For streaming data via TCP/IP by specifying a hostname and a port number. `StreamingContext.socketTextStream` is used for creating an input DStream
File stream	For reading files from a file system such as HDFS, NFS, and S3. `streamingContext.fileStream` or Python's `streamingContext.textFileStream(dataDirectory)` is used for creating the input DStream
Akka actors	For creating DStreams through Akka actors, `streamingContext.actorStream` is used for creating the DStream
Queue of RDDs	For testing a Spark Streaming application with a queue of RDDs, `streamingContext.queueStream` is used for creating DStream

Advanced sources

Let's take a look at some of the important custom sources:

Source	Description
Kafka	Kafka is the most widely-used source in any streaming application as it provides high reliability. It is a publish-subscribe messaging system which stores data as a distributed commit log and enables streaming applications to pull data. There are approaches for using Kafka: receiver-based approach and direct approach.
File stream	Flume is a reliable log collection tool, which is tightly integrated with Hadoop. Like Kafka, Flume also offers two approaches; regular push-based and a custom pull-based approach.
Kinesis	Kinesis is a service offered by **Amazon Web Services** (**AWS**), which is used for stream processing. The Kinesis receiver creates an input DStream using the **Kinesis Client Library** (**KCL**) provided by AWS.
Twitter	For streaming a public stream of tweets using the Twitter Streaming API. `TwitterUtils` uses `Twitter4j`.
ZeroMQ	ZeroMQ is another high performance asynchronous messaging system.
MQTT	MQTT is a publish-subscribe based messaging protocol for use on top of the TCP/IP protocol.

Custom sources

Input DStreams can also be created out of custom data sources of your own, by extending the API. Implement a user-defined receiver that can receive data from the new custom source. Python API does not support this functionality yet.

Receiver reliability

There are two types of receivers in Spark Streaming based on reliability:

- **Reliable receiver**: A reliable receiver sends acknowledgment to source systems after receiving the blocks and replicating in the Spark cluster. So, in case of failures of receivers, data is not lost.

- **Unreliable receiver**: An unreliable receiver does not acknowledge after receiving the blocks. So, in this case, if a receiver fails, data is lost.

So, depending on the type of the receiver, data can be received at-least-once or exactly-once. For example, while the regular Kafka API provides at-least-once semantics, the Kafka direct API provides exactly-once semantics. For unreliable receivers, to make sure that received blocks are not lost in case of driver failures, enabling WAL will help.

Output stores

Once the data is processed in the Spark Streaming application, it can be written to a variety of sinks such as HDFS, any RDBMS database, HBase, Cassandra, Kafka, or Elasticsearch, and so on. All output operations are processed one-at-a-time and they are executed in the same order they are defined in the application. Also, in some cases, the same record can be processed more than one time and will be duplicated in output stores.

It is important to understand at-most-once, at-least-once, and exactly-once guarantees offered by Spark Streaming. For example, using the Kafka direct API provides exactly once semantics, so a record is received, processed, and sent to the output store exactly once. Note that, irrespective of whether data is sent once or twice from the source, the Spark Streaming application processes any record exactly once. So, the outputs are affected by choosing the type of receiver. For NoSQL databases such as HBase, sending the same record twice will just update it with the new version. For updating the same record on HBase, the timestamp can be passed from source systems instead of HBase picking up a timestamp.

So, if the record is processed and sent multiple times to HBase, it will just replace the existing record because of the same timestamp. This concept is called **Idempotent updates**. However, for RDBMS databases, sending the same record twice may either throw an exception or insert the second record as a duplicate. Another way to achieve exactly once is to follow the **Transactional updates** approach to update exactly once.

Spark Streaming with Kafka and HBase

Apache Kafka is publish-subscribe messaging rethought as a distributed, partitioned, replicated commit log service. Kafka plays an important role in any streaming application. Let's see what happens without having Kafka in a streaming application. If the streaming application processing the streams is down for 1 minute for some reason, what will happen to the stream of data for that 1 minute? We will end up losing 1 minute's worth of data. Having Kafka as one more layer buffers incoming stream data and prevents any data loss. Also, if something goes wrong within the Spark Streaming application or target database, messages can be replayed from Kafka. Once the streaming application pulls a message from Kafka, acknowledgement is sent to Kafka only when data is replicated in the streaming application. This makes Kafka a reliable receiver.

There are two approaches to receive data from Kafka.

Receiver-based approach

Using the Kafka consumer API, receivers in a Spark Streaming application will receive data from Kafka partitions. As with all receivers, the data received from Kafka through a receiver is stored in Spark executors, and then jobs launched by Spark Streaming process the data. Offsets consumed by the receiver are stored in Zookeeper for tracking the progress. To ensure zero-data loss, you have to additionally enable WAL in Spark Streaming. This process is illustrated in *Figure 5.5*.

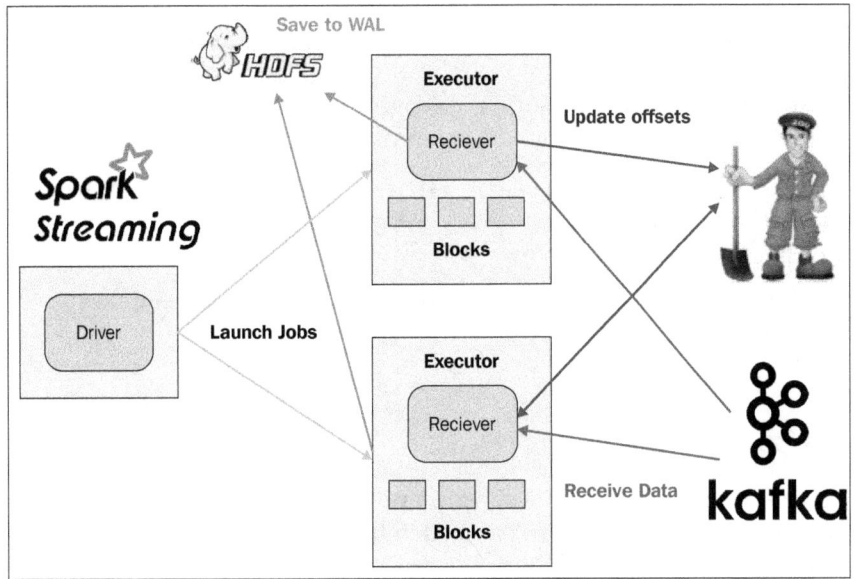

Figure 5.5: Spark Streaming with Kafka with receivers

Let's go through a Kafka word count example that is receiver-based and shipped with the Spark installation. The easiest way to work with Kafka is to install and start Kafka broker. Perform the following commands to download, unzip, and start the Kafka broker:

```
wget http://www.trieuvan.com/apache/kafka/0.8.2.0/kafka_2.10-0.8.2.0.tgz
tar xzvf kafka_2.10-0.8.2.0.tgz
cd kafka_2.10-0.8.2.0/
bin/kafka-server-start.sh config/server.properties
```

Open another terminal and create a topic called test with two partitions and the replication factor as 1:

```
bin/kafka-topics.sh --zookeeper quickstart.cloudera:2181 --topic test
--create --partitions 2 --replication-factor 1
```

Start a Kafka console producer to start sending messages to the topic test:

```
bin/kafka-console-producer.sh --broker-list localhost:9092 --topic test
```

Start another terminal and submit the Kafka wordcount job:

```
cd /usr/lib/spark/examples/lib/streaming
spark-submit --master local[*] --packages org.apache.spark:spark-
streaming-kafka_2.10:1.5.0 kafka_wordcount.py localhost:2181 test
```

Now, let's start entering some messages in the kafka console producer window; those should show up as wordcounts in the Kafka Streaming program.

For every message published in Kafka, it assigns an offset number. We can see the latest offset numbers with the following commands:

```
bin/kafka-run-class.sh kafka.tools.GetOffsetShell --broker-list
localhost:9092 --topic test -time -1 --partitions 0

test:0:18

bin/kafka-run-class.sh kafka.tools.GetOffsetShell --broker-list
localhost:9092 --topic test -time -1 --partitions 1

test:1:16
```

Role of Zookeeper

In the receiver-based approach, the consumer, which is a Spark Streaming program, maintains offsets in Zookeeper. We can watch the offsets by entering the zkCli shell. Use the following commands to check the offsets of the `spark-streaming-consumer` group:

```
/usr/lib/zookeeper/bin/zkCli.sh -server localhost:2181 get /consumers/
spark-streaming-consumer/offsets/test/0
```

```
/usr/lib/zookeeper/bin/zkCli.sh -server localhost:2181 get /consumers/
spark-streaming-consumer/offsets/test/1
```

The output of the previous commands will be similar to the output shown in the following. Note that `18` is the latest offset of the Spark Streaming consumer for the partition `0`. This offset number is exactly same as the offset in Kafka (see the previous result), which means that all the messages from Kafka are consumed:

```
WatchedEvent state:SyncConnected type:None path:null

18

cZxid = 0x44f

ctime = Sun Dec 20 15:47:14 PST 2015

mZxid = 0x4bd

mtime = Sun Dec 20 15:58:07 PST 2015

pZxid = 0x44f

cversion = 0

dataVersion = 1

aclVersion = 0

ephemeralOwner = 0x0

dataLength = 2

numChildren = 0
```

Let's check the lag between the offsets of Kafka and the Spark Streaming consumer using the following command:

```
bin/kafka-consumer-offset-checker.sh --zookeeper localhost:2181 --topic
test --group spark-streaming-consumer
Group                   Topic Pid Offset logSize Lag          spark-
streaming-consumer test  0     18     18      0              spark-
streaming-consumer test  1     16     16      0
```

> Note that the lag is 0 for both partitions.

Direct approach (no receivers)

This was introduced in Spark 1.3 to ensure exactly once semantics of receiving data even in case of failures. The direct approach periodically queries Kafka for the latest offsets in each topic and partition, and accordingly defines the offset ranges to process in each batch as shown in *Figure 5.6*.

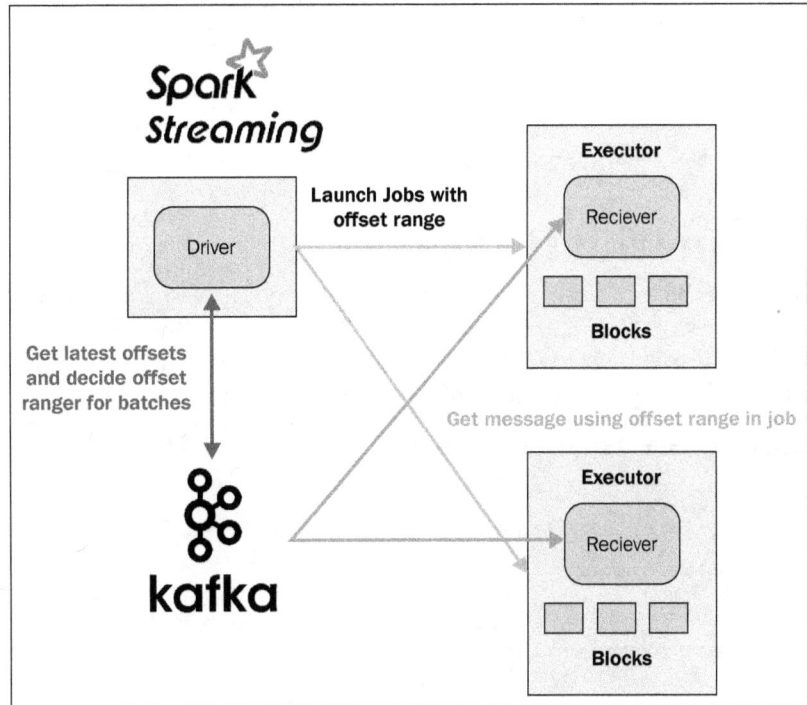

Figure 5.6: Spark Streaming with Kafka direct approach

This approach provides the following benefits:

- **Simplified parallelism**: This approach avoids creating multiple input streams and unionizing all of them. This will create a number of RDD partitions equal to the Kafka partitions to consume. This one-to-one mapping of Kafka partitions and RDD partitions makes it easier to understand and tune.

- **Efficiency**: No need for WAL.

- **Exactly-once semantics**: This approach eliminates inconsistencies between Zookeeper and Kafka. So each record is received by Spark Streaming effectively, exactly once despite failures in receiving.

Let's run a Kafka direct word count now. Use the same procedure as the previous to enter messages in the Kafka console producer and then start a Spark Streaming program with the following command. Note that this program takes an argument of Kafka broker while the earlier program takes an argument of Zookeeper. Offsets are not maintained within Zookeeper now:

```
cd /usr/lib/spark/examples/lib/streaming

spark-submit --master local[*] --packages org.apache.spark:spark-streaming-kafka_2.10:1.5.0 direct_kafka_wordcount.py localhost:9092 test
```

The number of records per second is controlled by setting the parameters `spark.streaming.receiver.maxRate` and `spark.streaming.kafka.maxRatePerPartition`.

Integration with HBase

Integration with HBase is fairly easy. Use `newAPIHadoopRDD` for reading HBase data and use `saveAsNewAPIHadoopDataset` for writing data to HBase. Let's go through a HBase write example by creating a table called `test` with column family `f1`. Then, run a Spark job to write data to the `test` table with `col1` and `value1`:

```
[cloudera@quickstart lib]$ hbase shell


hbase(main):002:0> create 'test', 'f1'
0 row(s) in 0.6460 seconds


cd /usr/lib/spark/examples/lib/
```

```
spark-submit --master local[*] --driver-class-path /usr/lib/spark/lib/
spark-examples.jar hbase_outputformat.py localhost test row1 f1 col1
value1
```

```
hbase(main):005:0> scan 'test'
ROW                 COLUMN+CELL
row1                column=f1:col1, timestamp=1450657755249, value=value1
1 row(s) in 0.0700 seconds
```

Similar logic from the previous example can be applied in Spark Streaming as well. Transform the RDD into a *(key,value)* pair with content as *(rowkey, [row key, column family, column name , value])*. Then write DStream to HBase. Alternatively, you can implement `foreachRDD` for writing data out.

> Note that the HBase native API provides `put`, `get`, `scan`, `filter`, and `coprocessor` methods. Hadoop provides `InputFormat` and `OutputFormat` to read and write data. The Hadoop API provides low performance while reading data from HBase rather than using the HBase native API. Using *Spark SQL on HBase* or *Spark connector for HBase* (introduced in *Chapter 4, Big Data Analytics with Spark SQL, DataFrames, and Datasets*) provides high performance with native HBase APIs and Spark's in-memory performance. It is the recommended approach to use Spark SQL on HBase or Spark connector for HBase for optimized performance.

Advanced concepts of Spark Streaming

Let's go through some of the important advanced concepts of Spark Streaming.

Using DataFrames

We learned Spark SQL and DataFrames in *Chapter 4, Big Data Analytics with Spark SQL, DataFrames, and Datasets*. There are many use cases where you want to convert DStream and DataFrame to do interactive analytics. RDDs generated by DStreams can be converted to DataFrames and queried with SQL internally within the program or from external SQL clients as well. Refer to the `sql_network_wordcount.py` program in `/usr/lib/spark/examples/lib/streaming` for implementing SQL in a Spark Streaming application. You can also start JDBC server within the application with the following code:

```
HiveThriftServer2.startWithContext(hiveContext)
```

Temporary tables can now be accessed from any SQL client such as beeline to query the data.

MLlib operations

It is easy to implement machine learning algorithms in Spark Streaming applications. The following Scala code trains a KMeans clustering model with training data offline and then applies the model on DStreams in real-time coming from Kafka:

```scala
val model = KMeans.train(training_data, ...)

val DStream = KafkaUtils.createDStream(...)
DStream.map { event => model.predict(featurize(event)) }
```

Caching/persistence

Persistence levels available on RDDs can be applied on DStreams as well using the persist() method. This is needed if multiple actions are applied on the same DStream multiple times.

With window-based operations and state-based operations like updateStateByKey, DStreams are automatically persisted in memory with serialization by default. DStreams created by receiving the data over the network are always replicated twice for fault tolerance.

Fault-tolerance in Spark Streaming

There are two kinds of failures in any Spark Streaming application: failure of executor or failure of driver. Let's understand how fault recovery is achieved in these two scenarios.

Failure of executor

Executors can fail because of hardware or software issues. If an executor fails, all tasks running on the executor will fail and all in-memory data stored in the executor JVM will be lost. If a receiver is running on this node, all the blocks that are buffered but not processed yet will be lost. Spark automatically handles these failures by placing a new receiver on a new node and tasks are restarted on block replicas as shown in *Figure 5.7*.

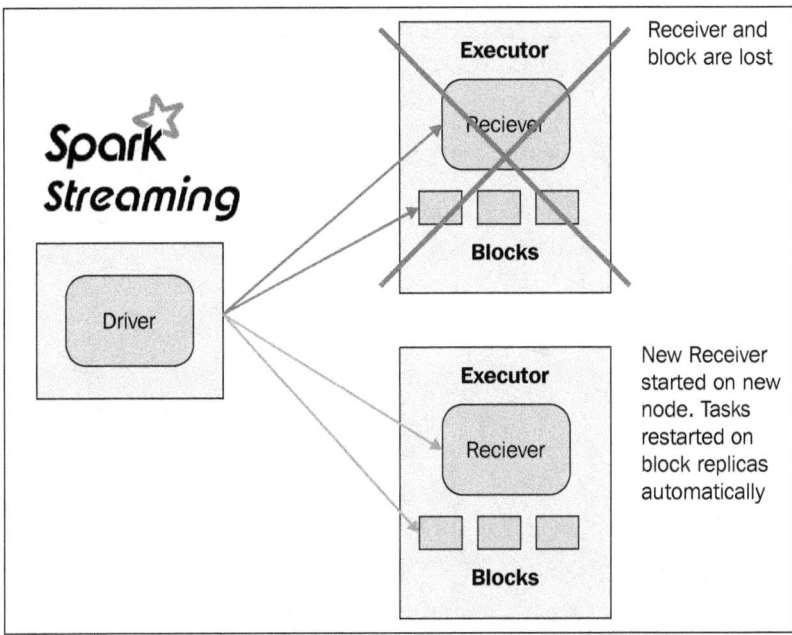

Figure 5.7: Spark Streaming behavior in executor failure

Failure of driver

If a driver fails, all executors will fail including the computation and replicated in-memory blocks. There are two ways to recover from driver failures: recovering with checkpoint and recovering with the WAL. Typically, both are needed for zero data loss.

Recovering with checkpointing

A Spark application must checkpoint data to a storage system like HDFS to recover from failures. There are two types of data stored in the checkpoint directory; metadata and data. Metadata is configuration for an application, DStream operations, and incomplete batch information. Data is nothing more than the storage of RDD content. Metadata checkpointing is for driver recovery and data checkpointing is for recovery of stateful transformations. Recovering driver failures with checkpointing is illustrated in *Figure 5.8*.

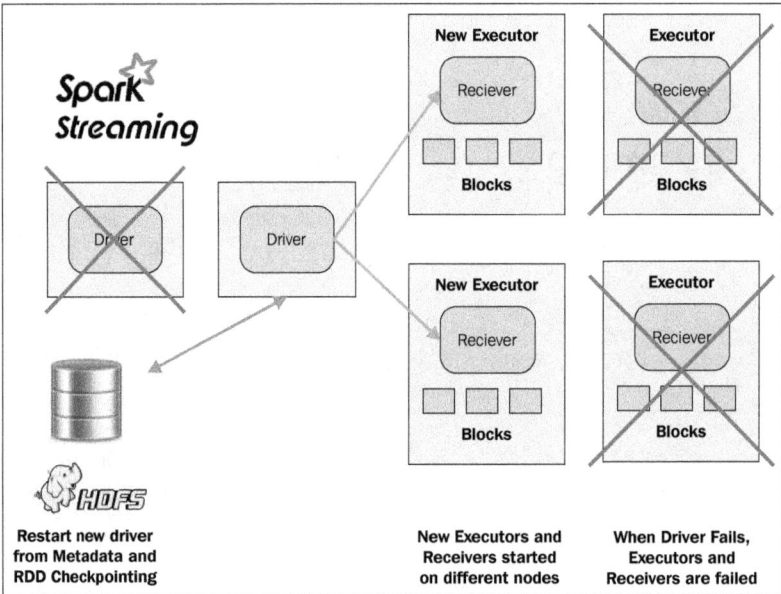

Figure 5.8: Spark Streaming behavior in driver failure with checkpointing

The following points must be considered when enabling checkpointing:

- Checkpointing RDDs to reliable, external storage slows down the processing time of the batches

- With a batch interval size of 1 second, checkpointing every batch will significantly slow down operation throughput

- Checkpointing too infrequently causes the lineage and task sizes to grow too large with detrimental effects

- Ensure that a checkpoint interval of 5-10 times the sliding interval has been set

- For stateful transformations, the default checkpoint interval will be at least 10 seconds and will be a multiple of the batch interval

A driver can be automatically restarted with the `--supervise` option in the standalone master. In YARN, the driver is automatically restarted with the configuration parameter `yarn.resourcemanager.am.max-attempts`.

Recovering with WAL

When a Spark Streaming application recovers from driver failure, blocks received, but not yet processed by the receiver, will be lost. Enabling WAL reduces this loss. To enable WAL, set the following configuration property:

```
sparkConf.set("spark.streaming.receiver.writeAheadLog.enable",
    "true")
```

Enabling WAL provides fault recovery, but it reduces the performance. Consider using the Kafka direct API wherever possible since it does not need WAL.

Performance tuning of Spark Streaming applications

Spark Streaming applications tuning is needed before deploying in production. Consider the following points for better performance:

- Batch window — Batch window depends on the needs of the application, input rate, and scheduling delay. Start with a batch window of x seconds and y input rate and check the total delay in the **streaming** tab of the spark UI. If total delay is stable, you can decrease batch window and increase input rate until you get an optimized batch window needed for the business.

- Increase throughput by increasing the number of receivers and increasing parallelism while processing.

- Garbage collection and memory usage:
    - Using CMS garbage collector `--conf spark.executor.extraJavaOptions=-XX:+UseConcMarkSweepGC`.
    - Caching RDDs in serialized form.
    - Using Kryo Serialization.
    - Using more executors with a smaller heap size to reduce garbage collector impact.
    - Estimate and allocate sufficient memory needed by the application. For example, if you are using a window operation for 5 minutes, you need to allocate memory for storing and processing 5 minutes' worth of data.

Use the following formulas as a rule of thumb for performance considerations:

Consumer parallelism = Number of consumers created

Spark parallelism = spark.cores.max - number of consumers

To maximize the chances of data locality, and even parallel execution, `spark.cores.max` should be a multiple of the number of consumers:

*Batch processing time = Number of tasks * scheduling cost + number of tasks * time -complexity per task / parallelism level*

*Number of tasks = Number of stages * Number of partitions*

Number of partitions in the RDDs created by DStream = batchInterval / spark.streaming. blockInterval multiplied by number of receivers

Monitoring applications

Spark Streaming jobs produce useful information for understanding the current state of the application. Broadly, there are two ways to monitor Spark Streaming jobs: using the UI and using external tools.

The Spark UI HTTP address is `http://driver-host-name:4040/`. When multiple SparkContexts run at the same time, they are bound to successive ports like 4041, 4042, and so on. The Spark UI provides useful information like event timeline and DAG visualizations as explained in *Chapter 3, Deep Dive into Apache Spark*. When a Spark Streaming application is running, a **streaming** tab appears on the UI, which provides information such as the number of batches completed, number of records processed, batch window time, total time of Spark Streaming application, input rate, scheduling delay, processing time, and total delay. The UI also shows the Kafka topic name, partition numbers, and offsets processed in a batch when using the Kafka direct API. This is really helpful and easy to debug in case of issues.

Spark provides integration with external tools such as Ganglia and Graphite.

>  For Streaming specific metrics, StreamingListener API can be used:
> `http://spark.apache.org/docs/latest/api/scala/`
> `index.html#org.apache.spark.streaming.scheduler.`
> `StreamingListener`

Introducing Structured Streaming

A streaming application is not just about doing some real-time computations on a stream of data. Generally, streaming will be part of a larger application that includes real-time, batch, and serving layers with machine learning, and so on. A continuous application is an end-to-end application that combines all these features in one application.

In Spark 2.0, the Structured Streaming API is introduced for building continuous applications. The Structured Streaming API addresses the following concerns of a typical streaming application:

- **Node delays**: Delay in a specific node can cause data inconsistency at the database layer. Ordering the guarantee of events is achieved using systems like Kafka in which events on the same key always go to the same Kafka partition. Streaming applications pull data from this partition and process them in the order they are received. However, while applying operations on streaming data, if one of the node delays processing, data consistency cannot be guaranteed on the database. In Structured Streaming, output from the streaming computation of a batch job will always be the same irrespective of any node delays. This provides strong consistency at the database level.

- **Node failures**: If one of the node fails, most streaming engines fail to provide strong exactly once semantics. Handling duplicate counts within computation or duplicate updates to a database is left to the user. Structured Streaming is designed to handle failures at any point with re-playable sources and idempotent sinks.

- **Late arrival of data**: It is pretty common to receive some events with a delay from the source. Creating a streaming application with an assumption of no delays will create issues with late events. Creating a streaming application that handles delays by maintaining a state might grow indefinitely. Structured Streaming handles this by providing a feature to drop the late events or process them and update in place using actual event-time, not the time when Spark received the event.

Structured Streaming application flow

Structured Streaming is built on top of the Spark SQL engine, so it inherits the performance benefits of datasets and DataFrames. Streaming computation can be done similar to batch computation on data at rest. The Spark SQL engine will process the incoming stream of data in batches incrementally and update the sinks. Structured Streaming is supported in the Java, Scala, and Python programming languages with dataset and DataFrame APIs. Structured Streaming is an alpha release in Spark 2.0 with limited capabilities. Upcoming releases will have fully-fledged capabilities, more sources, and sinks.

In Structured Streaming, the incoming stream of data is treated as a table that is continuously growing. All events coming in a batch window will be treated like new rows appended to the input table as shown in *Figure 5.9*.

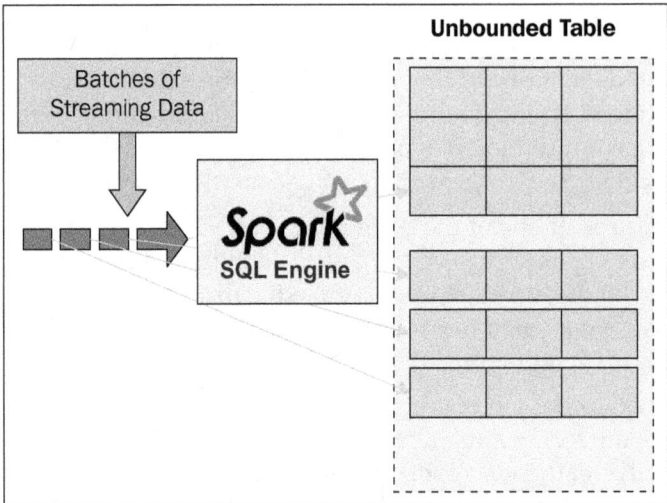

Figure 5.9: Spark Structured Streaming model

Queries are executed on the input table to produce the result set as shown in *Figure 5.10*. Queries are executed based on the trigger interval, which creates the result set, and then it is updated on sinks such as file systems or databases, and so on.

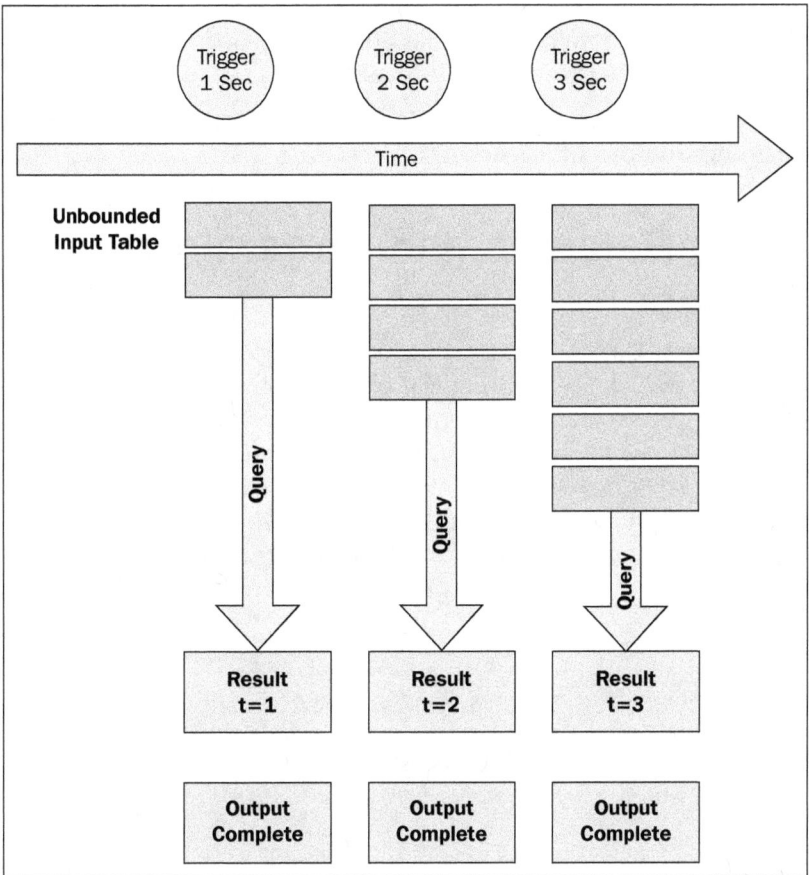

Figure 5.10: Spark Structured Streaming model

Valid output modes are `complete`, `append`, or `update`. `append` is the default mode.

When to use Structured Streaming?

Structured Streaming can be used in the following scenarios:

- To create a streaming application using Dataset and DataFrame APIs
- When providing data consistencies and exactly-once semantics even in cases of delays and failures at multiple levels
- Creating continuous applications that are integrated with batch queries, streaming, and machine learning

Streaming Datasets and Streaming DataFrames

Streaming Datasets or DataFrames are created using Spark session, which is introduced in Spark 2.0. For creating DataFrame from static data we use SparkSession.read whereas for creating Streaming DataFrame, we use SparkSession.readStream. Also, for writing DataFrame out, we use SparkSession.write whereas for writing Streaming DataFrames, we use SparkSession.writeStream. The following Scala example creates the SparkSession and then creates the stream by reading CSV files from a directory:

```
import org.apache.spark.sql.functions._
import org.apache.spark.sql.SparkSession

val spark = SparkSession
  .builder
  .appName("CSVStructuredStreaming")
  .getOrCreate()

val csvSchema = new StructType().add("emp_name",
  "string").add("emp_age", "integer")
val csv_df = spark
  .readStream
  .option("sep", ",")
  .schema(userSchema)
  .csv("HDFS Path")

csv_df
  .writeStream
  .format("parquet")
  .option("path","HDFS Path")
  .option("checkpointLocation","HDFS Path")
  .outputMode("append")
  .start()
```

Input sources and output sinks

Currently only two types of built-in sources are supported: file source and socket source. File source creates a stream by reading files from a directory as shown in the previous example. Spark 2.0 supports CSV, JSON, and Parquet formats. The socket source reads the data from a socket connection, which is used for testing purposes only.

Currently four types of output sinks are supported, `file` sink, `foreach` sink, `console` sink, and `memory` sink. Only the Parquet format is supported in `file` sink with `append` mode. The `foreach` mode can be used to write an arbitrary operation of output data and is supported in Scala and Java APIs. `console` and `memory` sinks are used for debugging purposes only.

Operations on Streaming Datasets and Streaming DataFrames

Most common operations like `filter`, `groupBy`, and `aggregation` are supported by streaming DataFrames. Streaming DataFrames can be converted to Streaming Datasets as well. Window operations are supported on streaming DataFrames and also streaming DataFrames can be joined with static DataFrames.

Let's create a Structured Streaming application using **Internet of Things (IOT)** use case where a few sensors are sending information about an active or inactive device at different intervals. Our goal is to find how many devices are active or inactive at different time intervals; the steps to do so are as follows:

1. Let's create three input datasets as shown here in JSON format. In the real-life project, data would automatically come to this directory. But, for our understanding, let's create these datasets manually:

   ```
   iot-file1.json
   {"device_id":1,"timestamp":1470009600,"status":"active"}
   {"device_id":2,"timestamp":1470013200,"status":"active"}
   {"device_id":3,"timestamp":1470016800,"status":"active"}
   {"device_id":4,"timestamp":1470020400,"status":"active"}
   {"device_id":5,"timestamp":1470024000,"status":"active"}
   {"device_id":1,"timestamp":1470009601,"status":"active"}
   {"device_id":2,"timestamp":1470013202,"status":"active"}
   {"device_id":3,"timestamp":1470016803,"status":"inactive"}
   {"device_id":4,"timestamp":1470020404,"status":"active"}
   {"device_id":5,"timestamp":1470024005,"status":"active"}

   iot-file2.json
   ```

```
{"device_id":1,"timestamp":1470027600,"status":"active"}
{"device_id":2,"timestamp":1470031200,"status":"active"}
{"device_id":3,"timestamp":1470034800,"status":"active"}
{"device_id":4,"timestamp":1470038400,"status":"active"}
{"device_id":5,"timestamp":1470042000,"status":"active"}
{"device_id":1,"timestamp":1470027601,"status":"active"}
{"device_id":2,"timestamp":1470031202,"status":"active"}
{"device_id":3,"timestamp":1470034803,"status":"active"}
{"device_id":4,"timestamp":1470038404,"status":"active"}
{"device_id":5,"timestamp":1470042005,"status":"active"}

iot-file3.json
{"device_id":1,"timestamp":1470027601,"status":"active"}
```

2. Create an HDFS directory and copy the first IOT events file:

   hadoop fs -mkdir iotstream

   hadoop fs -put iot-file1.json iotstream/

3. Start a Scala shell session, create the streaming DataFrame, and start the stream. bin/spark-shell starts the Scala shell, which creates a pre-configured Spark session called spark:

```
import org.apache.spark.sql.types._
import org.apache.spark.sql.functions._

val iotSchema = new StructType().add("device_id",
  LongType).add("timestamp", TimestampType).add("status",
  StringType)
val iotPath =
  "hdfs://quickstart.cloudera:8020/user/cloudera/iotstream"
val iotStreamingDataFrame =
  spark.readStream.schema(iotSchema)
  .option("maxFilesPerTrigger", 1).json(iotPath)
val iotStreamingCounts =
  iotStreamingDataFrame.groupBy($"status",
  window($"timestamp", "1 hour")).count()
iotStreamingCounts.isStreaming

val iotQuery =
  iotStreamingCounts.writeStream.format("memory")
  .queryName("iotstream").outputMode("complete").start()
```

4. Now query the in-memory `iotstream` table:

```
scala> spark.sql("select status, date_format(window.start, 'MMM-
dd HH:mm') as start_time, date_format(window.end, 'MMM-dd HH:mm')
as end_time, count from iotstream order by start_time,end_time,
status").show()
```

```
+--------+------------+------------+-----+
|  status|  start_time|    end_time|count|
+--------+------------+------------+-----+
|  active|Jul-31 17:00|Jul-31 18:00|    2|
|  active|Jul-31 18:00|Jul-31 19:00|    2|
|  active|Jul-31 19:00|Jul-31 20:00|    1|
|inactive|Jul-31 19:00|Jul-31 20:00|    1|
|  active|Jul-31 20:00|Jul-31 21:00|    2|
|  active|Jul-31 21:00|Jul-31 22:00|    2|
+--------+------------+------------+-----+
```

5. Now, copy the second `iot-file2.json` to the same HDFS directory; you can observe that the streaming query executes automatically and computes the counts. Let's run the same query again as we have seen previously:

```
hadoop fs -put iot-file2.json iotstream/
```

```
scala> spark.sql("select status, date_format(window.start, 'MMM-
dd HH:mm') as start_time, date_format(window.end, 'MMM-dd HH:mm')
as end_time, count from iotstream order by start_time,end_time,
status").show()
```

```
+--------+------------+------------+-----+
|  status|  start_time|    end_time|count|
+--------+------------+------------+-----+
|  active|Aug-01 00:00|Aug-01 01:00|    2|
|  active|Aug-01 01:00|Aug-01 02:00|    2|
|  active|Aug-01 02:00|Aug-01 03:00|    2|
|  active|Jul-31 17:00|Jul-31 18:00|    2|
|  active|Jul-31 18:00|Jul-31 19:00|    2|
|  active|Jul-31 19:00|Jul-31 20:00|    1|
|inactive|Jul-31 19:00|Jul-31 20:00|    1|
|  active|Jul-31 20:00|Jul-31 21:00|    2|
|  active|Jul-31 21:00|Jul-31 22:00|    2|
```

```
|   active|Jul-31 22:00|Jul-31 23:00|    2|
|   active|Jul-31 23:00|Aug-01 00:00|    2|
+--------+------------+------------+-----+
```

6. Now, copy the third `iot-file3.json` to the same HDFS directory, which has a late event. Once you execute the query you can observe that the late event is handled by updating the previous record:

```
hadoop fs -put iot-file3.json iotstream/

scala> spark.sql("select status, date_format(window.start, 'MMM-
dd HH:mm') as start_time, date_format(window.end, 'MMM-dd HH:mm')
as end_time, count from iotstream order by start_time,end_time,
status").show()
+--------+------------+------------+-----+
|  status|  start_time|    end_time|count|
+--------+------------+------------+-----+
|   active|Aug-01 00:00|Aug-01 01:00|    2|
|   active|Aug-01 01:00|Aug-01 02:00|    2|
|   active|Aug-01 02:00|Aug-01 03:00|    2|
|   active|Jul-31 17:00|Jul-31 18:00|    2|
|   active|Jul-31 18:00|Jul-31 19:00|    2|
|   active|Jul-31 19:00|Jul-31 20:00|    1|
| inactive|Jul-31 19:00|Jul-31 20:00|    1|
|   active|Jul-31 20:00|Jul-31 21:00|    2|
|   active|Jul-31 21:00|Jul-31 22:00|    2|
|   active|Jul-31 22:00|Jul-31 23:00|    3|
|   active|Jul-31 23:00|Aug-01 00:00|    2|
+--------+------------+------------+-----+
```

You can observe that late coming event is updated in place and incremented the count as 3. You can also copy the same datasets again to the same directory to see how counts are updated.

7. Finally, you can stop the job with the following command:

```
iotQuery.stop
```

Summary

Spark Streaming is based on a micro-batching model that is suitable for applications with throughput and high latency (> 0.5 seconds). Spark Streaming's DStream API provides transformations and actions for working with DStreams, including conventional transformations, window operations, output actions, and stateful operations such as `updateStateByKey`. Spark Streaming supports a variety of input sources and output sources used in the Big Data ecosystem. Spark Streaming supports the direct approach with Kafka, which really provides great benefits such as exactly once processing and avoiding WAL replication.

There are two types of failures in a Spark Streaming application; executor failure and driver failure. Executor failures are automatically taken care of by the Spark Streaming framework, but for handling driver failures, checkpointing and WAL must be enabled with high availability options for the driver such as `--supervise`.

Structured Streaming is a new paradigm shift in streaming computing, which enables building continuous applications with end-to-end exactly once guarantees and data consistency even in case of node delays and failures. Structured Streaming is introduced in Spark 2.0 as an alpha version and it is expected to become stable in upcoming versions.

The next chapter introduces an interesting topic; notebooks and data flows with Spark and Hadoop.

6
Notebooks and Dataflows with Spark and Hadoop

There are many tools available for interactive analytics and to provide visualizations on Spark and Hadoop platforms. Some of the more important tools are the IPython Notebook (Jupyter), Spark Notebook, Ispark, Hue, Spark Kernel, Jove Notebook, Beaker Notebook, and Databricks Cloud. All of these notebooks are open source, except Databricks Cloud. This chapter is aimed at introducing and using some of the important interactive analytics tools using notebooks and a dataflow engine called NiFi. This chapter is divided into the following subtopics:

- Introducing web-based notebooks
- Introducing Jupyter
- Introducing Apache Zeppelin
- Using the Livy REST job server and Hue Notebooks
- Introducing Apache NiFi for dataflows

Introducing web-based notebooks

We have worked with the Spark shell and applications in previous chapters. The shell provides great features, such as trying out code quickly and checking results interactively. However, when code becomes larger, it is difficult to edit some lines and re-execute the code. This is where applications are useful in which the entire script is saved in a file and submitted. However, in this way, you lose powerful **Read, Evaluate, Print, and Loop (REPL)** features of the shell. Notebooks solve this problem by providing features of both the shell and application in a web browser.

Web-based notebooks are files that contain the input code and output such as results and graphs from an interactive session. They also contain additional information, such as documentation, mathematical expressions, and media related to an interactive session. They are stored in the JSON format and can be shared with anybody across the organization or externally. It is easy to view the existing notebooks on the web using nbviewer or the ZeppelinHub Viewer. Notebooks are extremely useful for later executions and re-evaluations or sharing with anybody else without installing, setting up, and running the code.

Notebooks are nothing but *executable documents*, which will enhance developer productivity and reduce the complexity.

All programs in this chapter are executed on HDP 2.4 VM, except the *Hue notebook with Livy* program, which is executed on CDH 5.8 VM. For other environments, file paths might change. However, the concepts are the same in any environment.

Introducing Jupyter

The Jupyter Notebook supports over 40 languages and integrates with Spark and Hadoop to query interactively and visualize results with `ggplot2`, `matplotlib`, and others.

The Jupyter project evolved from the IPython project. The IPython project has accumulated many languages other than Python over a period of time. As a result, the IPython name became irrelevant for the project, so the name has been changed to Jupyter with inspiration from the Julia, Python, and R languages. IPython will continue to exist as a Python kernel for Jupyter. In simple words, IPython supports the Python language and Jupyter is language-agnostic. Jupyter provides the following features:

- An interactive shell for OS commands
- A Qt console for interactive shell-based analytics
- A browser-based notebook for interactive analytics on a web browser
- Kernels for different languages such as Python, Ruby, Julia, R, and so on
- The **nbconvert** tool to convert `.ipynb` to other formats such as `.html`, `.pdf`, `.markdown`, and others
- The **nbviewer** tool (`http://nbviewer.ipython.org/`) to view the notebooks with integration of GitHub to share notebooks in public

The Jupyter web-based notebook will automatically detect installed kernels such as Python, Scala, R, and Julia. Notebook users will be able to select the programming language of their choice for each individual notebook from a drop-down menu. The UI logic such as syntax highlighting, logos, and help menus, will automatically be updated on the notebook as the programming language of a notebook is changed.

Installing Jupyter

You need Python 3.3 and above or Python 2.7 for the installation of Jupyter. Once these requirements are met, installing Jupyter is quite easy with Anaconda or pip using the following commands:

```
conda install jupyter
```

```
pip3 install jupyter
```

The IPython kernel will be automatically installed with the Juypter installation. If you want to install other kernels, go to `https://github.com/ipython/ipython/wiki/IPython-kernels-for-other-languages`, click on the kernel, and follow the procedure. This page provides a list of all the available languages for Jupyter as well.

Let's follow this procedure for the installation of the Jupyter Notebook (if you are not using `conda`) on the Hortonworks Sandbox virtual machine. These instructions will work on other distributions (Cloudera and MapR) as well:

1. First of all, configure the dependencies with the following commands and then install and enable Python 2.7:

   ```
   yum install nano centos-release-SCL zlib-devel bzip2-devel
   openssl-devel ncurses-devel sqlite-devel readline-devel
   tk-devel gdbm-devel db4-devel libpcap-devel xz-devel
   libpng-devel libjpg-devel atlas-devel

   yum groupinstall "Development tools"

   yum install python27

   source /opt/rh/python27/enable
   ```

2. Now, let's install `pip` and then install the Jupyter Notebook:

   ```
   sudo yum -y install python-pip

   sudo pip install --upgrade pip
   ```

```
pip install numpy scipy pandas scikit-learn tornado pyzmq pygments
matplotlib jinja2 jsonschema

pip install jinja2 --upgrade

pip install jupyter
```

3. Once the profile is created, create the script to start the kernel. Create a file and enter the following content:

```
vi ~/start_ipython_notebook.sh

#!/bin/bash
source /opt/rh/python27/enable
IPYTHON_OPTS="notebook --port 8889 \
--notebook-dir='/usr/hdp/current/spark-client/' \
--ip='*' --no-browser" pyspark

chmod +x ~/start_ipython_notebook.sh
```

4. Finally, run the following command:

```
./start_ipython_notebook.sh
```

5. Go to the browser and open the page with the following address as an example. You should see a page similar to *Figure 6.1*. Change the IP address to the IP address of your sandbox:

```
http://192.168.139.165:8889/tree#
```

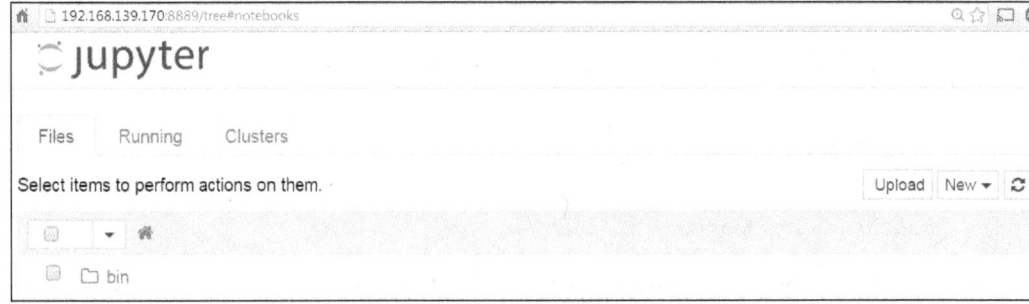

Figure 6.1: The Jupyter Notebook

Note that, by default, the Spark application starts in local mode. If you want to start with the YARN cluster manager, change your start command as follows:

```
[root@sandbox ~]# cat start_ipython_notebook.sh
#!/bin/bash
source /opt/rh/python27/enable
IPYTHON_OPTS="notebook --port 8889
--notebook-dir='/usr/hdp/current/spark-client/' --ip='*'
--no-browser" pyspark --master yarn
```

Hortonworks provides an unsupported Ambari service for Jupyter. The installation and management of Jupyter is easier with this service. Perform the following steps to install and start the Jupyter Service within Ambari:

```
git clone https://github.com/randerzander/jupyter-service
sudo cp -r jupyter-service /var/lib/
ambari-server/resources/stacks/HDP/2.4/services/
sudo ambari-server restart
```

Go to `ipaddressofsandbox:8080` and log in with `admin`/`admin` credentials. The Jupyter service is now included in the stack and can be added as a service. Click on **Actions** | **Add Service** | Select **Jupyter** | Customize service and deploy. Start the service; the notebook can be viewed at port number `9999` on the browser. You can also add a port forwarding rule for port `9999` so that the notebook can be accessed with the address hostname `9999`.

Change the port number in the configuration if it is already bound to another service.

Analytics with Jupyter

Before we get started with the analytics of Spark, let's learn some of the important features of the Jupyter Notebook.

Click on **New** in the upper right corner and select the **Python 2** kernel to start a new notebook. Notebooks provide cells and output areas. You need to write code in a cell and then click on the execute button or press *Shift + Enter*. You can run regular operating system commands such as `ls`, `mkdir`, `cp`, and others. Note that you get tab completion while typing the commands. IPython also provides magic commands that start with the `%` symbol. A list of magic commands is available with the `%lsmagic` command.

You can mark the cell with **Code, Markdown, Raw NBConvert,** or **Heading** with drop-down lists located on the toolbar. You can add rich text, links, mathematical formulas, code, and images in Markdown text to document within the notebook. Some of the example Markdowns are available at `https://guides.github.com/features/mastering-markdown/`. When you create a notebook, it is created with `untitled.ipynb`, but you can save it with a filename by clicking at the top of the page.

Now, let's get started with analytics using Spark. You can execute any exercise from *Chapter 3, Deep Dive into Apache Spark* to *Chapter 5, Real-Time Analytics with Spark Streaming and Structured Streaming.* Commands can be executed one by one or you can put all the code in one cell for entire code execution. You can open multiple notebooks and run them on the same SparkContext. Let's run a simple word count and plot the output with `matplotlib`:

```
from operator import add
words = sc.parallelize(["hadoop spark hadoop
                        spark mapreduce spark
                        jupyter ipython notebook
                        interactive analytics"])
counts = words.flatMap(lambda x: x.split(' ')) \
                .map(lambda x: (x, 1)) \
                .reduceByKey(add)    \
                .sortBy(lambda x: x[1])


%matplotlib inline
import matplotlib.pyplot as plt
def plot(counts):
    labels = map(lambda x: x[0], counts)
    values = map(lambda y: y[1], counts)
    plt.barh(range(len(values)), values, color='green')
    plt.yticks(range(len(values)), labels)
    plt.show()


plot(counts.collect())
```

You will see the result as shown in *Figure 6.2*:

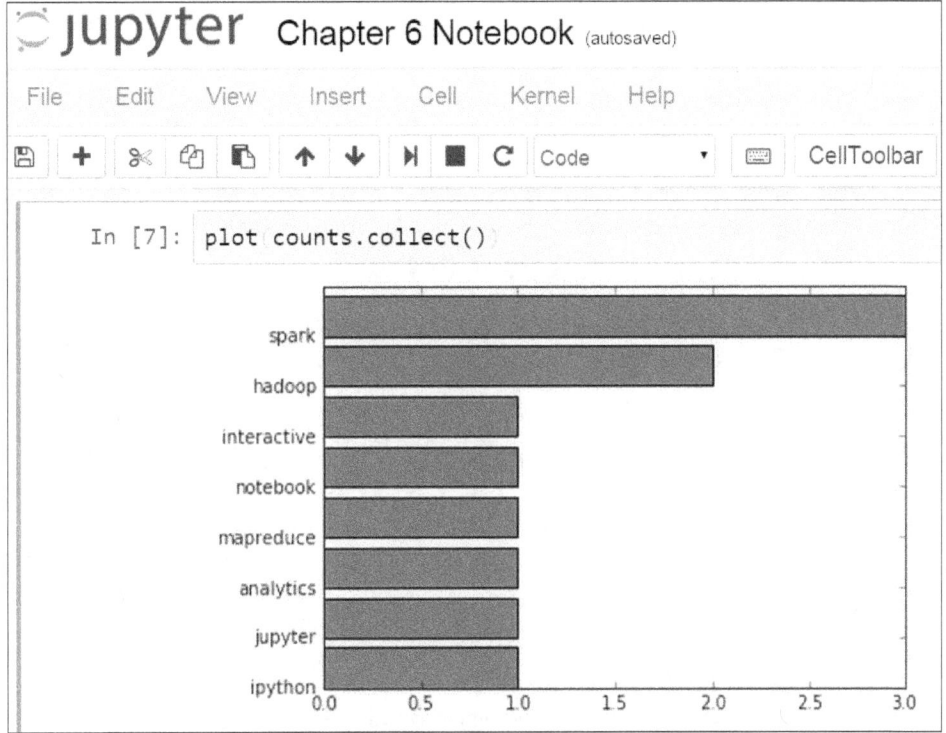

Figure 6.2: Visualizations in the Jupyter Notebook

Introducing Apache Zeppelin

Apache Zeppelin is a web-based notebook that enables data-driven, interactive analytics with built-in visualizations. It supports multiple languages with an interpreter framework. Currently, it supports interpreters such as Spark, Markdown, Shell, Hive, Phoenix, Tajo, Flink, Ignite, Lens, HBase, Cassandra, Elasticsearch, Geode, PostgreSQL, and Hawq. It can be used for data ingestion, discovery, analytics, and visualizations using notebooks similar to IPython Notebooks. Zeppelin notebooks recognize output from any language and visualize these using the same tools.

The Zeppelin project started as an incubator project in the Apache software foundation in December 2014 and became a top-level project in May 2016. Zeppelin mainly has four components, as shown in the architecture in *Figure 6.3*:

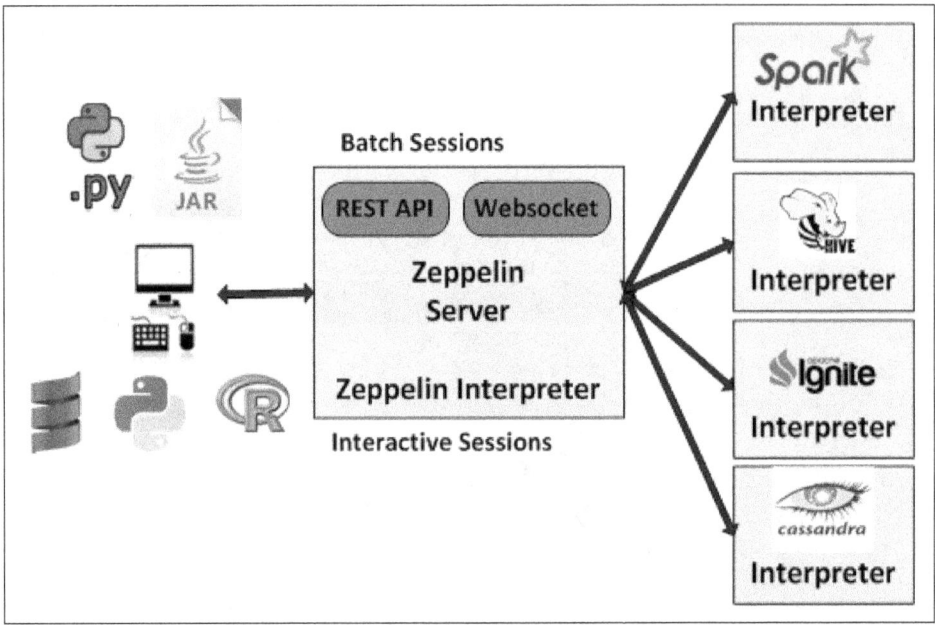

Figure 6.3: The Zeppelin architecture

The components in the Zeppelin architecture are described as follows:

- **Frontend**: This provides UI and shells to interact with humans and a display system to show data in tabular, graphical form, and export iframe.

- **Zeppelin Server**: This provides web sockets and the REST API to interact with the UI and access service remotely. There are two types of API calls — a REST API for notebooks and an Interpreter API for interpreters. The Notebook REST API is to interact with notebooks — creating paragraph, submitting paragraph job in batch, adding cron jobs, and so on. The Interpreter REST API is to change the configuration properties and restart the interpreter. For more information about the REST API, visit `https://github.com/apache/incubator-zeppelin/tree/master/docs/rest-api`.

- **Pluggable Interpreter System**: This is to interact with different interpreters such as Spark, Shell, Markdown, AngularJS, Hive, Ignite, Flink, and others.

- **Interpreters**: Each interpreter runs in a separate JVM to provide the functionality needed by the user.

Jupyter versus Zeppelin

Each product has its own strengths and weaknesses. We need to understand the differences in order to use the right tool for the right use case. The following table shows you the differences between Jupyter and Zeppelin:

	Jupyter	Zeppelin
Evolution	A long history, large community support, and stable	Relatively young
Type of software	Open source	Open source with Apache Releases
Visualization of results	Using tools such as matplotlib	Built-in tools in the notebook for graphs and charts
Customization of forms	No dynamic forms	Dynamic forms with user-provided inputs
Tab completion	Jupyter provides tab completion	Zeppelin does not provide tab completion yet
Languages/ components supported	Over 40+ languages including Python, Julia, and R	Interpreters such as Scala and Python with Apache Spark, Spark SQL, Hive, Markdown, Shell, HBase, Flink, Cassandra, Elasticsearch, Tajo, HDFS, Ignite, Lens, PostgreSQL, Hawq, Scalding, and Geode
Mixing multiple languages	Not easy to mix multiple languages in the same notebook.	It's quite easy to mix multiple languages in the same notebook
Implementation	Python-based	JVM-based
Environments	Jupyter is a generic tool that can be used in any environment	Zeppelin is more suitable for Hadoop and Spark installations

Installing Apache Zeppelin

The latest Hortonworks Sandbox provides a preconfigured Zeppelin service that can be used to quickly try out. If you want to install Zeppelin on a cluster, there are a couple of ways to do so. Use the Hortonworks Ambari service or the manual installation method. The Ambari service can be used for Hortonworks-based installations and the manual installation can be used for Hortonworks, Cloudera, and MapR distributions.

Ambari service

Use the following instructions to install, configure, and start the Zeppelin service on Ambari:

```
VERSION=`hdp-select status hadoop-client | sed 's/hadoop-client -
\([0-9]\.[0-9]\).*/\1/'`
```

```
sudo git clone https://github.com/hortonworks-gallery/
ambari-zeppelin-service.git   /var/lib/ambari-server/resources/stacks/
HDP/$VERSION/services/ZEPPELIN
```

```
sudo ambari-server restart
```

Go to `ipaddressofsandbox:8080` and log in with `admin`/`admin` credentials. The Apache Zeppelin service is now included in the stack and can be added as a service. At the bottom left of the Ambari page, click on **Actions**, click on **Add Service**, check **Zeppelin** service, configure it and deploy.

During the configuration step, change the following parameters as necessary:

- `spark.home`: Use the standard `/usr/hdp/current/spark` or any custom Spark version installed.
- `zeppelin.server.port`: This is the port number where the Zeppelin server listens. Use any unused port.
- `zeppelin.setup.prebuilt`: Make it `false` to get the latest code base.

The manual method

Use the following commands to install and configure the Apache Zeppelin service manually:

```
wget http://mirror.metrocast.net/apache/zeppelin/zeppelin-0.6.1/zeppelin-
0.6.1-bin-all.tgz
```

```
tar xzvf zeppelin-0.6.1-bin-all.tgz
```

```
cd zeppelin-0.6.1-bin-all/conf
```

To access the Hive metastore, copy `hive-site.xml` to the `conf` directory of Zeppelin:

```
cp /etc/hive/conf/hive-site.xml .
```

Copy the configuration template files as follows:

```
cp zeppelin-env.sh.template zeppelin-env.sh
cp zeppelin-site.xml.template zeppelin-site.xml
```

Add the following lines to the `zeppelin-env.sh` file:

```
export JAVA_HOME=/usr/lib/jvm/java
export MASTER=yarn-client
export HDAOOP_CONF_DIR=/etc/hadoop/conf
```

Add the following lines to `zeppelin-site.xml`:

```
<property>
  <name>zeppelin.server.addr</name>
  <value>sandbox.hortonworks.com</value>
  <description>Server address</description>
</property>

<property>
  <name>zeppelin.server.port</name>
  <value>9999</value>
  <description>Server port.</description>
</property>
```

Finally, start the Zeppelin service from the `bin` directory with the following command:

```
cd ../bin/
./zeppelin-daemon.sh start
```

Now you can access your notebook at `http://host.ip.address:9999`.

Analytics with Zeppelin

Zeppelin provides multiple interpreters in the same notebook. So, you can write Scala, Python, SQL, and others in the same notebook.

Click on the **Notebook** menu option at the top of the screen, and then click on **Create new note** and provide a meaningful name for the notebook. The newly created notebook can be opened from the main screen or from the **Notebook** menu option. Click on the newly created notebook and then on the interpreter binding button in the upper right corner. Click on the interpreters to bind or unbind the interpreters. You can change the order of interpreters by dragging and dropping them. The first one on the list will be the default interpreter in the notebook. Finally, click on the **Save** option at the bottom to save the changes.

Now, click on the **Interpreter** menu option at the top and then on **edit** to change Spark properties such as `master`, `spark.cores.max`, `spark.executor.memory`, and `args` as needed by the application. Click on **Save** to make changes to update and restart the interpreter with new settings. You can also restart any specific interpreter by clicking on the **restart** button.

You are now ready to code. As `%spark` is the first on the list of interpreter binding, you don't need to type `%spark` to write Scala code in the paragraph. However, in the paragraph, if you are writing any other code, say, PySpark, you need to type `%pyspark`. Provide a Markdown text in the first paragraph to provide information about the notebook. Write code in the next set of paragraphs. Finally, to visualize the result, write `%sql` or `%table` in a separate paragraph.

Write code from previous chapters or use the **Zeppelin Tutorial** notebook that comes along with Zeppelin for a quick start. You can use the following code to analyze Ambari agent logs:

```
%pyspark
words = sc.textFile('file:///var/log/ambari-agent/
  ambari-agent.log') \
 .flatMap(lambda x: x.lower().split(' ')) \
 .filter(lambda x: x.isalpha()).map(lambda x: (x, 1)) \
 .reduceByKey(lambda a,b: a+b)
sqlContext.registerDataFrameAsTable(sqlContext.createDataFrame(
  words, ['word', 'count']), 'words')

%sql select word, max(count) from words group by word
```

The output of the preceding code looks similar to *Figure 6.4*:

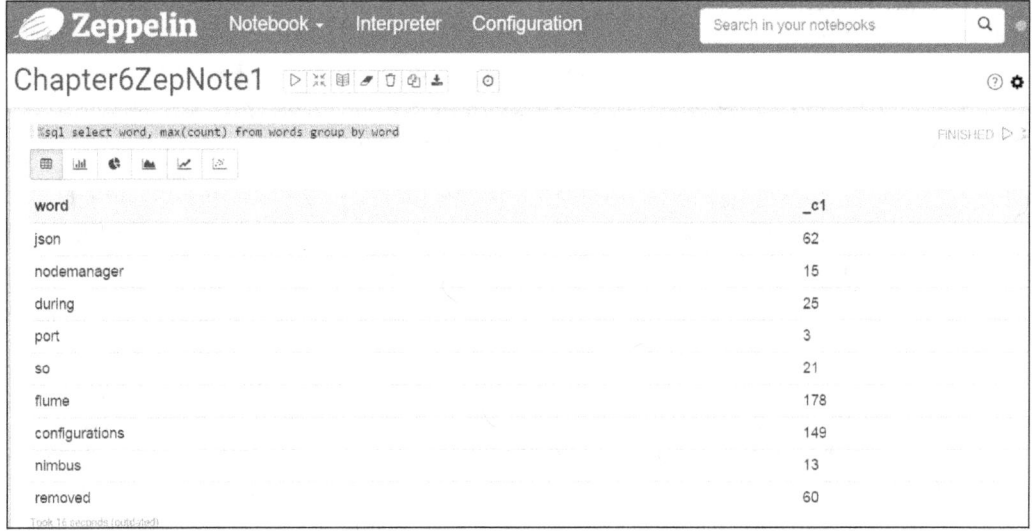

Figure 6.4: Zeppelin visualizations

If you get any errors, check the logs in the logs directory of Zeppelin.

Hortonworks Gallery has prebuilt notebooks at https://github.com/ hortonworks-gallery/zeppelin-notebooks to play with Spark, PySpark, Spark SQL, Spark Streaming, Hive, and so on.

Any existing notebook can be viewed at the ZeppelinHub Viewer:

https://www.zeppelinhub.com/viewer

There are multiple ways to share a notebook with others. Other users on the same cluster can access and run the notebook with the URL of the notebook. You can also share the notebook in report mode by clicking on the drop-down list in the upper right corner and then choosing **report**.

> If you get an error such as interpreter not found, click on the **interpreter binding** icon at the right-hand top corner in the notebook and then click on **Save** to resolve the issue.

The Livy REST job server and Hue Notebooks

Hadoop User Experience (**Hue**) introduced Spark-based notebooks, which are inspired by IPython Notebooks. The Spark Notebook works on the Livy REST job server backend to provide Spark as a service to end users.

Hue Notebooks are similar to IPython Notebooks or Zeppelin Notebooks, which are integrated well with Hadoop ecosystem components. Notebooks support Scala, Python, and R languages, and Hive and Impala queries. They can be shared with import/export and sharing features. Visualizations can be done with a variety of charts and graphs. Hue supports a multiuser environment with impersonation.

Livy is a Spark REST job server that can submit and interact with Spark jobs from anywhere. It is inspired by the popular IPython/Jupyter and Spark REST job server, but implemented to better integrate the Hadoop ecosystem with multiple users. With the Livy server, Spark can be offered as a service to users in the following two ways:

- Instead of every user creating their own shells, Livy creates a shell on the cluster while the end user will access them at their own convenience through a REST API

- Batch applications can also be submitted using a REST API remotely

- Livy creates several SparkContexts and RDDs for users that can be shared with multiple users

- With the YARN impersonation, jobs will be executed with the actual permissions of the users submitting them

Livy supports browser-based notebooks from Hue, Jupyter, or any REST clients. The output of the jobs is returned in a tabular format to visualize in charts in Hue. *Figure 6.5* shows you the architecture of the Livy REST job server and Hue, which has the following main components:

- The Livy web server that exposes a REST API

- The Session Manager creates, and manages sessions for users on YARN

- Pluggable Interpreters such as Scala, PySpark, and R to execute user programs

- Hue web-based notebooks for interactive sessions

- Users sending REST calls from any shell or programs in batch or interactive mode

SparkMagic (`https://github.com/jupyter-incubator/sparkmagic`) provides you with a set of tools to be used to connect to remote Spark clusters from Jupyter notebooks using Livy Server.

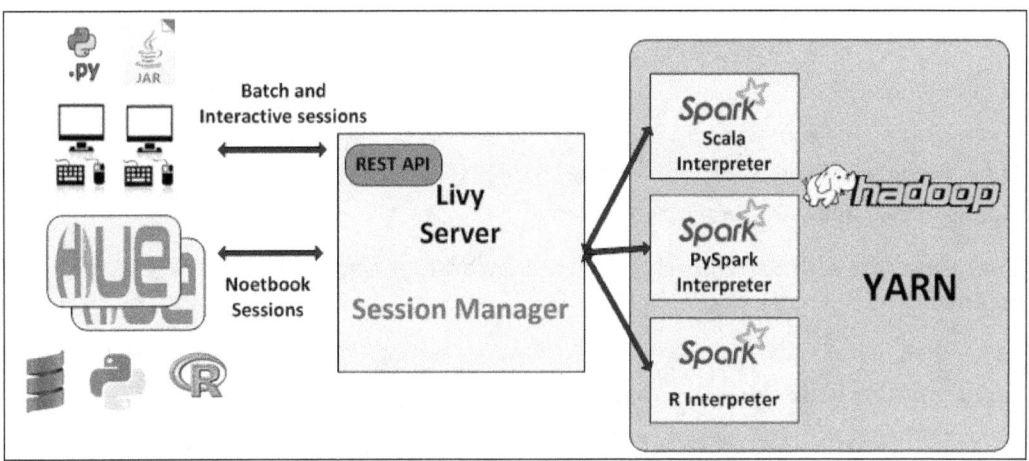

Figure 6.5: The Livy server is between clients and the Spark cluster

Installing and configuring the Livy server and Hue

The latest Livy version must be installed before using Hue Notebooks. Follow these instructions to install and configure the Livy job server on a CDH QuickStart VM or any CDH cluster. Note that the Livy server and Hue Notebooks are in alpha release mode as of writing this book.

You can download and unzip prebuilt binaries as follows:

```
wget  http://archive.cloudera.com/beta/livy/livy-server-0.2.0.zip
unzip livy-server-0.2.0.zip
cd livy-server-0.2.0
```

You can also download and compile the source, as shown in the following:

```
git clone https://github.com/cloudera/livy.git
cd livy
mvn -DskipTests clean package
mvn -Dspark.version=1.6.1 package (To build Livy against a specific
version of spark)
```

Once you are done with one of the preceding two methods, follow the steps:

```
cd conf/
```

Add the following configuration properties to `livy.conf` to enable a YARN impersonation of other users:

```
vi livy.conf
```

```
livy.impersonation.enabled = true
livy.server.session.factory = yarn
```

Create a script with the following parameters and then start the `livy-server` command:

```
cd ../bin
export SPARK_HOME=/usr/lib/spark/
export CLASSPATH=`hadoop classpath`
export HADOOP_CONF_DIR=/etc/hadoop/conf/
export LIVY_SERVER_JAVA_OPTS="-Dlivy.impersonation.enabled=true"
./livy-server
```

The REST server will start at the default port number `8998`. Change the port number to a different port number in the configuration if necessary.

Using the Livy server

There are multiple ways to use Livy's REST API. You can submit jobs interactively in a shell or in batch mode. SparkContext and RDDs created within SparkContext can be shared by multiple users. Let's understand these features with simple examples.

An interactive session

An interactive session is similar to Spark-shell or PySpark shell, where we interactively enter commands and check the result. However, instead of users creating the SparkContext, users will interact with Livy using a REST API, and the Livy server creates and manages the sessions for users. To check the existing sessions, run the following command from any terminal. This will return zero if no sessions are running:

```
curl localhost:8998/sessions | python -m json.tool
```

```
{"from": 0,"sessions": [],"total": 0}
```

Create a PySpark session with the following command, which will return the session ID number. In this example, the ID number is 0 with the status as starting. If you submit another similar command, a new session will be created by incrementing the session ID:

```
curl -X POST --data '{"kind": "pyspark"}' -H "Content-Type:
application/json" localhost:8998/sessions
```

```
{"id":0,"state":"starting","kind":"pyspark","log":[]}
```

Let's poll the status again with the following command. When the status becomes idle, a session will be ready to receive any interactive commands. This command displays the log output as well, so, if the state is in error, check the log in the JSON output:

```
curl localhost:8998/sessions/0 | python -m json.tool
```

```
"state": "idle"
```

We are now ready to submit interactive commands. Let's submit a simple PySpark code and check the output:

```
curl localhost:8998/sessions/0/statements -X POST -H 'Content-Type:
application/json' -d '{"code":"sc.parallelize(range(1000)).map(lambda
x: 2 * x).take(10)"}'
```

```
{"id":2,"state":"running","output":null}
```

From the preceding result, id will become the statement number. So, run the following command to view the output:

```
curl localhost:8998/sessions/0/statements/2 | python -m json.tool
```

```
{
    "id": 2,
    "output": {
        "data": {
            "text/plain": "[0, 2, 4, 6, 8, 10, 12, 14, 16, 18]"
        },
        "execution_count": 2,
        "status": "ok"
    },
```

```
    "state": "available"
}
```

The computation result is shown as [0, 2, 4, 6, 8, 10, 12, 14, 16, 18]. You can submit any Spark code snippet in the code block. Once you are done with the session, delete the session as follows:

```
curl localhost:8998/sessions/0 -X DELETE
```

```
{"msg":"deleted"}
```

A batch session

A batch session is similar to submitting applications using spark-submit. As the first step, copy all the JARs or Python files to the HDFS filesystem to execute them:

```
hadoop fs -put /usr/lib/spark/lib/spark-examples.jar

sudo tar xzvf /usr/lib/spark/examples/lib/python.tar.gz

hadoop fs -put /usr/lib/spark/examples/lib/pi.py

curl -X POST --data '{"file": "/user/cloudera/spark-examples.jar",
"className": "org.apache.spark.examples.SparkPi", "args": ["100"]}'
-H "Content-Type: application/json" localhost:8998/batches
```

```
{"id":1,"state":"running","log":[]}
```

Check the status of the job at the resource manager UI, http://quickstart.cloudera:8088/cluster, or check with the following REST call:

```
curl localhost:8998/batches/1 | python -m json.tool
```

To delete a running job, use the following command:

```
curl -X DELETE localhost:8998/batches/1
{"msg":"deleted"}
```

To run a PySpark batch job, use the following command:

```
curl -X POST --data '{"file": "user/cloudera/pi.py"}' -H
"Content-Type: application/json" localhost:8998/batches
```

```
{"id":2,"state":"starting","log":[]}
```

Command-line arguments can be passed args, as shown in the first example. The entire batch API can be found at https://github.com/cloudera/hue/tree/master/apps/spark/java#post-batches.

Sharing SparkContexts and RDDs

Usually, multiple users will create their own sessions and won't share with each other. This will waste the resources of the Spark cluster. If all users are talking to the same session, they would interact with the same SparkContext. This context would itself manage several RDDs, which can be shared by multiple users. Users simply need to use the same session ID, for example, 0, and issue commands there.

They can be accessed from any shell, program, or notebook. Here is an example:

User1 creates an RDD with the name `sharedRDD` in session 0. Then, both User1 and User2 access the same RDD using the same session ID, as shown here:

User1 uses the following command:

```
curl localhost:8998/sessions/0/statements -X POST -H 'Content-Type:
application/json' -d '{"code":"sharedRDD.collect()"}'
```

User2 uses the following command:

```
curl localhost:8998/sessions/0/statements -X POST -H 'Content-Type:
application/json' -d '{"code":"sharedRDD.take(5)"}'
```

Using Livy with Hue Notebook

As the Spark Notebooks in Hue are in the beta mode, it is not enabled by default in Hue. To enable the Spark Notebooks in Hue, make the following changes in Cloudera Manager:

1. Navigate to **Hue** service | **Configuration** | **Advanced** | **Hue Service Advanced Configuration Snippet (Safety Valve) for hue_safety_valve.ini** and enter the following lines:

   ```
   [desktop]
   app_blacklist=

   [notebook]
   show_notebooks=true
   ```

2. In the **Hue Server Advanced Configuration Snippet (Safety Valve) for hue_safety_valve_server.ini**, enter the following lines:

   ```
   [spark]
   server_url=http://quickstart.cloudera:8998/
   livy_server_host=quickstart.cloudera
   livy_server_port=8998
   livy_server_session_kind=yarn
   livy_impersonation_enabled=false
   livy_server_session_timeout=3600000
   ```

3. In the **HDFS Service | Configuration | Service-Wide-Advanced | Cluster-wide Advanced Configuration Snippet (Safety Valve) for core-site.xml**, enter the following key value pairs:

```
hadoop.proxyuser.livy.groups *
hadoop.proxyuser.livy.hosts *
```

4. Save the configuration changes and restart HDFS and Hue.

Before using the Hue Notebook, stop the Livy server by pressing *Ctrl + C* in the terminal where the Livy server is running. Start the Livy server by disabling impersonation to avoid errors in Hue:

```
CLASSPATH=`hadoop classpath` SPARK_HOME=/usr/lib/spark/ HADOOP_CONF_
DIR=/etc/hadoop/conf/ LIVY_SERVER_JAVA_OPTS="-Dlivy.impersonation.
enabled=false" ./livy-server
```

Log in to Hue using `cloudera/cloudera` credentials at `http://quickstart.cloudera:8888/about/`. Hue ships sample tables along with the Hue installation. Go to Hue's main screen, click on **Step 2: Examples**, and then import all examples. This will create the `web_logs` table, which can be used with Impala queries.

Navigate to **Notebooks** menu and then open a new notebook or an existing notebook.

The notebook look and feel, execution, and general notebook operations will be similar to IPython or Zeppelin Notebooks.

Figure 6.6 shows you the available snippets from the Spark Notebook application. It shows PySpark, R, Hive, Impala, and Scala snippets. For more snippets, click on **select snippet** on the plus symbol that will show more snippets, such as **Spark Submit Jar** and **Spark Submit Python**, and so on:

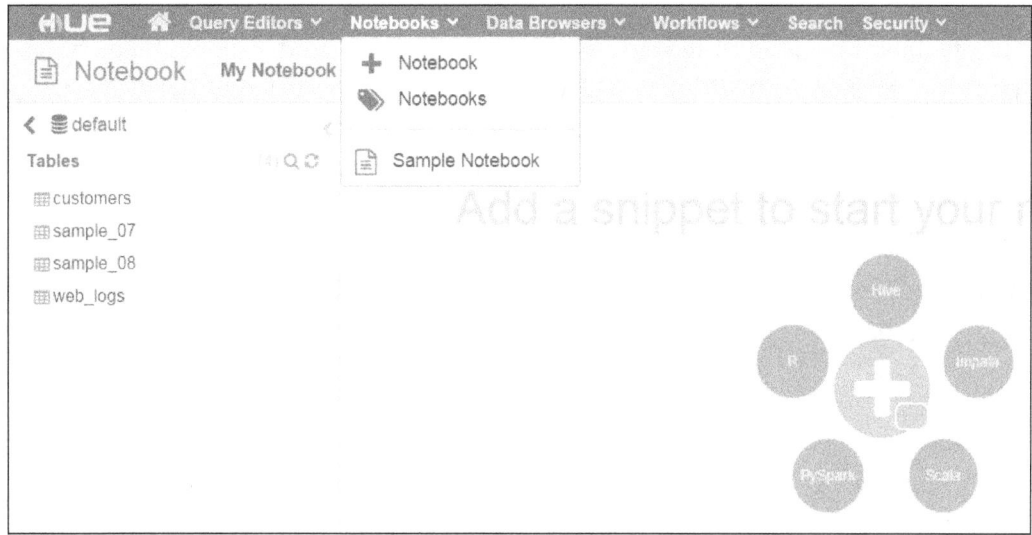

Figure 6.6: The Hue Notebook

For a new notebook, click on **PySpark,** enter the name of the notebook, and enter the following code. Note that it takes more time on the first execution as the SparkContext has not started yet. The next set of commands will be quickly executed:

```
sc.parallelize(range(1000)).map(lambda x: x * x).take(10)
```

Figure 6.7 shows you the typical execution of PySpark code in the Hue notebook. Notice that a job is running in the job browser with the name as `livy-session-0`, application type as `SPARK,` and user as `cloudera`. Click on the job ID and then on the URL of the jobs, which will take you to the Spark UI. The jobs submitted in Hue will appear on this Spark UI:

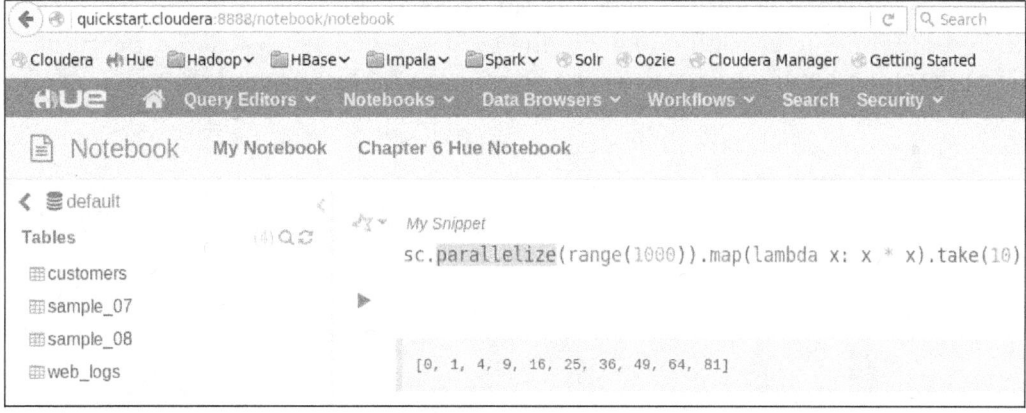

Figure 6.7: The Hue PySpark notebook

Now click on the drop-down menu in front of the PySpark icon and select **Impala**. Install Impala examples from step 2 of HUE quick start wizard. Run the following query and select **gradient map** from the drop-down list. Select **country_code3** as **REGION** and **count(*)** as **VALUE**.

```
invalidate metadata;

select country_code3, count(*) from web_logs group by country_code3;
```

Results will be shown on the world map, as shown in *Figure 6.8*:

Figure 6.8: HUE visualizations

Using Livy with Zeppelin

Apache Zeppelin provides an interpreter for Livy server. So, Apache Spark jobs can be executed interactively from a Zeppelin notebook. Configure `livy.spark.master` and `zeppelin.livy.url` in Livy interpreter settings before using it. External libraries to be configured with the `livy.spark.jars.packages` property. The interpreter bindings to be used are `%livy.spark`, `%livy.pyspark`, and `%livy.sparkr`. For more information, refer to `https://zeppelin.apache.org/docs/0.6.0/interpreter/livy.html`.

Introducing Apache NiFi for dataflows

Apache NiFi automates dataflows by receiving data from any source, such as Twitter, Kafka, databases, and so on, and sends it to any data processing system, such as Hadoop or Spark, and then finally to data storage systems, such as HBase, Cassandra, and other databases. There can be multiple problems at these three layers, such as systems being down, or data production and consumption rates are not in sync. Apache NiFi addresses the dataflow challenges by providing the following key features:

- Guaranteed delivery with write-ahead logs

- Data buffering with Back Pressure and Pressure Release

- Prioritized queuing with the oldest first, newest first, or largest first, and so on

- Configurations for low latency, high throughput, loss tolerance, and so on

- Data provenance records all data events for later discovery or debugging

- Data is rolled off as it ages

- Visual Command and Control provides dataflow visualizations and enables making changes to the existing dataflows without stopping them

- XML-based flow templates make it easy to version control and share

- High security with encryption such as two-way SSL

- Designed for extension at all levels

- Clustering for scale-out architecture

Hortonworks supports Apache NiFi in their product **Hortonworks DataFlow (HDF)**.

Installing Apache NiFi

Hortonworks' latest sandbox VM has a pre-configured NiFi setup. The NiFi service should be added from Ambari. Go to `ipaddressofsandbox:8080` and log in with `admin`/`admin` credentials. On the bottom left of the Ambari page, navigate to **Actions | Add Service**, check the NiFi service, then configure and deploy.

Configure the port number and other properties in the `nifi.properties` as needed during the configuration stage.

Log in to the NiFi UI at `ipaddressofsandbox:9090/nifi`.

If you want to download HDF, instructions for downloading, installing, and running the service can be found at `http://docs.hortonworks.com/HDPDocuments/HDF1/HDF-1.2.0.1/bk_HDF_GettingStarted/content/ch_HDF_GettingStarted.html`.

Dataflows and analytics with NiFi

There are prebuilt NiFi templates that can be downloaded and tested in your NiFi environment. Templates are available at `https://cwiki.apache.org/confluence/display/NIFI/Example+Dataflow+Templates`. Download the necessary templates to your machine.

In the NiFi window, you need to click on the **Templates** link in the upper right corner. Click on **Browse**, select the template, click on **Open**, and then import it.

Drag the template from the upper left-hand side menu to the main screen and then select the template to create the workflow from an XML document. Follow the instructions mentioned for every template in the preceding link. Right-click on the processors and verify the configurations. Click on the play button at the top to start the workflow.

More information on how to create and manage dataflows is available at `https://nifi.apache.org/docs.html`.

Let's create a simple dataflow in NiFi by getting data from Kafka and writing to a Spark Streaming application and HDFS. The goal of this application is to analyze Ambari logs and produce a number of INFO, WARN, and ERROR messages in a given timeframe. Perform the following commands to create a Kafka topic and start sending the Ambari agent log data to the topic to analyze in the Spark Streaming application:

```
cd /usr/hdp/current/kafka-broker/bin/
```

```
./kafka-topics.sh --zookeeper localhost:2181 --topic ambarilogs --create
--partitions 2 --replication-factor 1
```

```
tail -f /var/log/ambari-agent/ambari-agent.log | ./kafka-console-
producer.sh --broker-list sandbox.hortonworks.com:6667 --topic ambarilogs
```

Download `spark-reciever` and site-to-site client jars. Check the NiFi version and download compatible versions. This example downloads 0.5.1 version related jars:

```
mkdir /opt/spark-receiver
```

```
cd /opt/spark-receiver
```

```
wget http://central.maven.org/maven2/org/apache/nifi/nifi-site-to-site-
client/0.5.1/nifi-site-to-site-client-0.5.1.jar
```

```
wget http://central.maven.org/maven2/org/apache/nifi/nifi-spark-
receiver/0.5.1/nifi-spark-receiver-0.5.1.jar
```

In Ambari, go to Spark service configurations and add the following two properties in custom `spark-defaults` and then restart Spark service:

`spark.driver.allowMultipleContexts true`

```
spark.driver.extraClassPath /opt/spark-receiver/nifi-spark-receiver-
0.5.1.jar:/opt/spark-receiver/nifi-site-to-site-client-0.5.1.jar:/
opt/nifi-0.5.1.1.1.2.0-32/lib/nifi-api-0.5.1.1.1.2.0-32.jar:/opt/
nifi-0.5.1.1.1.2.0-32/lib/bootstrap/nifi-utils-0.5.1.1.1.2.0-32.
jar:/opt/nifi-0.5.1.1.1.2.0-32/work/nar/framework/nifi-framework-
nar-0.5.1.1.1.2.0-32.nar-unpacked/META-INF/bundled-dependencies/nifi-
client-dto-0.5.1.1.1.2.0-32.jar
```

In Ambari NiFi configurations, change the following site-to-site configurations and restart the service:

```
nifi.remote.input.socket.host=
nifi.remote.input.socket.port=8055
nifi.remote.input.secure=false
```

On the NiFi UI (`ipaddressofsandbox:9090/nifi`), drag a processor and choose and add **GetKafka** processor. Right-click on the processor and click on **configure**. Enter the Zookeeper connection string as `ipaddressofsandbox:2181` (for example, `192.168.139.167:2181`) and topic as `ambarilogs`. Add another **PutHDFS** processor and configure to write to the `/tmp/kafka` directory and specify the configuration resources as `/etc/hadoop/conf/core-site.xml` and `/etc/hadoop/conf/hdfs-site.xml`. Set auto terminate relationships in HDFS processor. Also, drag an output port and name it as `Data for Spark`. Connect the processors and start the dataflow. Make sure to remove all warnings that are shown at the top of the processor.

Now, let's create a Scala Spark streaming application `ambari-logs.sh` with the following code to pull data from NiFi workflow:

`cd /opt/spark-receiver`

`vi ambari-logs.sh`

The code is as follows:

```
import org.apache.nifi._
import java.nio.charset._
import org.apache.nifi.spark._
import org.apache.nifi.remote.client._
import org.apache.spark._
import org.apache.nifi.events._
import org.apache.spark.streaming._
import org.apache.spark.streaming.StreamingContext._
import org.apache.nifi.remote._
```

```
import org.apache.nifi.remote.client._
import org.apache.nifi.remote.protocol._
import org.apache.spark.storage._
import org.apache.spark.streaming.receiver._
import java.io._
import org.apache.spark.serializer._
import org.apache.nifi.remote.client.SiteToSiteClient
import org.apache.nifi.spark.{NiFiDataPacket, NiFiReceiver}
import org.apache.spark.SparkConf
import org.apache.spark.storage.StorageLevel
import org.apache.spark.streaming.dstream.{DStream,
ReceiverInputDStream}
import org.apache.spark.streaming.{Seconds, StreamingContext}

object SparkNiFiAmbari {
  def main(args: Array[String]) {
  val conf = new
    SiteToSiteClient.Builder().url("http://localhost:9090/nifi")
    .portName("Data for Spark").buildConfig()
  val config = new SparkConf().setAppName("Ambari Log Analyzer")
  val ssc = new StreamingContext(config, Seconds(30))
  val packetStream: ReceiverInputDStream[NiFiDataPacket] =
      ssc.receiverStream(new NiFiReceiver(conf,
      StorageLevel.MEMORY_ONLY))
      val lines: DStream[String] = packetStream.flatMap(packet =>
        new String(packet.getContent).split("\n"))
      val pairs: DStream[(String, Int)] = lines.map(line =>
        (line.split(" ")(0), 1))
      val wordCounts: DStream[(String, Int)] =
        pairs.reduceByKey(_ + _)

      wordCounts.print()

  ssc.start()
  }
}
SparkNiFiAmbari.main(Array())
```

Start the Spark shell by passing the program to it:

```
spark-shell -i ambari-logs.sh
```

The output will appear on the screen as follows:

```
-------------------------------------------
Time: 1471091460000 ms
-------------------------------------------
(INFO,46)
(WARN,4)
(ERROR,1)
```

Check the HDFS directory (`/tmp/kafka`) to see whether the data is being written from Kafka. The NiFi dataflow looks similar to *Figure 6.9*. Note that data buffering occurs if you stop the Spark Streaming application, and data will not be lost:

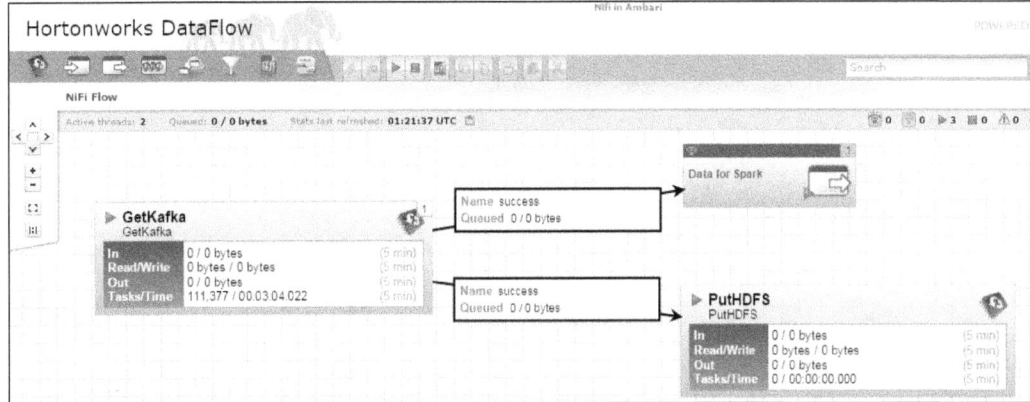

Figure 6.9: The NiFi workflow

We are now ready to play with the various notebooks and dataflow tools.
Happy coding!

Summary

Web-based notebooks are really helpful because they provide rich visualizations and high developer productivity and make it easy to share with others. While there are many open source-based notebooks available, the most popular notebooks are Jupyter and Apache Zeppelin. The Jupyter Notebook is very mature, supports over 40 languages, and integrates with Spark and Hadoop to query interactively and visualize results. Apache Zeppelin is a web-based notebook that enables data-driven, interactive analytics with built-in visualizations. There are many similarities between Jupyter and Zeppelin, but Zeppelin is tightly integrated with Spark and Hadoop, and it is also possible to include multiple languages in the same notebook.

Hue 3.8 introduced Spark-based notebooks, which are inspired by IPython Notebooks that provide built-in visualizations. The Spark Notebook works on the Livy REST job server backend to provide Spark as a service to end users. The Livy job server exposes both batch and interactive REST APIs. It enables users to share SparkContexts and RDDs.

Apache NiFi automates dataflows by receiving data from any source, such as Twitter, Kafka, databases, and so on, and sends it to any data processing system, such as Hadoop and Spark, and then finally to data storage systems, such as HBase, Cassandra, and other databases.

In the next chapter, you will start learning machine learning on Spark and Hadoop.

7
Machine Learning with Spark and Hadoop

We have discussed a typical life cycle of a data science project in *Chapter 1, Big Data Analytics at a 10,000-Foot View*. This chapter, however, is aimed at learning more about machine learning techniques used in data science with Spark and Hadoop.

Data science is all about extracting deep meaning from data and creating data products. This requires both tools and methods such as statistics, machine learning algorithms, and tools for data collection and data cleansing. Once the data is collected and cleansed, it is analyzed using exploratory analytics to find patterns and build models with the aim of extracting deep meaning or creating a data product.

So, let's understand how these patterns and models are created. This chapter is divided into the following subtopics:

- Introducing machine learning
- Machine learning on Spark and Hadoop
- Machine learning algorithms
- Examples of machine learning algorithms
- Building machine learning pipelines
- Machine learning with H2O and Spark
- Introducing Hivemall
- Introducing Hivemall for Spark

Introducing machine learning

Machine learning is the science of making machines work without programming predefined rules. Let's go through a simple example of how a program is written with a regular approach and a machine learning approach. For example, if you are developing a spam filter. You need to identify all possible parameters at design time and hardcode them within the program as follows:

```
spam_words = ("No investment", "Why pay more?",
              "You are a winner!", "Free quote")

import sys
for line in sys.stdin:
    if spam_words in line:
        print "Spam Found"
    else:
        process_lines()
```

In machine learning, computers will learn from the data we provide and make a decision on these spam words. Machine learning is similar to human learning. Let's understand how humans learn.

Humans learn something by doing a task over and over again, which is known as practice. Humans gain experience by practicing something. They get better at the task with more and more practice. Humans are considered to have learned something when they can repeat a task with some expected level of accuracy. However, human learning is not scalable as it has to consider a variety of things.

In machine learning, you typically provide **training data** with **features**, such as the type of words with **output variables** such as spam or ham. Once this data is fed to machine learning algorithms, such as **classification** or **regression**, it learns a model of correlation between features and output variables. You can predict that the e-mail is a spam or ham by providing input e-mails called **test data** to the model. You can refine the model by providing more and more **training data** to improve accuracy. You can see a spam detection example with machine learning in the next section.

The advantages of machine learning are as follows:

- It is more accurate than human learning as it is data-driven. The bigger the data, a better accuracy level is achieved as it learns from the data.

- Machine learning can be automated to automatically predict or recommend products.

- Machine learning algorithms can produce answers in milliseconds, which enables us to create real-time applications.
- Machine learning algorithms are scalable and able to process all data.

The disadvantages of machine learning are as follows:

- You need to acquire the right data (labeled data) and enrich it
- It is usually impossible to get 100% accuracy

Machine learning on Spark and Hadoop

MLlib is a machine learning library on top of Spark that provides major machine learning algorithms and utilities. It is divided into two separate packages:

- `spark.mllib`: This is the original machine learning API built on top of **Resilient Distributed Datasets (RDD)**. As of Spark 2.0, this RDD-based API is in maintenance mode and is expected to be deprecated and removed in upcoming releases of Spark.
- `spark.ml`: This is the primary machine learning API built on top of DataFrames to construct machine learning pipelines and optimizations.

`spark.ml` is preferred over `spark.mllib` because it is based on the DataFrames API that provides higher performance and flexibility.

Apache Mahout was a general machine learning library on top of Hadoop. Mahout started out primarily as a Java MapReduce package to run machine learning algorithms. As machine learning algorithms are iterative in nature, MapReduce had major performance and scalability issues. So, Mahout stopped the development of MapReduce-based algorithms and started supporting new platforms such as Spark, H2O, and Flink with a new package called Samsara. The Apache Mahout integration with Spark is explained in *Chapter 8, Building Recommendation Systems with Spark and Mahout*.

The **Sparkling Water** project allows H2O project's powerful machine learning algorithms to be used on a Spark cluster. It is an open source system that offers the ability to develop machine learning applications in Java, Scala, Python, and R. It also has the ability to interface with HDFS, Amazon S3, SQL, and NoSQL databases as well. Sparkling Water is explained in detail in the *Getting started with Sparkling Water* section of this chapter.

Machine learning algorithms

The following table provides a list of algorithms supported by MLlib with classifications such as the type of machine learning and the type of algorithm:

Type of machine learning	Type of algorithm	Algorithm name
Supervised learning	Classification	Naive Bayes
		Decision Trees
		Random Forests
		Gradient-Boosted Trees
	Regression	Linear Regression
		Logistic Regression
		Support Vector Machines
Unsupervised learning	Clustering	K-Means
		Gaussian mixture
		Power Iteration Clustering (PIC)
		Latent Dirichlet Allocation (LDA)
		Streaming k-means
	Dimensionality reduction	**Singular Value Decomposition (SVD)**
		Principal Component Analysis (PCA)
Recommender systems	Collaborative filtering	User-based collaborative filtering
		Item-based collaborative filtering
		Alternating Least Squares (ALS)
Feature extraction	Feature extraction and transformation	TF-IDF
		Word2Vec
		Standard Scaler
		Normalizer
		Chi-Square Selector
Optimization	Optimization	Stochastic Gradient Descent
		Limited-memory BFGS

Let's understand these algorithms now.

Supervised learning

Supervised learning deals with labeled training data. For example, historical e-mail training data will have e-mails marked as ham or spam. This data is used to train a model that can predict and classify future e-mails as ham or spam. Supervised learning problems can be broadly categorized into two major types—classification and regression:

Classification predicts categorical variables or classes. A couple of examples are spam detection and predicting customer churn. This target variable is discrete and has a predefined set of values. The classification algorithms are as follows:

- **Naive Bayes**: This algorithm makes predictions based on the conditional probability distribution of a label given an observation. This assumes that features are mutually independent of each other.

- **Decision Trees**: This algorithm uses a decision tree as a predictive model, which maps observations about an item to conclusions about the item's target value.

- **Ensembles of trees (Random Forests** and **Gradient-Boosted Trees)**: Ensemble algorithms combine base decision tree models in order to build a robust model. They are intuitive and very successful for classification and regression tasks.

Regression deals with a target variable and is continuous. For example, to predict house prices, the target variable price is continuous and doesn't have a predefined set of values. The regression algorithms are as follows:

- **Regression Models (Linear Regression, Logistic Regression,** and **Support Vector Machines)**: Regression algorithms are expressed as convex optimization problems aiming to minimize an objective function based on a vector of weight variables. An objective function controls the complexity of the model through the regularized part of the function, and the error of the model through the loss part of the function.

Unsupervised learning

Unsupervised learning deals with unlabeled data. The objective is to observe structure in the data and find patterns. Tasks such as cluster analysis, association rule mining, outlier detection, dimensionality reduction, and so on can be modeled as unsupervised learning problems.

The clustering algorithms are as follows:

- **K-Means**: This is the task of grouping similar objects (called a cluster) together to partition n observations into k clusters, for example, grouping similar customers together to target them separately, detecting abnormal data, and clustering of text documents.

- **Gaussian mixure**: This is a probabilistic model that is also used for data clustering such as k-means.

- **Power Iteration Clustering (PIC)**: This algorithm groups vertices of a graph based on pairwise edge similarities.

- **Latent Dirichlet Allocation (LDA)**: This algorithm is used to group collections of text documents into topics.

- **Streaming K-Means**: This algorithm clusters streaming data dynamically using a windowing function on the incoming data. This is a really useful algorithm in Spark Streaming applications.

Dimensionality Reduction algorithms aim to reduce the number of features under consideration. This reduces noise in the data and focuses on key features. This type of algorithms include the following:

- **Singular Value Decomposition (SVD)**: This algorithm breaks the matrix that contains the data into simpler meaningful pieces. It factorizes the initial matrix into three matrices.

- **Principal Component Analysis (PCA)**: This algorithm approximates a high dimensional dataset with a low dimensional subspace.

Recommender systems

Recommender systems are used to recommend products or information to users. Examples are video recommendations on YouTube or Netflix.

Collaborative filtering forms the basis for recommender systems. It creates a user-item association matrix and aims to fill the gaps. Based on other users and items, along with their ratings, it recommends an item that the target user has no ratings for. In Spark, one of the most useful algorithms is Alternating Least Squares, which is described as follows:

- **Alternating Least Squares (ALS)**: ALS models the rating matrix (**R**) as the multiplication of low-rank user (**U**) and product (**V**) factors and learns these factors by minimizing the reconstruction error of the observed ratings. Input data can be of two types—explicit feedback or implicit feedback from users. In explicit feedback, the relationship between a set of user-item pairs is directly known, for example, the presence of movie ratings from different users on movies. In implicit feedback, the relationship does not exist directly. A recommender system has to infer user preferences from the presence or absence of movies watched or not, purchases, and click or search events. An implicit feedback problem is much harder than an explicit feedback problem. This is discussed in detail in *Chapter 8, Building Recommendation Systems with Spark and Mahout*.

Feature extraction and transformation

Feature extraction and transformation are essential techniques to process large text documents and other datasets. It has the following techniques:

- **Term frequency**: Search engines use TF-IDF to score and rank document relevance in a vast corpus. It is also used in machine learning to determine the importance of a word in a document or corpus. **term frequency** (**TF**) statistically determines the weight of a term relative to its frequency in the corpus. **Inverse Document Frequency** (**IDF**) provides the specificity or measure of the amount of information, whether the term is rare or common across all documents in the corpus.

- **Word2Vec**: This method computes the distributed vector representation of words. It includes two models—**skip-gram** and **continuous bag of words**. The skip-gram model predicts neighboring words in sliding windows of words. The continuous bag of words model predicts the current word given the neighboring words.

- **Standard Scaler**: As part of preprocessing the dataset, it must often be standardized by mean removal and variance scaling. This computes the mean and standard deviation on the training data and applies the same transformation to the test data.

- **Normalizer**: This scales the individual samples to have a unit norm.

- **Chi-Square Selector**: This is a statistical method to measure the independence of two events.

Optimization

Optimization algorithms of MLlib focus on techniques of gradient descent. Spark provides an implementation of gradient descent on a distributed cluster of machines. This is compute-intensive as it iterates through all the data available. The optimization algorithms include the following:

- **Stochastic Gradient Descent**: This minimizes an objective function that is the sum of differentiable functions. Stochastic Gradient Descent uses only a sample of the training data in order to update a parameter in a particular iteration. It is used for large-scale and sparse machine learning problems, such as text classification.

- **Limited-memory BFGS (L-BFGS)**: As the name says, L-BFGS uses limited memory and suits the distributed optimization algorithm implementation of Spark MLlib.

Spark MLlib data types

MLlib supports four data types used in MLlib algorithms—local vector, labeled point, local matrix, and distributed matrix:

We need to install numpy to work with MLlib data types and algorithms, so use the following commands to install numpy:

 All programs in this chapter are executed on CDH 5.8 VM. For other environments, file paths might change, but the concepts are the same in any environment.

```
[cloudera@quickstart ~]$ sudo yum -y install python-pip
[cloudera@quickstart ~]$ sudo pip install --upgrade pip
[cloudera@quickstart ~]$ sudo pip install 'numpy==1.8.1'
[cloudera@quickstart ~]$ sudo pip install 'scipy==0.9.0'
```

- **Local vector**: This can be a dense or sparse vector that is stored on a single machine.

  A dense vector is a traditional array of doubles:

  ```
  >>> import numpy as np
  >>> import scipy.sparse as sps
  >>> from pyspark.mllib.linalg import Vectors
  >>> dv1 = np.array([2.0, 0.0, 5.0])
  >>> dv1
  array([ 2.,   0.,   5.])
  ```

  A sparse vector uses integer indices and double values:

  ```
  >>> sv1 = Vectors.sparse(2, [0, 3], [5.0, 1.0])
  >>> sv1
  SparseVector(2, {0: 5.0, 3: 1.0})
  ```

- **Labeled point**: This can be a dense or sparse vector with a label used in supervised learning:

  ```
  >>> from pyspark.mllib.linalg import SparseVector
  >>> from pyspark.mllib.regression import LabeledPoint

  # Labeled point with a positive label and a dense feature vector
  >>> lp_pos = LabeledPoint(1.0, [4.0, 0.0, 2.0])
  >>> lp_pos
  LabeledPoint(1.0, [4.0,0.0,2.0])

  # Labeled point with a negative label and a sparse feature vector
  >>> lp_neg = LabeledPoint(0.0, SparseVector(5, [1, 2], [3.0, 5.0]))
  >>> lp_neg
  LabeledPoint(0.0, (5,[1,2],[3.0,5.0]))
  ```

- **Local matrix**: This is a matrix with integer type indices and double type values. This is also stored on a single machine.

  ```
  from pyspark.mllib.linalg import Matrix, Matrices
  # Dense matrix ((1.0, 2.0, 3.0), (4.0, 5.0, 6.0))
  dMatrix = Matrices.dense(2, 3, [1, 2, 3, 4, 5, 6])
  # Sparse matrix ((9.0, 0.0), (0.0, 8.0), (0.0, 6.0))
  sMatrix = Matrices.sparse(3, 2, [0, 1, 3], [0, 2, 1], [9, 6, 8])
  ```

- **Distributed matrix**: This matrix is stored distributively in one or more RDDs on multiple machines. There are four types of distributed matrix available— `RowMatrix`, `IndexedRowMatrix`, `CoordinateMatrix`, and `BlockMatrix`:
    - ○ `RowMatrix`: This is a distributed matrix of rows with meaningless indices created from an RDD of vectors.
    - ○ `IndexedRowMatrix`: Row indices are meaningful in this matrix. The RDD is created with indexed rows using the `IndexedRow` class and then `IndexedRowMatrix` is created.
    - ○ `CoordinateMatrix`: This matrix is useful for very large and sparse matrices. `CoordinateMatrix` is created from RDDs of the `MatrixEntry` points, represented by a tuple of the `long` or `float` type.
    - ○ `BlockMatrix`: `BlockMatrix` is created from RDDs of sub-matrix blocks.

An example of machine learning algorithms

This section shows you an example of building a machine learning application for spam detection using RDD-based API. The next section shows an example based on DataFrame-based API.

Logistic regression for spam detection

Let's use two algorithms to build a spam classifier:

- `HashingTF` to build term frequency feature vectors from a text of spam and ham e-mails
- `LogisticRegressionWithSGD` to build a model to separate the type of messages, such as spam or ham

As you have learned how to use notebooks in *Chapter 6, Notebooks and Dataflows with Spark and Hadoop*, you may execute the following code in the IPython Notebook or Zeppelin Notebook. You can execute the code from the command line as well:

1. First of all, let's create some sample spam and ham e-mails:

```
[cloudera@quickstart ~]$ cat spam_messages.txt
$$$ Send money
100% free
Amazing stuff
Home based
```

```
Reverses aging
No investment
Send SSN and password


[cloudera@quickstart ~]$ cat ham_messages.txt
Thank you for attending conference
Message from school
Recommended courses for you
Your order is ready for pickup
Congratulations on your anniversary
```

2. Copy both files to HDFS:

```
[cloudera@quickstart ~]$ hadoop fs -put spam_messages.txt
[cloudera@quickstart ~]$ hadoop fs -put ham_messages.txt
```

3. Get into the PySpark shell with the following command. You can change the `master` to `yarn-client` to execute on YARN:

```
[cloudera@quickstart ~]$ pyspark --master local[*]
```

4. Import all dependencies as the first step:

```
>>> from pyspark import SparkContext
>>> from pyspark.mllib.regression import LabeledPoint
>>> from pyspark.mllib.classification import
LogisticRegressionWithSGD
>>> from pyspark.mllib.feature import HashingTF
```

5. Create RDDs for spam and ham messages:

```
>>> spam_messages = sc.textFile("spam_messages.txt")
>>> ham_messages = sc.textFile("ham_messages.txt")
```

6. Create a `HashingTF` instance to map the e-mail text to vectors of `100` features. Split each e-mail into words and then map each word to one feature:

```
>>> from pyspark.mllib.feature import HashingTF
>>> tf = HashingTF(numFeatures = 100)
>>> spam_features = spam_messages.map(lambda email:
tf.transform(email.split(" ")))
>>> ham_features = ham_messages.map(lambda email:
tf.transform(email.split(" ")))
```

7. Create `LabeledPoint` datasets for positive (spam) and negative (ham) examples. `LabeledPoint` consists simply of a label and features vector:

    ```
    >>> positive_examples = spam_features.map(lambda features:
    LabeledPoint(1, features))
    ```

    ```
    >>> negative_examples = ham_features.map(lambda features:
    LabeledPoint(0, features))
    ```

8. Create training data and cache it as logistic regression in an iterative algorithm. Examine the training data with the collect action:

    ```
    >>> training_data = positive_examples.union(negative_examples)
    ```

    ```
    >>> training_data.cache()
    ```

    ```
    >>> training_data.collect()
    ```

    ```
    [LabeledPoint(1.0, (100,[29,50,71],[1.0,1.0,1.0]))
    , LabeledPoint(1.0, (100,[0,34,38],[1.0,1.0,1.0])),
    LabeledPoint(1.0, (100,[0,86,91],[1.0,1.0,1.0])),
    LabeledPoint(1.0, (100,[1,48],[1.0,1.0])), LabeledPoint(1.0,
    (100,[65,93],[1.0,1.0])), LabeledPoint(1.0,
    (100,[85,91],[1.0,1.0])), LabeledPoint(1.0, (100,[50,55,76,79
    ],[1.0,1.0,1.0,1.0])), LabeledPoint(0.0, (100,[20,25,57,82],
    [1.0,1.0,1.0,2.0])), LabeledPoint(0.0, (100,[46,66,92],[1.0,1
    .0,1.0])), LabeledPoint(0.0, (100,[25,82,94],[1.0,2.0,1.0])),
    LabeledPoint(0.0, (100,[1,25,62,78,82,92],[1.0,1.0,1.0,1.0,1.0,1.0
    ])), LabeledPoint(0.0, (100,[21,81,88,89],[1.0,1.0,1.0,1.0]))]
    ```

9. Run logistic regression using the SGD optimizer and then check the model contents:

    ```
    >>> model = LogisticRegressionWithSGD.train(training_data)
    ```

    ```
    >>> model
    ```

    ```
    (weights=[0.747245937607,0.312621971183,0.0,0.0,0.0,0.0,0.0,0.0,
    0.0,0.0,0.0,0.0,0.0,0.0,0.0,0.0,0.0,0.0,0.0,0.0,-0.182791053614,
    -0.396071137454,0.0,0.0,0.0,-0.616391394849,0.0,0.0,0.0,0.0,
    0.399792136011,0.0,0.0,0.0,0.0,0.400316310041,0.0,0.0,0.0,0.0,
    0.400316310041,0.0,0.0,0.0,0.0,0.0,0.0,0.0,-0.412567752266,
    0.0,0.548276952195,0.0,0.754346808086,0.0,0.0,0.0,0.0,0.0,
    0.354554672075,0.0,-0.182791053614,0.0,0.0,0.0,0.0,
    -0.235654981013,0.0,0.0,0.508145068107,-0.412567752266,
    0.0,0.0,0.0,0.0,0.399792136011,0.0,0.0,0.0,0.0,0.354554672075,
    0.0,-0.235654981013,0.354554672075,0.0,-0.396071137454,
    -0.997127808685,0.0,0.0,0.454803011847,0.346929627566,0.0,
    -0.396071137454,-0.396071137454,0.0,0.801732639413,
    -0.648222733279,0.508145068107,-0.197945360222,0.0,0.0,0.0,0.0,
    0.0], intercept=0.0)
    ```

10. Test on a positive example (which is a spam) and a negative one (which is a ham). Apply the same `HashingTF` feature transformation algorithm used on the training data:

```
>>> pos_example = tf.transform("No investment required".split("
"))
>>> neg_example = tf.transform("Data Science courses recommended
for you".split(" "))
```

11. Now use the learned model to predict spam/ham for new e-mails:

```
>>> print "Prediction for positive test: %g" % model.predict(pos_
example)
Prediction for positive test: 1
>>> print "Prediction for negative test: %g" % model.predict(neg_
example)
Prediction for negative test: 0
```

Try other messages and check the accuracy of the algorithm. If you provide more training data to the algorithm, the accuracy will improve.

Building machine learning pipelines

Spark ML is an API built on top of the DataFrames API of Spark SQL to construct machine learning pipelines. Spark ML is inspired by the scikit-learn project, which makes it easier to combine multiple algorithms into a single pipeline. The following are the concepts used in ML pipelines:

- **DataFrame**: A DataFrame is used to create rows and columns of data just like an RDBMS table. A DataFrame can contain text, feature vectors, true labels, and predictions in columns.

- **Transformer**: A Transformer is an algorithm to transform a DataFrame into another DataFrame. The ML model is an example of a Transformer that transforms a DataFrame with features into a DataFrame with predictions.

- **Estimator**: This is an algorithm to produce a Transformer by fitting on a DataFrame. Generating a model is an example of an Estimator.

- **Pipeline**: As the name indicates, a pipeline creates a workflow by chaining multiple Transformers and Estimators together.

- **Parameter**: This is an API to specify parameters.

An example of a pipeline workflow

Let's see how a pipeline works with a simple document workflow. *Figure 7.1* illustrates the workflow during training time:

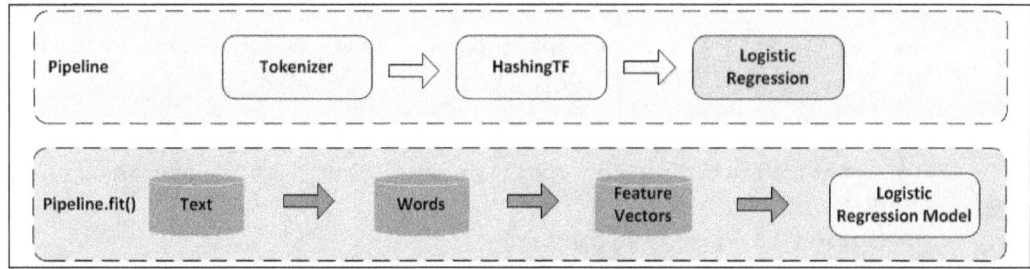

Figure 7.1: An ML pipeline during training

The pipeline workflow to create `PipelineModel` can be understood with the following points:

- The top box shows a **Pipeline** with three stages. The first two stages are Transformers and the third one is an Estimator.

- The bottom box shows data flowing through the pipeline to produce a logistic regression model. Each stage produces a DataFrame.

- The `Pipeline.fit()` method is called on the first DataFrame with raw documents.

- The `Tokenizer.transform()` method splits the raw text documents into words and then adds a new column with words to the DataFrame.

- The `HashingTF.transform()` method converts the words to feature vectors by adding a new column with the vectors to the DataFrame.

- The pipeline first calls `LogisticRegression.fit()` to produce a logistic regression model.

- After a pipeline's `fit()` method runs, it produces `PipelineModel`, which is a Transformer.

This `PipelineModel` is used at test time. *Figure 7.2* illustrates the usage at test time:

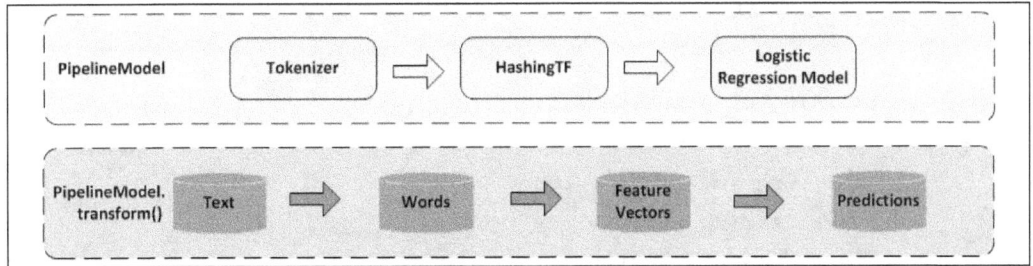

Figure 7.2: An ML Pipeline during testing

The `PipelineModel` can be understood with the following points:

- The number of stages for `PipelineModel` and the original pipeline are the same, but all Estimators in the original pipeline are changed as Transformers.

- Once the `transform()` method is called on a test dataset, the dataset is passed through the fitted pipeline in order.

- The `transform()` method updates the dataset at every stage and passes it to the next stage, as shown in the preceding image.

- Pipelines and `PipelineModels` ensure that training and testing data go through the same feature processing steps.

Building an ML pipeline

This following example follows the simple text document pipeline, illustrated in the preceding images:

1. Get into the PySpark shell and import all dependencies as follows:

   ```
   >>> from pyspark.ml import Pipeline
   >>> from pyspark.ml.classification import LogisticRegression
   >>> from pyspark.ml.feature import HashingTF, Tokenizer
   >>> from pyspark.sql import Row
   ```

2. Prepare a training document DataFrame from a list of id, text, and label tuples:

   ```
   >>> LabeledDocument = Row("id", "text", "label")

   >>> training_df = spark.createDataFrame([
           (0L, "apache spark rdd memory", 1.0),
           (1L, "mllib pipeline", 0.0),
   ```

```
        (2L, "hadoop mahout", 1.0),
        (3L, "mapreduce iterative", 0.0)], ["id", "text",
"label"])


>>> training_df.printSchema()
root
 |-- id: long (nullable = true)
 |-- text: string (nullable = true)
 |-- label: double (nullable = true)


>>> training_df.show()
```

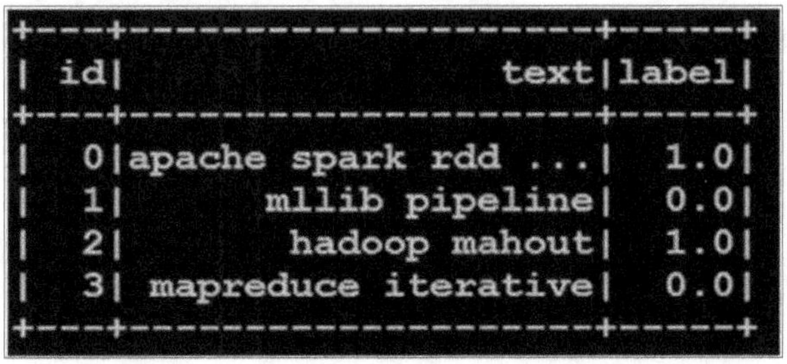

```
+---+--------------------+-----+
| id|                text|label|
+---+--------------------+-----+
|  0|apache spark rdd ...|  1.0|
|  1|     mllib pipeline|  0.0|
|  2|     hadoop mahout|  1.0|
|  3| mapreduce iterative|  0.0|
+---+--------------------+-----+
```

Figure 7.3: A screenshot of the training DataFrame

3. Configure an ML pipeline which consists of three stages — Tokenizer,
    HashingTF, and LogisticRegression:

```
>>> tokenizer_split = Tokenizer(inputCol="text",
outputCol="words")
>>> hashingTF_vectors = HashingTF(inputCol=tokenizer_split.
getOutputCol(), outputCol="features")
>>> log_reg = LogisticRegression(maxIter=10, regParam=0.01)
>>> pipeline = Pipeline(stages=[tokenizer_split, hashingTF_
vectors, log_reg])
>>>
>>> model = pipeline.fit(training_df)
```

4. Prepare the test documents which are unlabeled id, and text tuples:

```
>>> test_df = spark.createDataFrame([
        (4L, "p q r"),
        (5L, "mllib pipeline"),
        (6L, "x y z"),
```

```
         (7L, "hadoop mahout")], ["id", "text"])
```

```
>>> test_df.show()
```

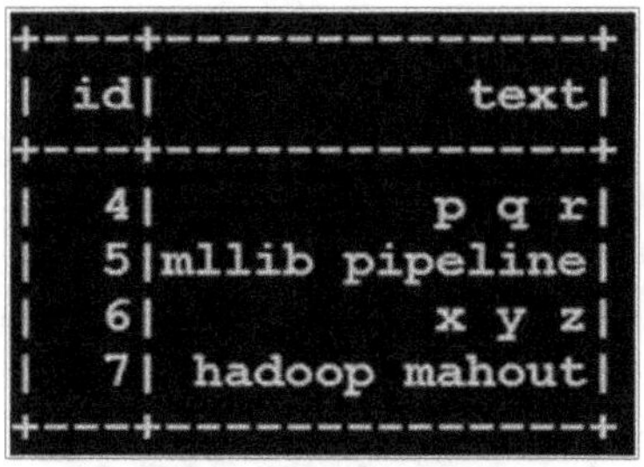

```
+---+--------------+
| id|          text|
+---+--------------+
|  4|         p q r|
|  5|mllib pipeline|
|  6|         x y z|
|  7| hadoop mahout|
+---+--------------+
```

Figure 7.4: A screenshot of the test DataFrame

5. Make predictions on the test documents and print columns of interest:

```
>>> prediction = model.transform(test_df)
```

```
>>> prediction
```

```
DataFrame[id: bigint, text: string, words: array<string>,
features: vector, rawPrediction: vector, probability: vector,
prediction: double]
```

```
>>> selected = prediction.select("id", "text","probability",
"prediction")
```

```
>>> selected
```

```
DataFrame[id: bigint, text: string, probability: vector,
prediction: double]
```

```
>>> for row in selected.collect():
        print(row)
```

```
Row(id=4, text=u'p q r', probability=DenseVector([0.6427,
0.3573]), prediction=0.0)
Row(id=5, text=u'mllib pipeline', probability=DenseVector([0.9833,
0.0167]), prediction=0.0)
Row(id=6, text=u'x y z', probability=DenseVector([0.6427,
0.3573]), prediction=0.0)
Row(id=7, text=u'hadoop mahout', probability=DenseVector([0.0218,
0.9782]), prediction=1.0)
```

You can try predictions with different sets of test data.

Saving and loading models

Models and pipelines can be saved to storage systems and loaded back into machine learning programs later. Use the following commands to save and load models:

```
model.save("/user/cloudera/spark-lr-model")
pipeline.save("/user/cloudera/unfit-lr-model")


from pyspark.ml import Pipeline, PipelineModel
lodeadModel = PipelineModel.load("/user/cloudera/spark-lr-model")
```

Machine learning with H2O and Spark

H2O is an open source system for machine learning. It offers a rich set of machine learning algorithms and a web-based data processing user interface. It offers the ability to develop machine learning applications in Java, Scala, Python, and R. It also has the ability to interface with Spark, HDFS, Amazon S3, SQL, and NoSQL databases. H2O also provides an **H2O Flow**, which is an IPython-like notebook that allows you to combine code execution, text, mathematics, plots, and rich media into a single document. Sparkling Water is a product of H2O on Spark.

Why Sparkling Water?

Sparkling Water combines the best of both worlds of Spark and H2O:

- Spark provides the best APIs, RDDs, and multitenant contexts
- H2O provides speed, columnar-compression, machine learning, and deep learning algorithms
- Both Spark and H2O Contexts reside in a shared executor JVM and shared Spark RDDs and H2O RDDs

An application flow on YARN

The steps involved in a Sparkling Water application submitted on YARN are as follows:

1. When the Sparkling Water application is submitted with spark-submit, the YARN resource manager allocates a container to launch the application master. The Spark driver runs in a client when submitted in the `yarn-client` mode. The Spark driver runs in the same container as the application master when submitted in yarn-cluster mode.

2. The application master negotiates resources with the resource manager to spawn Spark executor JVMs.

3. The Spark executor starts an H2O instance within the JVM.

4. When the Sparkling Water cluster is ready, HDFS data can be read by H2O or Spark. The H2O flow interface can be accessed when the cluster is ready. Data is shared across Spark RDDs and H2O RDDs.

5. All jobs can be monitored and visualized in the resource manager UI and Spark UI as well.

Once the job is finished, YARN will free up resources for other jobs. *Figure 7.5* illustrates a Sparkling Water application flow on YARN:

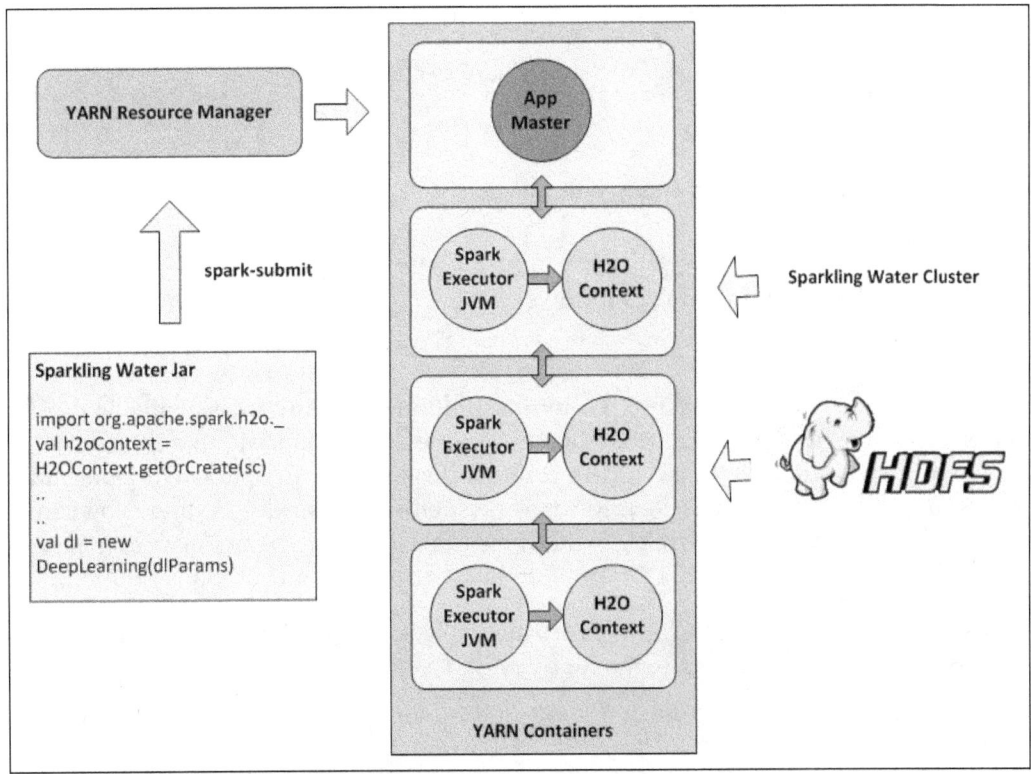

Figure 7.5: A Sparkling Water application on YARN

Getting started with Sparkling Water

The recommended system versions that should be used with H2O are available at `http://h2o.ai/product/recommended-systems-for-h2o/`. To get started, download the Sparkling Water binaries, set up environment variables, and start using it.

Go to `http://www.h2o.ai/download/sparkling-water/choose` to choose the Sparkling Water version that you want to use with Spark. Download the chosen version (1.6.5 in this case) as follows:

```
wget http://h2o-release.s3.amazonaws.com/sparkling-water/rel-1.6/5/
sparkling-water-1.6.5.zip
```

```
unzip sparkling-water-1.6.5.zip
```

```
cd sparkling-water-1.6.5
```

```
export SPARK_HOME=/usr/lib/spark
```

```
export MASTER=yarn-client
```

For Python shell, use the following command:

```
bin/pysparkling
```

For Scala shell, the command is as follows:

```
bin/sparkling-shell
```

The `bin` directory of the Sparkling Water installation has many tools available. You will see `launch-spark-cloud.sh`, which is used to start a standalone master and three worker nodes. The `pysparkling` command is used for PySpark with Sparkling Water and `sparkling-shell` is used for Scala shell with Sparkling Water. You can interactively execute the Sparkling Water programs in `pysparkling` or `sparkling-shell`. The `run-pynotebook.sh` command is used to start an IPython Notebook.

Step-by-step, deep learning examples are available at `https://github.com/h2oai/sparkling-water/tree/master/examples`.

Introducing Hivemall

Hivemall is a scalable machine learning library built on top of Apache Hive and Hadoop. It is a collection of machine learning algorithms that are created as **User Defined Functions** (UDFs) and **User Defined Table Functions** (UDTFs). Hivemall offers the following benefits:

- Easy to use: Existing users of Hive can implement machine learning algorithms using the well-known Hive QL language. There is no need to compile programs and create executable jars as in MLlib or H2O. Just add UDFs or UDTFs and execute Hive queries.

- Scalability: It provides the scalability benefits of Hadoop and Hive with additional features to provide scalability to any number of training and testing instances and also any number of features.

- It offers a variety of algorithms including Classification, Regression, K-Means, Recommendation, Anomaly Detection, and Feature engineering.

Follow this procedure to get started:

1. Download the compatible JAR and functions from `https://github.com/myui/hivemall/releases`:

   ```
   [cloudera@quickstart ~]$ wget https://github.com/myui/hivemall/
   releases/download/v0.4.2-rc.2/hivemall-core-0.4.2-rc.2-with-
   dependencies.jar
   ```

2. Start Hive and issue the following commands:

   ```
   hive>   add jar hivemall-core-0.4.2-rc.2-with-dependencies.jar;

   hive>   source define-all.hive;
   ```

3. Execute examples from `https://github.com/myui/hivemall/wiki`.

Introducing Hivemall for Spark

Apache Hive supports three execution engines — MapReduce, Tez, and Spark. Though Hivemall does not support Spark natively, the **Hivemall for Spark** project (`https://github.com/maropu/hivemall-spark`) implements a wrapper for Spark. This wrapper enables you to use Hivemall UDFs in SparkContext, DataFrames, or Spark Streaming. It is really easy to get started with Hivemall for Spark. Follow this procedure to start a Scala shell, load UDFs, and execute SQLs:

1. Download the `define-udfs` script:

   ```
   [cloudera@quickstart ~]$ wget https://raw.githubusercontent.com/
   maropu/hivemall-spark/master/scripts/ddl/define-udfs.sh --no-
   check-certificate
   ```

2. Start a Scala shell with the `packages` option:

```
[cloudera@quickstart ~]$ spark-1.6.0-bin-hadoop2.6/bin/spark-shell
--master local[*] --packages maropu:hivemall-spark:0.0.6
```

3. Create Hivemall functions as follows. Hivemall for Spark does not support Python yet:

```
scala> :load define-udfs.sh
```

4. Now you can execute examples from:

```
https://github.com/maropu/hivemall-spark/tree/master/tutorials
```

Summary

Machine learning is the science of making machines work without programming predefined rules and learn from data. It is used to build regression, classification, clustering, anomaly detection, and recommender-based systems. It involves training or fitting a model on historical data and using the trained model to make predictions for new data.

Spark provides you with the MLlib library which is a RDD based API and ML pipelines which is a DataFrames based API to build machine learning applications. MLlib is in maintenance mode from version 2.0 and it will be deprecated and discontinued in upcoming releases. ML pipelines will be the mainstream API. Apache Mahout was a machine learning library built on top of Hadoop, which is now integrated with Spark to provide in-memory performance and avoid scalability issues. H2O is an open source project that has powerful machine learning and deep learning algorithms that provide integration with Spark as a Sparkling Water product.

Both Hadoop and Spark platforms provide higher scalability and performance to machine learning algorithms.

In the next chapter, we will build recommendation systems.

8
Building Recommendation Systems with Spark and Mahout

Machine learning-based recommendation systems have become very popular and necessary in recent years in a variety of applications, such as movies, music, books, news, search queries, and products. They have brought in a dramatic change in how people buy products and find information. Recommendation systems usually recommend products to users based on their tastes and preferences. Users typically find relevant products and information that they did not know existed or did not know how to ask for.

This chapter is designed for you to understand and create recommendation systems, and will cover the following topics:

- Building recommendation systems
- Building a recommendation system with MLlib
- Building a recommendation system with Mahout and Spark

Building recommendation systems

The input to a recommendation system is the feedback of likes and dislikes, and the output is recommended items based on the feedback. Some of the examples of recommendation systems, are as follows:

- **Netflix/YouTube**: Movie/video recommendations
- **Amazon.com**: Customers Who Bought This Item Also Bought section
- **Spotify**: Music recommendations
- **Google**: News recommendations

Broadly, there are two approaches to build recommendation systems: content-based filtering and collaborative filtering. Let's understand these approaches.

Content-based filtering

Content-based filtering systems build recommenders based on item attributes. Examples of item attributes in movies are the genre, actor, director, producer, and hero. A user's taste identifies the values and weights for an attribute, which are provided as an input to the recommender system. This technique is purely domain-specific and the same algorithm cannot be used to recommend other types of products.

One simple example of content-based filtering is to recommend movies in the western genre to a user who watches many cowboy movies.

Collaborative filtering

Collaborative filtering systems recommend items based on similarity measures between items or users. Items preferred by similar users will be recommended to another user. Collaborative filtering is similar to how you get recommendations from your friends. This technique is not domain-specific and does not know anything about the items, and the same algorithm can be used for any type of product such as movies, music, books, and so on.

There are two types of collaborative filtering: user-based and item-based. Let's understand these two types in detail.

User-based collaborative filtering

A user-based recommender system is based on the similarities between users.

The idea behind this algorithm is that similar users share similar preferences. For example, in the following table, **User1** and **User3** rated **Movie1** and **Movie4** with similar ratings (**4** and **5**). This indicates that the taste of User1 and User3 is the same. Based on this, we can recommend Movie2 to User1, which is rated **5** by **User3**. Similarly, Movie3 can be recommended for User3.

	User1	User2	User3
Movie1	4	4	5
Movie2		4	5
Movie3	4	2	
Movie4	4		5

So, we are creating a user-item matrix from the user data and then predicting the missing entries by finding similar user preferences.

Item-based collaborative filtering

Item-based recommendation is based on similarities between items. The idea behind this algorithm is that a user will have a similar preference for similar items.

The item-based algorithm works like this. For every *I* item that a user *U* has no preference for, compute the similarity between *I* and every other item that *U* has a preference for. Calculate a weighted average, where the weighted preference is the product of the similarity of item *I* with any other items that *U* has expressed a preference for, with the preference value for that item. Adding this weighted preference for all items that *U* has a preference for gives the weighted sum, and dividing it by the number of such items gives the weighted average of preference value *P*. The *P* value is the preference for item *I* for user *U*, and if this is above a particular threshold, we can recommend the item to *U*. To build an item-based recommender, we need preference data and a notion of similarity between items.

Scalability of item-based collaborative filtering systems is much better than user-based filtering, and item-based recommendation systems are most widely used. Most successful companies have more users than products (items).

It is possible to combine content-based filtering and collaborative filtering to achieve optimized results. For example, you can predict the rating with the content-based approach and collaborative filtering, and then average the values to create a hybrid prediction.

Limitations of a recommendation system

Recommendation systems have some limitations. Understanding these limitations is important in order to build a successful recommendation system:

- **The cold-start problem**: Collaborative filtering systems are based on the action of available data from similar users. If you are building a brand new recommendation system, you would have no user data to start with. You can use content-based filtering first and then move on to the collaborative filtering approach.

- **Scalability**: As the number of users grow, the algorithms suffer scalability issues. If you have 10 million customers and 100,000 movies, you would have to create a sparse matrix with one trillion elements.

- **The lack of right data**: Input data may not always be accurate because humans are not perfect at providing ratings. User behavior is more important than ratings. Item-based recommendations provide a better answer in this case.

A recommendation system with MLlib

Spark's MLlib implements a collaborative filtering algorithm called **Alternating Least Squares (ALS)** to build recommendation systems.

ALS models the rating matrix (R) as the multiplication of a low-rank user (U) and product (V) factors, and learns these factors by minimizing the reconstruction error of the observed ratings. The unknown ratings can subsequently be computed by multiplying these factors. In this way, we can recommend products based on the predicted ratings. Refer to the following quote at `https://databricks.com/blog/2014/07/23/scalable-collaborative-filtering-with-spark-mllib.html`:

> *"ALS is an iterative algorithm. In each iteration, the algorithm alternatively fixes one factor matrix and solves for the other, and this process continues until it converges. MLlib features a blocked implementation of the ALS algorithm that leverages Spark's efficient support for distributed, iterative computation. It uses native LAPACK to achieve high performance and scales to billions of ratings on commodity clusters."*

This is illustrated in *Figure 8.1*:

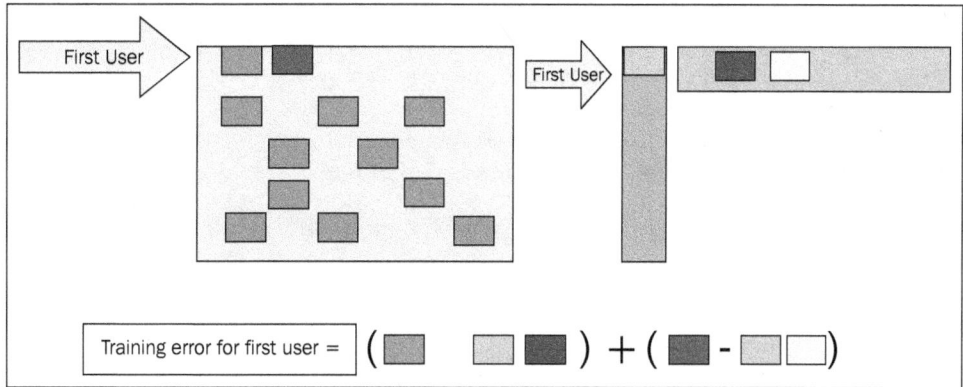

Figure 8.1: The ALS algorithm

Let's implement a recommendation system for movies using this ALS algorithm.

 All programs in this chapter are executed on CDH 5.8 VM. For other environments, file paths might change, but the concepts are the same in any environment.

Preparing the environment

We need to install NumPy, as it is a requirement for the ALS algorithm. Refer to *Chapter 7, Machine Learning with Spark and Hadoop*, for installation procedure of NumPy.

Let's download a public movielens data with one million ratings from 6,040 users on 3,706 movies from http://files.grouplens.org/datasets/movielens/ml-1m. zip. Once downloaded, copy the files to HDFS:

```
wget http://files.grouplens.org/datasets/movielens/ml-1m.zip
unzip ml-1m.zip
cd ml-1m
hadoop fs -put movies.dat movies.dat
hadoop fs -put ratings.dat ratings.dat
```

The `movies.dat` file has a format of the movie ID, movie name, and movie genre, as shown in the following snippet:

```
1::Toy Story (1995)::Animation|Children's|Comedy
2::Jumanji (1995)::Adventure|Children's|Fantasy
3::Grumpier Old Men (1995)::Comedy|Romance
4::Waiting to Exhale (1995)::Comedy|Drama
5::Father of the Bride Part II (1995)::Comedy
```

The `ratings.dat` file has a format of the user ID, movie ID, rating, and timestamp as shown in the following snippet:

```
1::1193::5::978300760
1::661::3::978302109
1::914::3::978301968
1::3408::4::978300275
1::2355::5::978824291
```

Creating RDDs

Now, let's get into the PySpark shell to work interactively with these datasets and build a recommendation system. Alternatively, you can use the IPython or Zeppelin Notebook to execute the following commands. For execution in YARN mode, change the master to yarn-client:

```
pyspark --master local[*]
```

Once you are in the shell, import ALS algorithm-related dependencies and create functions to parse the movies and ratings datasets:

```
>>> from pyspark.mllib.recommendation import ALS,
MatrixFactorizationModel, Rating


>>> def parseMovie(line):
    fields = line.strip().split("::")
    return int(fields[0]), fields[1]


>>> def parseRating(line):
    fields = line.strip().split("::")
    return int(fields[0]), int(fields[1]), float(fields[2])
```

Create RDDs for movies and ratings by parsing them using the preceding parse functions. Calculate the number of ratings, users, and movies:

```
>>> moviesRDD = sc.textFile("movies.dat").map(parseMovie)
>>> ratingsRDD = sc.textFile("ratings.dat").map(parseRating)

>>> numRatings = ratingsRDD.count()
>>> numUsers = ratingsRDD.map(lambda r:r[0]).distinct().count()
>>> numMovies = ratingsRDD.map(lambda r: r[1]).distinct().count()

>>> print "Ratings dataset has %d ratings from %d users on %d movies." %
(numRatings, numUsers, numMovies)
Ratings dataset has 1000209 ratings from 6040 users on 3706 movies.
```

Exploring the data with DataFrames

Now, let's create DataFrames for the movies and ratings RDDs to explore the datasets interactively using SQL:

```
>>> movieSchema = ['movieid', 'name']
>>> ratingsSchema = ['userid', 'movieid', 'rating']
>>> moviesDF  = moviesRDD.toDF(movieSchema)
>>> ratingsDF = ratingsRDD.toDF(ratingsSchema)

>>> moviesDF.printSchema()
root
 |-- movieid: long (nullable = true)
 |-- name: string (nullable = true)

>>> ratingsDF.printSchema()
root
 |-- userid: long (nullable = true)
 |-- movieid: long (nullable = true)
 |-- rating: double (nullable = true)
```

Let's register the DataFrames as temporary tables:

```
>>> ratingsDF.createOrReplaceTempView("ratings")
>>> moviesDF.createOrReplaceTempView("movies")
```

Now, get the maximum and minimum ratings along with the count of users who have rated a movie:

```
>>> ratingStats = spark.sql(
    """select movies.name, movieratings.maxrtng, movieratings.minrtng,
movieratings.cntusr
    from(SELECT ratings.movieid, max(ratings.rating) as maxrtng,
    min(ratings.rating) as minrtng, count(distinct(ratings.userid)) as
cntusr
    FROM ratings group by ratings.movieid ) movieratings
    join movies on movieratings.movieid=movies.movieId
    order by movieratings.cntusr desc""")
```

```
>>> ratingStats.show(5)
```

The output is shown in the following screenshot:

```
+--------------------+-------+-------+------+
|                name|maxrtng|minrtng|cntusr|
+--------------------+-------+-------+------+
|American Beauty (...|    5.0|    1.0|  3428|
|Star Wars: Episod...|    5.0|    1.0|  2991|
|Star Wars: Episod...|    5.0|    1.0|  2990|
|Star Wars: Episod...|    5.0|    1.0|  2883|
|Jurassic Park (1993)|    5.0|    1.0|  2672|
+--------------------+-------+-------+------+
only showing top 5 rows
```

Figure 8.2: A screenshot of ratingStats

Show the top 10 most active users and how many times they rated a movie:

```
>>> mostActive = spark.sql(
    """SELECT ratings.userid, count(*) as cnt from ratings
        group by ratings.userid order by cnt desc limit 10""")
```

```
>>> mostActive.show(5)
```

The output of the preceding command is shown in the following screenshot:

```
+------+----+
|userid| cnt|
+------+----+
|  4169|2314|
|  1680|1850|
|  4277|1743|
|  1941|1595|
|  1181|1521|
+------+----+
only showing top 5 rows
```

Figure 8.3: A screenshot of the most active users

As per the preceding result, `userid` `4169` is the most active user. Let's find the movies that user `4169` rated higher than `4`:

```
>>> user4169 = spark.sql("""SELECT ratings.userid, ratings.movieid,
    ratings.rating, movies.name FROM ratings JOIN movies
    ON movies.movieId=ratings.movieid
    where ratings.userid=4169 and ratings.rating > 4""")
>>> user4169.show(5)
```

The output is shown in the following screenshot:

```
+------+-------+------+--------------------+
|userid|movieid|rating|                name|
+------+-------+------+--------------------+
|  4169|   1231|   5.0|Right Stuff, The ...|
|  4169|    232|   5.0|Eat Drink Man Wom...|
|  4169|   3632|   5.0|Monsieur Verdoux ...|
|  4169|   1233|   5.0|Boat, The (Das Bo...|
|  4169|   1834|   5.0|Spanish Prisoner,...|
+------+-------+------+--------------------+
only showing top 5 rows
```

Figure 8.4: A screenshot of user 4169

Creating training and testing datasets

Now, let's use the MLlib's ALS algorithm to create a model. First, we need to separate the ratings data into two parts—training (80%) and testing (20%). We need to predict the recommendations for the training data and then compare the predictions with the testing data for cross-validation. This process of cross-validation will reveal the accuracy of the model. Usually, this process is done in multiple iterations with different sets of data to improve the accuracy of the model. In this exercise of building a recommendation engine, we will do only one such iteration.

Use the `randomSplit()` method to create training data and testing data, and cache them so that the iterative ALS algorithm will perform better:

```
>>> RDD1, RDD2 = ratingsRDD.randomSplit([0.8, 0.2])
>>> trainingRDD = RDD1.cache()
>>> testRDD = RDD2.cache()
>>> trainingRDD.count()
800597
>>> testRDD.count()
199612
```

Creating a model

Let's create the model by running the ALS algorithm that takes `trainingRDD` (user ID, movie ID, and rating) as input with `rank` (number of latent factors in the model) and number of iterations to run:

```
>>> rank = 10
>>> numIterations = 10
>>> model = ALS.train(trainingRDD, rank, numIterations)
```

Let's examine the available methods on this model. You can see methods such as `predict`, `predictAll`, `recommendProducts`, and `recommendUsers`. We will use the `predictAll` method. Additionally, you can save the model using the `save` method and *load* it for later use:

```
>>> dir(model)
```

The output is shown as follows:

```
>>> dir(model)
['__class__', '__del__', '__delattr__', '__dict__', '__doc__', '__format
__', '__getattribute__', '__hash__', '__init__', '__module__', '__new__
', '__reduce__', '__reduce_ex__', '__repr__', '__setattr__', '__sizeof__'
, '__str__', '__subclasshook__', '__weakref__', '_java_loader_class', '_
java_model', '_load_java', '_sc', 'call', 'load', 'predict', 'predictAll
', 'productFeatures', 'rank', 'recommendProducts', 'recommendUsers', 'sa
ve', 'userFeatures']
```

Figure 8.5: A screenshot of model methods

Note that the preceding model is created with RDD API. It can be created with DataFrame API as well and can be used with Pipeline API as explained in *Chapter 7, Machine Learning with Spark and Hadoop.*

Making predictions

Now, get the top five movie predictions for user `4169` from the model generated:

```
>>> user4169Recs = model.recommendProducts(4169, 5)
```

```
>>> user4169Recs
```

```
[Rating(user=4169, product=128, rating=5.6649367937005231),
Rating(user=4169, product=2562, rating=5.526190642914254),
Rating(user=4169, product=2503, rating=5.2328684996745327),
Rating(user=4169, product=3245, rating=5.1980663524880235),
Rating(user=4169, product=3950, rating=5.0785092078435197)]
```

Evaluating the model with testing data

Let's evaluate the model by comparing the predictions generated with the real ratings in `testRDD`. First, remove the ratings from `testRDD` to create user ID and movie ID pairs only. Once these movie ID and user ID pairs are passed to the model, it will generate the predicted ratings:

```
>>> testUserMovieRDD = testRDD.map(lambda x: (x[0], x[1]))
```

```
>>> testUserMovieRDD.take(2)
[(1, 661), (1, 3408)]
```

```
>>> predictionsTestRDD = model.predictAll(testUserMovieRDD).map(lambda r:
((r[0], r[1]), r[2]))
```

```
>>> predictionsTestRDD.take(2)
[((4904, 1320), 4.3029711294149289), ((4904, 3700), 4.3938405710892967)]
```

Let's transform `testRDD` into the key, value ((user ID, movie ID), rating)) format and then join with the predicted ratings as follows:

```
>>> ratingsPredictions = testRDD.map(lambda r: ((r[0], r[1]), r[2])).
join(predictionsTestRDD)
```

```
>>> ratingsPredictions.take(5)
[((5636, 380), (3.0, 2.5810444309550147)), ((5128, 480), (4.0,
3.8897996775001684)), ((5198, 248), (1.0, 1.9741132086395059)),
((2016, 3654), (4.0, 4.2239704909063338)), ((4048, 256), (4.0,
4.1190428484234198))]
```

The preceding prediction result indicates that, for user ID 5636 and movie ID 380, the actual rating from the testing data was 3.0 and the predicted rating was 2.5. Similarly, for user ID 5128 and movie ID 480, the actual rating was 4.0 and the predicted rating was 3.8.

Checking the accuracy of the model

Now, let's check the model to see how many bad predictions were generated by finding the predicted ratings that were >= 4 when the actual test rating was <= 1:

```
>>> badPredictions = ratingsPredictions.filter(lambda r: (r[1][0] <= 1
and r[1][1]) >= 4)
```

```
>>> badPredictions.take(2)
[((2748, 1080), (1.0, 4.0622434036284556)), ((4565, 175), (1.0,
4.728689683016448))]
```

```
>>> badPredictions.count()
395
```

So, there are 395 bad predictions out of 199612 test ratings. Next, let's evaluate the model using **Mean Squared Error (MSE)**. MSE is the difference between the predicted and the actual target:

```
>>> MeanSquaredError = ratingsPredictions.map(lambda r: (r[1][0] - r[1]
[1])**2).mean()
```

```
>>> print("Mean Squared Error = " + str(MeanSquaredError))
Mean Squared Error = 0.797355258111
```

The lower the MSE number, the better the predictions are.

Explicit versus implicit feedback

Input data can be of two types—explicit feedback or implicit feedback from users. In explicit feedback, users rate items as we have seen in the preceding example. The relationship between a set of user-item pairs is directly known in this case.

In many application domains and real-world cases, ratings are not available. We have access to implicit feedback only. We need to consider the presence or absence of events such as movies watched or not.

The Spark MLlib ALS algorithm provides you with a way to deal with implicit feedback. This model tries to relate ratings to the level of confidence from user preferences.

The following method is used to build a model using implicit feedback from users:

model = ALS.trainImplicit(ratings, rank, numIterations, alpha=0.01)

The Mahout and Spark integration

Apache Mahout was a general machine learning library built on top of Hadoop. Mahout started out primarily as a Java MapReduce package to run machine learning algorithms. As machine learning algorithms are iterative in nature, MapReduce had major performance and scalability issues, so Mahout stopped the development of MapReduce-based algorithms and started supporting new platforms, such as Spark, H2O, and Flink, with a new package called **Samsara**.

Let's install Mahout, explore the Mahout shell with Scala bindings, and then build a recommendation system.

Installing Mahout

The latest version of Spark does not work well with Mahout yet, so I used the Spark 1.4.1 version with the Mahout 0.12.2 version. Download the Spark prebuilt binary from the following location and start Spark daemons:

```
wget http://d3kbcqa49mib13.cloudfront.net/spark-1.4.1-bin-hadoop2.6.tgz

tar xzvf spark-1.4.1-bin-hadoop2.6.tgz

cd spark-1.4.1-bin-hadoop2.6
```

Now, let's download the Mahout binaries and unpack them as shown here:

```
wget http://mirrors.sonic.net/apache/mahout/0.12.2/apache-mahout-
distribution-0.12.2.tar.gz

tar xzvf apache-mahout-distribution-0.12.2.tar.gz
```

Now, export the following environment variables and start the Mahout shell:

```
export MAHOUT_HOME=/home/cloudera/apache-mahout-distribution-0.12.2
export SPARK_HOME=/home/cloudera/spark-1.4.1-bin-hadoop2.6
export MAHOUT_LOCAL=true
export MASTER=yarn-client
export JAVA_TOOL_OPTIONS="-Xmx2048m -XX:MaxPermSize=1024m -Xms1024m"
cd ~/apache-mahout-distribution-0.12.2
bin/mahout spark-shell
```

Exploring the Mahout shell

The following two Scala imports are typically used to enable Mahout Scala DSL Bindings for linear algebra:

```
import org.apache.mahout.math._
import scalabindings._
import MatlabLikeOps._
```

The two types of vectors supported by Mahout shell are as follows:

- **Dense vector**: A dense vector is a vector with relatively few zero elements. On the Mahout command line, type the following command to initialize a dense vector:

  ```
  mahout> val denseVector1: Vector = (3.0, 4.1, 6.2)
  denseVector1: org.apache.mahout.math.Vector = {0:3.0,1:4.1,2:6.2}
  ```

- **Sparse vector**: A sparse vector is a vector with a relatively large number of zero elements. On the Mahout command line, type the following command to initialize a sparse vector:

  ```
  mahout> val sparseVector1 = svec((6 -> 1) :: (9 -> 2.0) :: Nil)
  sparseVector1: org.apache.mahout.math.RandomAccessSparseVector = {9:2.0,6:1.0}
  ```

Access the elements of a vector:

```
mahout> denseVector1(2)
res0: Double = 6.2
```

Set values to a vector:

```
mahout> denseVector1(2)=8.2
mahout> denseVector1
res2: org.apache.mahout.math.Vector = {0:3.0,1:4.1,2:8.2}
```

The following are the vector arithmetic operations:

```
mahout> val denseVector2: Vector = (1.0, 1.0, 1.0)
denseVector2: org.apache.mahout.math.Vector = {0:1.0,1:1.0,2:1.0}

mahout> val addVec=denseVector1 + denseVector2
addVec: org.apache.mahout.math.Vector = {0:4.0,1:5.1,2:9.2}

mahout> val subVec=denseVector1 - denseVector2
subVec: org.apache.mahout.math.Vector = {0:2.0,1:3.0999999999999996,2:7.1
99999999999999}
```

Similarly, multiplication and division can be done as well.

The result of adding a scalar to a vector is that all elements are incremented by the value of the scalar. For example, the following command adds 10 to all the elements of the vector:

```
mahout> val addScalr=denseVector1+10
addScalr: org.apache.mahout.math.Vector = {0:13.0,1:14.1,2:18.2}

mahout> val addScalr=denseVector1-2
addScalr: org.apache.mahout.math.Vector = {0:1.0,1:2.0999999999999996,2:6
.19999999999999}
```

Now let's see how to initialize the matrix. The inline initialization of a matrix, either dense or sparse, is always performed row-wise:

- The dense matrix is initialized as follows:

  ```
  mahout> val denseMatrix = dense((10, 20, 30), (30, 40, 50))
  denseMatrix: org.apache.mahout.math.DenseMatrix =
  {
    0 => {0:10.0,1:20.0,2:30.0}
    1 => {0:30.0,1:40.0,2:50.0}
  }
  ```

- The sparse matrix is initialized as follows:

```
mahout> val sparseMatrix = sparse((1, 30) :: Nil, (0, 20) :: (1,
20.5) :: Nil)
sparseMatrix: org.apache.mahout.math.SparseRowMatrix =
{
  0 => {1:30.0}
  1 => {0:20.0,1:20.5}
}
```

- The diagonal matrix is initialized as follows:

```
mahout> val diagonalMatrix=diag(20, 4)
diagonalMatrix: org.apache.mahout.math.DiagonalMatrix =
{
  0 => {0:20.0}
  1 => {1:20.0}
  2 => {2:20.0}
  3 => {3:20.0}
}
```

- The identity matrix is initialized as follows:

```
mahout> val identityMatrix = eye(4)
identityMatrix: org.apache.mahout.math.DiagonalMatrix =
{
  0 => {0:1.0}
  1 => {1:1.0}
  2 => {2:1.0}
  3 => {3:1.0}
}
```

Access the elements of a matrix as follows:

```
mahout> denseMatrix(1,1)
res5: Double = 40.0
```

```
mahout> sparseMatrix(0,1)
res18: Double = 30.0
```

Fetch a row of a vector as follows:

```
mahout> denseMatrix(1,::)
res21: org.apache.mahout.math.Vector = {0:30.0,1:40.0,2:50.0}
```

Fetch a column of a vector as follows:

```
mahout> denseMatrix(::,1)
res22: org.apache.mahout.math.Vector = {0:20.0,1:40.0}
```

Set a matrix row as follows:

```
mahout> denseMatrix(1,::)=(99,99,99)
res23: org.apache.mahout.math.Vector = {0:99.0,1:99.0,2:99.0}
mahout> denseMatrix
res24: org.apache.mahout.math.DenseMatrix =
{
  0 => {0:10.0,1:20.0,2:30.0}
  1 => {0:99.0,1:99.0,2:99.0}
}
```

Matrices are assigned by reference and not as a copy. See the following example:

```
mahout> val newREF = denseMatrix
newREF: org.apache.mahout.math.DenseMatrix =
{
  0 => {0:10.0,1:20.0,2:30.0}
  1 => {0:99.0,1:99.0,2:99.0}
}
mahout> newREF += 10.0
res25: org.apache.mahout.math.Matrix =
{
  0 => {0:20.0,1:30.0,2:40.0}
  1 => {0:109.0,1:109.0,2:109.0}
}
mahout> denseMatrix
res26: org.apache.mahout.math.DenseMatrix =
{
  0 => {0:20.0,1:30.0,2:40.0}
  1 => {0:109.0,1:109.0,2:109.0}
}
```

If you want a separate copy, you can clone it:

```
mahout> val newClone = denseMatrix clone
newClone: org.apache.mahout.math.Matrix =
{
 0 => {0:20.0,1:30.0,2:40.0}
 1 => {0:109.0,1:109.0,2:109.0}
}
mahout> newClone += 10
res27: org.apache.mahout.math.Matrix =
{
 0 => {0:30.0,1:40.0,2:50.0}
 1 => {0:119.0,1:119.0,2:119.0}
}
mahout> newClone
res28: org.apache.mahout.math.Matrix =
{
 0 => {0:30.0,1:40.0,2:50.0}
 1 => {0:119.0,1:119.0,2:119.0}
}
mahout> denseMatrix
res29: org.apache.mahout.math.DenseMatrix =
{
 0 => {0:20.0,1:30.0,2:40.0}
 1 => {0:109.0,1:109.0,2:109.0}
}
```

Building a universal recommendation system with Mahout and search tool

Mahout provides you with recommendation algorithms such as `spark-itemsimilarity` and `spark-rowsimilarity` to create recommendations. When these recommendations are combined with a search tool, such as Solr or Elasticsearch, the recommendations will be personalized for individual users.

Figure 8.6 is a recommendation application with lambda architecture to create and update the model in batch mode and a search engine playing the real-time serving role. All user interactions are collected in real time and stored on HBase. In Solr, two collections are created — one for user history and one for item indicators. Indicators are user interactions created by **spark-mahout correlation** algorithms.

A recommender application queries Solr directly to get recommendations. There can be two actions from users such as purchase which is a primary action and secondary actions such as product detail-views or add-to-wishlists. The primary action from the user history with its co-occurrence and cross-co-occurrence indicators are usually recommended. However, recommendations can be customized with secondary actions.

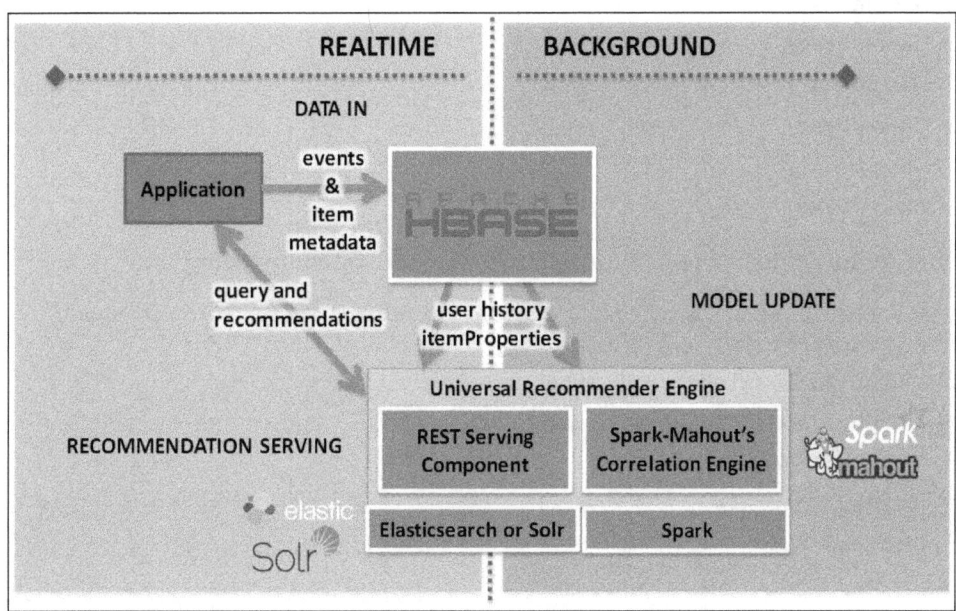

Figure 8.6: A universal recommendation engine with Spark and Mahout

Let's learn how to create a similarity matrix and cross-similarity matrix using the `spark-itemsimilarity` algorithm. Create a file called `infile` with the following content. Note that you can directly provide a log file as an input by providing delimiters:

```
[cloudera@quickstart ~]$ cat infile
u1,purchase,iphone
u1,purchase,ipad
u2,purchase,nexus
u2,purchase,galaxy
```

```
u3,purchase,surface
u4,purchase,iphone
u4,purchase,galaxy
u1,view,iphone
u1,view,ipad
u1,view,nexus
u1,view,galaxy
u2,view,iphone
u2,view,ipad
u2,view,nexus
u2,view,galaxy
u3,view,surface
u3,view,nexus
u4,view,iphone
u4,view,ipad
u4,view,galaxy
```

Then, run the `spark-itemsimilarity` job with the following command:

```
[cloudera@quickstart apache-mahout-distribution-0.12.2]$ bin/mahout
spark-itemsimilarity \
    --input /home/cloudera/infile          \
    --output /home/cloudera/outdir            \
    --master local[*]        \
    --filter1 purchase     \
    --filter2 view         \
    -ic 2                  \
    -rc 0                  \
    -fc 1
```

The previous command line options are explained as follows:

- `-f1` or `--filter1`: Datum for the primary item set
- `-f2` or `--filter2`: Datum for the secondary item set
- `-ic` or `--itemIDColumn`: Column number for item ID. Default is 1.
- `-rc` or `--rowIDColumn`: Column number for row ID. Default is 0.
- `-fc` or `--filterColumn`: Column number for filter string. Default is -1 for no filter.

Note that the `--master` parameter can be changed to a standalone master or yarn.

This program will produce the following output:

```
[cloudera@quickstart apache-mahout-distribution-0.12.2]$$ cd ~/outdir/
[cloudera@quickstart outdir]$ ls -R
.:
cross-similarity-matrix   similarity-matrix


./cross-similarity-matrix:
part-00000   part-00001   part-00002   _SUCCESS


./similarity-matrix:
part-00000   _SUCCESS


[cloudera@quickstart outdir]$ cat similarity-matrix/part-00000
galaxy nexus:1.7260924347106847
ipad iphone:1.7260924347106847
surface
iphone ipad:1.7260924347106847
nexus galaxy:1.7260924347106847


[cloudera@quickstart outdir]$ cat cross-similarity-matrix/part-0000*
galaxy galaxy:1.7260924347106847 ipad:1.7260924347106847
iphone:1.7260924347106847 nexus:1.7260924347106847
ipad galaxy:0.6795961471815897 ipad:0.6795961471815897
iphone:0.6795961471815897 nexus:0.6795961471815897
surface surface:4.498681156950466 nexus:0.6795961471815897
iphone galaxy:1.7260924347106847 ipad:1.7260924347106847
iphone:1.7260924347106847 nexus:1.7260924347106847
nexus galaxy:0.6795961471815897 ipad:0.6795961471815897
iphone:0.6795961471815897 nexus:0.6795961471815897
```

Based on the previous result, on the site for the page displaying the iPhone, we can now show that the iPad as a recommendation that was purchased by similar people. The current user's purchase history will be used to personalize the recommendations on Solr.

Summary

The goal of any recommendation system is to recommend products, such as movies, music, books, news, search queries, and products, to targeted users. Broadly, there are two approaches to build recommendation systems—content-based filtering and collaborative filtering. While content-based filtering is based on item attributes, collaborative filtering is based on users and items.

Spark's MLlib implements a collaborative filtering algorithm called **Alternating Least Squares** (**ALS**) to build recommendation systems with explicit feedback or implicit feedback from users. Recommendation systems with lambda architecture can be built using Mahout and Solr, which are used for real-time recommendations.

The next chapter introduces graph analytics with GraphX.

Graph Analytics with GraphX

Graph analytics enables finding relationship patterns in data. This chapter is aimed at introducing graph processing techniques that are generally used in page ranking, search engines, finding relationships in social networks, finding the shortest paths between two places, recommending products, and many more applications.

In this chapter, we will cover the following topics:

- Introducing graph processing
- Getting started with GraphX
- Analyzing flight data using GraphX
- Introducing GraphFrames

Introducing graph processing

As the number of users increases to millions in large organizations, traditional relational database performance will be degraded while finding relationships between these users. For example, finding relationships between two friends results in a simple join SQL query. But, if you have to find a relationship with a friend of a friend, six levels deep, you have to join the tables six times in a SQL query which leads to poor performance. Graph processing finds relationships without performance degradation as the size of the graph grows. In relational databases, relationships are established only by joining tables. In graph databases, relationships are first-class citizens. Let's understand what a graph is and how they are created and processed.

What is a graph?

A graph is a collection of vertices connected to each other using edges as shown in the following *Figure 9.1*. Vertex is a synonym for node, which can be a place or person with associated relationships expressed using edges. **Jacob, Jessica,** and **Emily** in the figure are vertices and their relationships are edges. This is a simple example of a social graph. Just imagine expressing the whole of Facebook as a social graph. Finding relationships between them can be a very complex task. In *Chapter 3, Deep Dive into Apache Spark*, we learned about creating the **Directed Acyclic Graph (DAG)** for Spark jobs that consist of **Resilient Distributed Datasets (RDD)** which are nothing but vertices, and transformations, which are nothing but edges. There are multiple ways to go from one place to another place. If we create places as vertices and roads as edges, graph processing can provide an optimized shortest path between these two places:

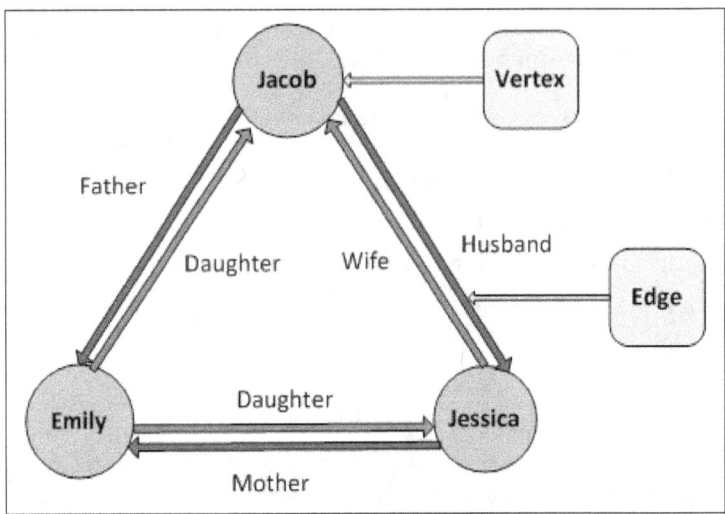

Figure 9.1: Representation of a family relationship graph

Weights in a graph provide strength to an edge, for example the distance between two cities can be closer or more distant. Graphs can be directed or undirected. RDD's DAG is directed because it goes only in one direction. Graphs can be cyclic or acyclic. For example, in a social network, you can start with one friendship and circle between different friends to get back to the original person.

Graphs are everywhere and almost everything can be represented as graphs. Graph processing can be implemented in telecoms, aviation, bio informatics, social networks, and many more fields.

Graph databases versus graph processing systems

There are two types of technologies in graph processing; graph databases and graph processing systems. Graph databases can be seen as OLTP databases that provide transactions, updates, deletes, and query language. Graph processing systems can be seen as OLAP systems that provide offline analytic capabilities. The following table shows the important graph databases and graph processing systems:

Graph databases	Graph processing systems
Neo4J, Titan, OrientDB, AllegroGraph, GraphBase, Oracle Spatial, and Graph. NoSQL databases such as HBase and Cassandra can also be used for storing graphs.	GraphX, Apache Giraph, GraphLab, Apache Hama, and Microsoft's Graph Engine.

The GraphLab framework implements the **Message Passing Interface** (**MPI**) model to run complex graph algorithms using data in HDFS. Apache Giraph and Apache Hama are based on the **Bulk Synchronous Parallel** (**BSP**) model inspired by Google's Pregel project. GraphX is built on top of Spark and supports a variant of the Pregel API as well. This chapter focuses on graph processing systems and especially GraphX.

Apache Giraph, born at LinkedIn, is a stable system that can process a trillion edges on top of Hadoop, but Apache Giraph is not supported by all major Hadoop vendors. If your use case is a pure graph-related problem, you can use Apache Giraph as a robust and stable solution, but if graph processing is just a part of the solution, GraphX on top of Spark provides a great unified solution with the power of Spark core capabilities.

Introducing GraphX

GraphX is a graph processing system built on top of Apache Spark, which can be easily integrated with other Spark modules to unify ETL, exploratory analytics, and graph analytics. GraphX creates graphs as another type of RDD such as VertexRDD and EdgeRDD. Spark's GraphX features such as speed of iterative processing and in-memory capabilities removed the issues of MapReduce that Apache Giraph and Pregel were designed to address. GraphX stores a graph's edges in one file and vertices in another file. This allows graph algorithms implemented in GraphX to view graphs either as graphs or as collections of edges or vertices to efficiently combine multiple processing types within the same program.

Typically, graphs would be too large to fit on a single machine and must use distributed systems such as HDFS and S3.

Graph algorithms

GraphX provides the following algorithms out-of-the-box in version 2.0. Some of these algorithms are practically implemented in the next section of this chapter:

- Connected components
- Label propagation
- PageRank
- SVD++
- Shortest Path
- Strongly connected components
- Triangle count

Getting started with GraphX

You don't need any additional installation of software to get started with GraphX. GraphX is included within the Spark installation. This section introduces how to create and explore graphs using a simple family relationship graph. The family graph created will be used in all operations within this section.

Basic operations of GraphX

GraphX does not support the Python API yet. For easy understanding, let's use `spark-shell` to interactively work with GraphX. First of all, let's create input data (vertex and edge files) needed for our GraphX operations and then store it on HDFS.

 All programs in this chapter are executed on CDH 5.8 VM. For other environments, file paths might change, but the concepts are the same in any environment.

Creating a graph

We can create a graph using the following steps:

1. Create a vertex file with vertex ID, name, and age as shown here:

   ```
   [cloudera@quickstart ~]$ cat vertex.csv
   1,Jacob,48
   2,Jessica,45
   3,Andrew,25
   4,Ryan,53
   5,Emily,22
   6,Lily,52
   ```

2. Create an edge file with vertex ID, destination vertex ID, and relationship as follows:

   ```
   [cloudera@quickstart ~]$ cat edges.csv
   6,1,Sister
   1,2,Husband
   2,1,Wife
   5,1,Daughter
   5,2,Daughter
   3,1,Son
   3,2,Son
   4,1,Friend
   1,5,Father
   1,3,Father
   2,5,Mother
   2,3,Mother
   ```

3. Now, let's copy both files to HDFS:

   ```
   [cloudera@quickstart ~]$ hadoop fs -put vertex.csv
   [cloudera@quickstart ~]$ hadoop fs -put edges.csv
   ```

4. Start a Scala shell with the master as yarn-client and then import GraphX and RDD dependencies. Note that GraphX is not supported in the Python language:

```
[cloudera@quickstart ~]$ spark-shell --master yarn


scala> sc.master
res0: String = yarn


scala> import org.apache.spark.graphx._
scala> import org.apache.spark.rdd.RDD
```

5. Create an RDD for both vertex and edge files:

```
scala> val vertexRDD = sc.textFile("vertex.csv")


vertexRDD: org.apache.spark.rdd.RDD[String] = MapPartitionsRDD[1]
at textFile at <console>:25


scala> vertexRDD.collect()


res1: Array[String] = Array(1,Jacob,48, 2,Jessica,45, 3,Andrew,25,
4,Ryan,53, 5,Emily,22, 6,Lily,52)


scala> val edgeRDD =  sc.textFile("edges.csv")
edgeRDD: org.apache.spark.rdd.RDD[String] = MapPartitionsRDD[3] at
textFile at <console>:25


scala> edgeRDD.collect()
res2: Array[String] = Array(6,1,Sister, 1,2,Husband, 2,1,Wife,
5,1,Daughter, 5,2,Daughter, 3,1,Son, 3,2,Son, 4,1,Friend,
1,5,Father, 1,3,Father, 2,5,Mother, 2,3,Mother)
```

6. Let's create the VertexRDD with VertexId and strings to represent the person's name and age:

```
scala> val vertices: RDD[(VertexId, (String, String))] =
        vertexRDD.map { line =>
        val fields = line.split(",")
      ( fields(0).toLong, ( fields(1), fields(2) ) )
        }
```

```
vertices: org.apache.spark.rdd.RDD[(org.apache.spark.graphx.
VertexId, (String, String))] = MapPartitionsRDD[4] at map at
<console>:28
```

```
scala> vertices.collect()
```

```
res3: Array[(org.apache.spark.graphx.VertexId, (String, String))]
= Array((1,(Jacob,48)), (2,(Jessica,45)), (3,(Andrew,25)),
(4,(Ryan,53)), (5,(Emily,22)), (6,(Lily,52)))
```

7. Let's create the EdgeRDD with source and destination vertex IDs converted to `Long` values and the relationship as String. Each record in this RDD is now an Edge record:

```
scala> val edges: RDD[Edge[String]] =

        edgeRDD.map { line =>

        val fields = line.split(",")

        Edge(fields(0).toLong, fields(1).toLong, fields(2))

    }
```

```
edges: org.apache.spark.rdd.RDD[org.apache.spark.graphx.
Edge[String]] = MapPartitionsRDD[5] at map at <console>:28
```

```
scala> edges.collect()
```

```
res4: Array[org.apache.spark.graphx.Edge[String]] =
Array(Edge(6,1,Sister), Edge(1,2,Husband), Edge(2,1,Wife),
Edge(5,1,Daughter), Edge(5,2,Daughter), Edge(3,1,Son),
Edge(3,2,Son), Edge(4,1,Friend), Edge(1,5,Father),
Edge(1,3,Father), Edge(2,5,Mother), Edge(2,3,Mother))
```

8. We should define a default value in case a connection or a vertex is missing. The graph is then constructed from these RDDs—vertices, edges, and the default record:

```
scala> val default = ("Unknown", "Missing")
```

```
default: (String, String) = (Unknown,Missing)
```

```
scala> val graph = Graph(vertices, edges, default)
```

```
graph: org.apache.spark.graphx.Graph[(String, String),String] =
org.apache.spark.graphx.impl.GraphImpl@284ee98f
```

This creates a GraphX-based structure called `graph`, which can now be used for multiple operations. Remember that, although these data samples are small, you can create extremely large graphs using this approach. Many of these algorithms are iterative applications, for instance, PageRank and triangle count, and as a result the programs will generate many iterative Spark jobs. Just like Spark's RDDs, graphs can be cached and un-cached in memory for better performance in iterative processing.

Counting

It is easy to count the number of vertices and edges in a graph with the following functions:

```scala
scala> println( "vertices count : " + graph.vertices.count )
vertices count : 6
scala> println( "edges count : " + graph.edges.count )
edges count : 12
```

Alternatively, counting can be done as follows:

```scala
scala> println(s"The graph has ${graph.numVertices} vertices")
The graph has 6 vertices
scala> println(s"The graph has ${graph.numEdges} edges")
The graph has 12 edges
```

Filtering

We can filter graphs to create sub-graphs. For example, filter the vertices to filter people whose age is greater than 40 years as shown here:

```scala
scala> val cnt1 = graph.vertices.filter { case (id, (name, age)) => age.toLong > 40 }.count
cnt1: Long = 4

scala> println( "Vertices count : " + cnt1 )
Vertices count : 4
```

Now, filter the edges on the relationship property of `Mother` or `Father` and then print the output:

```scala
scala> val cnt2 = graph.edges.filter { case Edge(from, to, property) => property == "Father" | property == "Mother" }.count
```

```
cnt2: Long = 4
```

```
scala> println( "Edges count : " + cnt2 )
Edges count : 4
```

inDegrees, outDegrees, and degrees

GraphX also defines a special data structure for node degree as `inDegrees`, `outDegrees`, and `degrees`. The degree of a node represents the number of links it has to other nodes. We can find the incoming degree of a node, or an in-degree, which is the number of its incoming links. Also, we can find the outgoing degree, or out-degree, which is the number of nodes that it points to. Let's compute the `max` degrees by defining a `reduce` operation to compute the highest degree vertex:

```
scala> def max(a: (VertexId, Int), b: (VertexId, Int)): (VertexId,
Int) = {
        if (a._2 > b._2) a else b
    }
max: (a: (org.apache.spark.graphx.VertexId, Int), b: (org.apache.spark.
graphx.VertexId, Int))(org.apache.spark.graphx.VertexId, Int)
```

```
scala> val maxInDegree: (VertexId, Int)  = graph.inDegrees.reduce(max)
maxInDegree: (org.apache.spark.graphx.VertexId, Int) = (1,5)
```

```
scala> val maxOutDegree: (VertexId, Int) = graph.outDegrees.reduce(max)
maxOutDegree: (org.apache.spark.graphx.VertexId, Int) = (1,3)
```

```
scala> val maxDegrees: (VertexId, Int)   = graph.degrees.reduce(max)
maxDegrees: (org.apache.spark.graphx.VertexId, Int) = (1,8)
```

We can define a minimum function to find people with the minimum out-degrees as follows:

```
scala> val minDegrees = graph.outDegrees.filter(_._2 <= 1)
minDegrees: org.apache.spark.graphx.VertexRDD[Int] = VertexRDDImpl[62] at
RDD at VertexRDD.scala:57
scala> minDegrees.collect()
Array[(org.apache.spark.graphx.VertexId, Int)] = Array((4,1), (6,1))
```

Triplets

GraphX also exposes a triplet view, which logically joins the vertex and edge properties yielding an RDD[EdgeTriplet[VD, ED]]. *Figure 9.2* expresses a triplet join graphically:

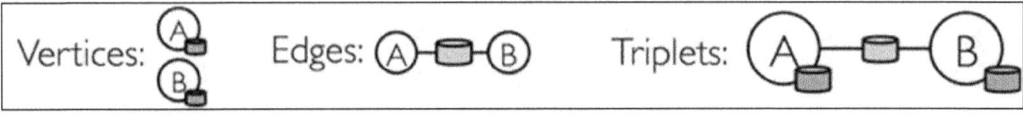

Figure 9.2: Triplet view of a graph

Let's print the triplets of our graph by using the srcAttr, attr, and dstAttr members:

```scala
scala> graph.triplets.map(
    triplet => triplet.srcAttr._1 + " is the " + triplet.attr + " of " +
triplet.dstAttr._1).collect.foreach(println)


Jacob is the Husband of Jessica

Jessica is the Wife of Jacob

Andrew is the Son of Jacob

Emily is the Daughter of Jacob

Emily is the Daughter of Jessica

Lily is the Sister of Jacob

Jacob is the Father of Andrew

Jacob is the Father of Emily

Jessica is the Mother of Andrew

Jessica is the Mother of Emily

Andrew is the Son of Jessica

Ryan is the Friend of Jacob
```

Transforming graphs

Graph operators can be used to either change the properties of graph elements or modify the structure of graphs. All the operators that we use in this section are methods that are invoked on a graph and return a new graph. Let's examine join methods to combine graph data with other datasets and perform data operations on VertexRDD and EdgeRDD.

Transforming attributes

The map is one of the main transformation functions for transforming RDDs in Spark. Similarly, graphs also have three map operators as follows:

```
class Graph[VD, ED] {
  def mapVertices[VD2](mapFun: (VertexId, VD) => VD2):
    Graph[VD2, ED]
  def mapEdges[ED2](mapFun: Edge[ED] => ED2): Graph[VD, ED2]
  def mapTriplets[ED2](mapFun: EdgeTriplet[VD, ED] => ED2):
    Graph[VD, ED2] }
```

Each of these methods is called on a graph with the vertex attribute type, VD and edge attribute type, ED. Each of them also takes a user-defined mapping function, say myMap, that performs one of the following:

- For mapVertices, myMap takes a pair of (VertexId, VD) as input and returns a transformed vertex attribute of type VD2

- For mapEdges, myMap takes an Edge object as input and returns a transformed edge attribute of type ED2

- For mapTriplets, myMap takes an EdgeTriplet object as input and returns a transformed edge attribute of type ED2

Modifying graphs

The GraphX library also provides four useful methods for changing the structure of graphs. Their method signatures are listed as follows:

```
class Graph[VD, ED] {
  def reverse: Graph[VD, ED]
  def subgraph(epred: EdgeTriplet[VD,ED] => Boolean,
               vpred: (VertexId, VD) => Boolean): Graph[VD, ED]
  def mask[VD2, ED2](other: Graph[VD2, ED2]): Graph[VD, ED]
  def groupEdges(merge: (ED, ED) => ED): Graph[VD,ED]
}
```

The operators used in the preceding code are explained as follows:

- reverse: If you want to reverse the edge directions, the reverse operator can be used. This does not cause any data movement and also does not change vertex or edge properties. This is useful for inverse PageRank as an example.

- subgraph: The subgraph operator is useful for filtering graphs that take two predicate functions as arguments, which return Boolean values. The first predicate epred takes an EdgeTriplet and returns true when the triplet satisfies the predicate. The second predicate vpred takes a pair of (VertexId, VD) and returns true when the vertex satisfies the predicate condition.

- mask: Just like subgraph, the mask operator also filters a graph. But, mask does not take predicate functions as arguments. It takes another graph as an argument and then the expression graph1.mask(graph2) constructs a sub-graph of graph1 by returning a graph that contains the vertices and edges that are also found in graph2. This is typically used together with the subgraph operator to filter a graph based on the properties in another related graph.

- groupEdges: The groupEdges operator merges duplicate edges between each pair of nodes into a single edge. This reduces the size of the graph in many applications.

Joining graphs

GraphX also provides APIs for joining RDD datasets with graphs as well. This is really useful when we want to add extra information or merge vertex attributes to any vertex attributes. These tasks can be accomplished using the joinVertices and outerJoinVertices join operators. Let's explore an example of joining the movies RDD with the graph we previously created:

```scala
scala> case class MoviesWatched(Movie: String, Genre: String)

scala>  val movies: RDD[(VertexId, MoviesWatched)] = sc.parallelize(List(
(1, MoviesWatched("Toy Story 3", "kids")), (2, MoviesWatched("Titanic",
"Love")), (3, MoviesWatched("The Hangover", "Comedy")))))

scala>  val movieOuterJoinedGraph = graph.outerJoinVertices(movies)
((_,name, movies) => (name,movies))

scala> movieOuterJoinedGraph.vertices.map(t => t).collect.
foreach(println)

(4,((Ryan,53),None))
(6,((Lily,52),None))
(2,((Jessica,45),Some(MoviesWatched(Titanic,Love))))
(1,((Jacob,48),Some(MoviesWatched(Toy Story 3,kids))))
(3,((Andrew,25),Some(MoviesWatched(The Hangover,Comedy))))
(5,((Emily,22),None))
```

You can see that movie information is added for `Jacob`, `Andrew`, and `Jessica`. We can use the `getOrElse` method to provide default attribute values for the vertices that are not present in the passed vertex:

```scala
scala> val movieOuterJoinedGraph = graph.outerJoinVertices(movies)
((_,name, movies) => (name,movies.getOrElse(MoviesWatched("NA","NA"))))

scala> movieOuterJoinedGraph.vertices.map(t=>t).collect.foreach(println)

(4,((Ryan,53),MoviesWatched(NA,NA)))
(6,((Lily,52),MoviesWatched(NA,NA)))
(2,((Jessica,45),MoviesWatched(Titanic,Love)))
(1,((Jacob,48),MoviesWatched(Toy Story 3,kids)))
(3,((Andrew,25),MoviesWatched(The Hangover,Comedy)))
(5,((Emily,22),MoviesWatched(NA,NA)))
```

VertexRDD and EdgeRDD operations

All of the graph operations in previous sections are invoked on a graph and return a new graph object. In this section, let's learn about operations that transform VertexRDD and EdgeRDD collections. The types of these collections are subtypes of `RDD[(VertexID, VD)]` and `RDD[Edge[ED]]` respectively.

Mapping VertexRDD and EdgeRDD

`mapValues` takes a `map` function as input and transforms each vertex attribute in the VertexRDD to return a new VertexRDD object while preserving the original vertex indices. `mapValues` is overloaded so that the `map` function can take two inputs, `VD` or `(VertexId, VD)`. The type of the new vertex attributes can be different to `VD`:

```scala
def mapValues[VD2](map: VD => VD2): VertexRDD[VD2]
def mapValues[VD2](map: (VertexId, VD) => VD2): VertexRDD[VD2]
```

Similarly, transform the edge attributes while preserving the structure:

```scala
def mapValues[ED2](f: Edge[ED] => ED2): EdgeRDD[ED2]
```

Filtering VertexRDDs

The `filter` method filters VertexRDD collections by not changing the vertex indexing. The `filter` method is not overloaded and the type of the predicate must be `(VertexId, VD) => Boolean`:

```scala
def filter(pred: (VertexId, VD) => Boolean): VertexRDD[VD]
```

The `diff` operation that follows also filters vertices inside a VertexRDD collection. It removes vertices from a set that appears in another set:

```
def diff(another: VertexRDD[VD]): VertexRDD[VD]
```

The `minus` operation returns vertices that are unique to a set based on their `VertexId`:

```
def minus(another: RDD[(VertexId, VD)])
```

Joining VertexRDDs

Two join operations, `innerJoin` and `leftJoin`, are optimized for VertexRDD collections with internal indexing to accelerate joins:

```
def innerJoin[U, VD2](other: RDD[(VertexId, U)])(f: (VertexId, VD,
  U) => VD2): VertexRDD[VD2]
def leftJoin[U, VD2](other: RDD[(VertexId, VD2)])(f: (VertexId,
  VD, Option[U]) => VD2): VertexRDD[VD2]
```

Joining EdgeRDDs

The `innerJoin` operator can be applied for joining two EdgeRDDs as well:

```
def innerJoin[ED2, ED3](other: EdgeRDD[ED2])(f: (VertexId,
  VertexId, ED, ED2) => ED3): EdgeRDD[ED3]
```

This is similar to the `innerJoin` method for VertexRDD, except that now its input function is different and `innerJoin` uses the same partitioning strategy as the original EdgeRDD.

Reversing edge directions

We have seen the reverse operation in the *Modifying graphs* section, that reverses all the edges of graph. If reversing a subset of edges in a graph is the requirement, the following `reverse` method defined as EdgeRDD objects is useful:

```
def reverse: EdgeRDD[ED]
```

GraphX algorithms

GraphX provides many algorithms out-of-the-box in version 1.6. Let's learn about PageRank, triangle counting, and connected components using the graph we created in the previous section.

PageRank measures the importance of each vertex in a graph. It creates a tolerance value, and calls the graph's `pageRank` method using it. The vertices are then ranked into a new value ranking. In order to make the ranking more meaningful, the ranking values are joined with the original vertices RDD. The `rankByPerson` value then contains the rank, vertex ID, and person's name.

Make sure to allocate additional memory (with the `--driver-memory` parameter) to avoid an out-of-memory exception. You can execute it in local mode by assigning more memory to the driver as well, as shown in the following command. If you are restarting the shell, make sure to reconstruct the graph by executing commands shown in the *Creating a graph* section:

```
spark-shell --master local[*] --driver-memory 3G


scala> val tolerance = 0.0001
scala> val ranking = graph.pageRank(tolerance).vertices


scala> val rankByPerson = vertices.join(ranking).map {
        case (id, ( (person,age) , rank )) => (rank, id, person)
        }
```

The PageRank result, held in `rankByPerson`, is then printed record by record, using a `case` statement to identify the record contents, and a format statement to print the contents:

```
Scala> rankByPerson.collect().foreach {
        case (rank, id, person) =>
        println ( f"Rank $rank%1.2f for id $id person $person")
    }
```

The output from the application is then shown here. As expected, Jacob and Jessica have the highest rank, as they have the most relationships:

```
Rank 0.15 for id 4 person Ryan
Rank 0.15 for id 6 person Lily
Rank 1.62 for id 2 person Jessica
Rank 1.82 for id 1 person Jacob
Rank 1.13 for id 3 person Andrew
Rank 1.13 for id 5 person Emily
```

Triangle counting

The triangle count algorithm provides a vertex-based count of the number of triangles associated with a vertex. For instance, vertex Jacob (1) is connected to Emily (5), who is connected to Jessica (2). Jessica is connected to Jacob (1) and so, a triangle is formed. This can be useful for route finding, where minimum, triangle-free, spanning tree graphs need to be generated for route planning:

```scala
scala> val tCount = graph.triangleCount().vertices
scala> println( tCount.collect().mkString("\n") )
(4,0)
(6,0)
(2,2)
(1,2)
(3,1)
(5,1)
```

The results of the application job show that the vertices called Lily (6) and Ryan (4) have no triangles, whereas Jacob (1) and Jessica (2) have the most, as expected, as they have the most relationships.

Connected components

When a large graph is created from the data, it might contain unconnected subgraphs that are isolated from each other and contain no connecting edges between them. This algorithm provides a measure of this connectivity. Depending upon your processing, it is important to know that all the vertices are connected. Let's use two graph methods, connectedComponents and stronglyConnectedComponents, for this algorithm. The strong method required a maximum iteration count, which has been set to 1000. These counts are acting on the graph vertices:

```scala
scala> val iterations = 1000
scala> val connected = graph.connectedComponents().vertices
scala> val connectedS = graph.stronglyConnectedComponents(iterations).
vertices
```

The vertex counts are then joined with the original vertex records, so that the connection counts can be associated with vertex information, such as the person's name:

```scala
scala> val connByPerson = vertices.join(connected).map {
case (id, ( (person,age) , conn )) => (conn, id, person)
}
```

```scala
scala> val connByPersonS = vertices.join(connectedS).map {
case (id, ( (person,age) , conn )) => (conn, id, person)
}
```

The results are then output using a `case` statement and formatted, printing:

```scala
scala> connByPerson.collect().foreach {
        case (conn, id, person) =>
        println ( f"Weak $conn $id $person" )
    }
```

```
Weak 1 4 Ryan
Weak 1 6 Lily
Weak 1 2 Jessica
Weak 1 1 Jacob
Weak 1 3 Andrew
Weak 1 5 Emily
```

As expected for the `connectedComponents` algorithm, the results show that, for each vertex, there is only one component.

The `stronglyConnectedComponents` algorithm gives a measure of the connectivity in a graph, taking into account the direction of the relationships between them:

```scala
scala> connByPersonS.collect().foreach {
        case (conn, id, person) =>
        println ( f"Strong $conn $id $person" )
    }
```

The result for the `stronglyConnectedComponents` algorithm output is as follows:

```
Strong 4 4 Ryan
Strong 6 6 Lily
Strong 1 2 Jessica
Strong 1 1 Jacob
Strong 1 3 Andrew
Strong 1 5 Emily
```

So, the strong method output shows that, for most vertices, there is only one graph component signified by the 1 in the second column. However, vertices 4 and 6 are not reachable due to the direction of their relationship, and so they have a vertex ID instead of a component ID.

Analyzing flight data using GraphX

Let's analyze flight data by representing the airports as vertices and routes as edges. Let's do some basic graph analytics to find out departures and arrivals and also analyze the data with the Pregel API to find out the cheapest fares. Download the flight data from the following location:

```
http://www.transtats.bts.gov/DL_SelectFields.asp?Table_ID=236&DB_
Short_Name=On-Time
```

The steps to analyze the data are as follows:

1. Select **OriginAirportID**, **Origin**, **DestAirportID**, **Dest**, and **Distance** then click **Download**. Copy the ZIP file onto the cluster, unzip it, and then copy the contents to HDFS:

    ```
    unzip 355968671_T_ONTIME.zip
    ```

    ```
    hadoop fs -put 355968671_T_ONTIME.csv
    ```

2. Get into the Scala shell using the `spark-shell` command and then import all dependencies, as follows:

    ```
    scala> import org.apache.spark.graphx._
    scala> import org.apache.spark.rdd.RDD
    ```

3. Define a Scala `case` class for the flight schema corresponding to the CSV data file:

    ```
    scala> case class Flight(org_id:Long, origin:String, dest_id:Long,
    dest:String, dist:Float)
    ```

4. Let's define a function to parse CSV data into the `Flight` class:

    ```
    scala> def parseFlightCsv(str: String): Flight = {
      val line = str.split(",")
      Flight(line(0).toLong, line(1), line(2).toLong, line(3),
    line(4).toFloat)
    }
    ```

5. Let's create `csvRDD` by reading the input file and then remove the header:

    ```
    scala> val csvRDD = sc.textFile("355968671_T_ONTIME.csv")
    scala> val noHdrRDD = csvRDD.mapPartitionsWithIndex { (idx, iter)
    => if (idx == 0) iter.drop(1) else iter }

    scala> val flightsRDD = noHdrRDD.map(parseFlightCsv)
    ```

6. Let's define airports as vertices (Airport ID and Airport name) and a default vertex called `nowhere`. Map the airport ID to the three-letter code for mapping later:

```scala
scala> val airports = flightsRDD.map(flight => (flight.org_id,
flight.origin)).distinct
```

```scala
scala> airports.take(3)
res26: Array[(Long, String)] = Array((14122,"PIT"), (10141,"ABR"),
(13158,"MAF"))
```

```scala
scala> val default = "nowhere"
```

```scala
scala> val airportMap = airports.map { case ((org_id), name) =>
(org_id -> name) }.collect.toList.toMap
```

7. The edges are the routes between airports in this case. An edge must have a source, a destination, and property such as the distance in this case:

```scala
scala> val flightRoutes = flightsRDD.map(flight => ((flight.org_
id, flight.dest_id), flight.dist)).distinct
```

```scala
scala> val edges = flightRoutes.map {

case ((org_id, dest_id), distance) =>Edge(org_id.toLong, dest_
id.toLong, distance) }
```

```scala
scala> edges.take(1)
```

```scala
// Array(Edge(10299,10926,160))
```

8. Create a graph using VertexRDD, EdgeRDD, and a default vertex:

```scala
scala> val graph = Graph(airports, edges, default)
```

9. Let's do some basic analytics using this graph. Find which airports have the most incoming flights:

```scala
scala> val maxIncoming = graph.inDegrees.collect.sortWith(_._2 >
_._2).map(x => (airportMap(x._1), x._2)).take(3)
```

```scala
scala> maxIncoming.foreach(println)
(ATL,152)
(ORD,145)
(DFW,143)
```

10. Now, let's find out which airport has the most outgoing flights:

```
scala> val maxout= graph.outDegrees.join(airports).sortBy(_._2._1,
ascending=false).take(3)

scala> maxout.foreach(println)
(10397,(153,ATL))
(13930,(146,ORD))
(11298,(143,DFW))
```

11. Find the top three flights from a source airport to a destination airport:

```
scala> graph.triplets.sortBy(_.attr, ascending=false).map(triplet
=> "There were " + triplet.attr.toInt + " flights from " +
triplet.srcAttr + " to " + triplet.dstAttr + ".").take(3)
.foreach(println)

There were 4983 flights from "JFK" to "HNL".
There were 4983 flights from "HNL" to "JFK".
There were 4962 flights from "EWR" to "HNL".
```

Pregel API

Many important graph algorithms are iterative algorithms, since the properties of vertices depend on the properties of their neighbors, which depend on the properties of their neighbors. Pregel is an iterative graph processing model, developed at Google, which uses a sequence of iterations of message passing between vertices in a graph. GraphX implements a Pregel-like bulk-synchronous message-passing API.

With the Pregel implementation in GraphX, vertices can only send messages to neighboring vertices.

The Pregel operator is executed in a series of super steps. In each super step:

- The vertices receive the sum of their inbound messages from the previous super step
- Compute a new value for the vertex property
- Send messages to their neighboring vertices in the next super step

When there are no more messages remaining, the Pregel operator will end the iteration and the final graph is returned. The following code computes the cheapest airfare using the Pregel API:

```scala
scala> val sourceId: VertexId = 13024 //  starting vertex
```

A graph with edges containing an airfare cost calculation as $50 + distance / 20$ is as follows:

```scala
scala> val gg = graph.mapEdges(e => 50.toDouble + e.attr.toDouble/20  )
```

Initialize the graph; all vertices except source have the distance as infinity:

```scala
scala> val initialGraph = gg.mapVertices((id, _) => if (id == sourceId)
0.0 else Double.PositiveInfinity)
```

Now, call `pregel` on the graph:

```scala
scala> val sssp = initialGraph.pregel(Double.PositiveInfinity)(
   // Vertex Program
  (id, dist, newDist) => math.min(dist, newDist),
  triplet => {
  // Send Message
   if (triplet.srcAttr + triplet.attr < triplet.dstAttr) {
     Iterator((triplet.dstId, triplet.srcAttr + triplet.attr))
   } else {
     Iterator.empty
   }
 },
 // Merge Message
 (a,b) => math.min(a,b)
)
```

Now, print the routes with the lowest flight cost:

```scala
scala> println(sssp.edges.take(4).mkString("\n"))
Edge(10135,10397,84.6)
Edge(10135,13930,82.7)
Edge(10140,10397,113.45)
Edge(10140,10821,133.5)
```

Find the routes with airport codes and the lowest flight cost:

```scala
scala> sssp.edges.map{ case ( Edge(org_id, dest_id,price))=> (
(airportMap(org_id), airportMap(dest_id), price)) }.takeOrdered(10)
(Ordering.by(_._3))


Array((WRG,PSG,51.55), (PSG,WRG,51.55), (CEC,ACV,52.8), (ACV,CEC,52.8),
(ORD,MKE,53.35), (IMT,RHI,53.35), (MKE,ORD,53.35), (RHI,IMT,53.35),
(STT,SJU,53.4), (SJU,STT,53.4))
```

Find airports with the lowest flight cost:

```scala
scala> println(sssp.vertices.take(4).mkString("\n"))


(10208,277.79)

(10268,260.7)

(14828,261.65)

(14698,125.25)
```

Find airport codes sorted by the lowest flight cost:

```scala
scala> sssp.vertices.collect.map(x => (airportMap(x._1), x._2)).
sortWith(_._2 < _._2)
res21: Array[(String, Double)] = Array(PDX,62.05), (SFO,65.75),
(EUG,117.35)
```

Introducing GraphFrames

While the GraphX framework is based on the RDD API, GraphFrames is an external
Spark package built on top of the DataFrames API. It inherits the performance
advantages of DataFrames using the catalyst optimizer. It can be used in the Java,
Scala, and Python programming languages. GraphFrames provides additional
functionalities over GraphX such as motif finding, DataFrame-based serialization,
and graph queries. GraphX does not provide the Python API, but GraphFrames
exposes the Python API as well.

It is easy to get started with GraphFrames. On a Spark 2.0 cluster, let's start a Spark shell with the packages option using the same data used to create the graph in the *Creating a graph* section of this chapter:

```
$SPARK_HOME/bin/spark-shell --packages graphframes:graphframes:0.2.0-
spark2.0-s_2.11


import org.graphframes._


val vertex = spark.createDataFrame(List(
    ("1","Jacob",48),
    ("2","Jessica",45),
    ("3","Andrew",25),
    ("4","Ryan",53),
    ("5","Emily",22),
    ("6","Lily",52)
)).toDF("id", "name", "age")


val edges = spark.createDataFrame(List(
    ("6","1","Sister"),
    ("1","2","Husband"),
    ("2","1","Wife"),
    ("5","1","Daughter"),
    ("5","2","Daughter"),
    ("3","1","Son"),
    ("3","2","Son"),
    ("4","1","Friend"),
    ("1","5","Father"),
    ("1","3","Father"),
    ("2","5","Mother"),
    ("2","3","Mother")
)).toDF("src", "dst", "relationship")


val graph = GraphFrame(vertex, edges)
```

Once a graph is created, all graph operations and algorithms can be executed. Some of the basic operations are shown as follows:

```scala
scala> graph.vertices.show()
+---+-------+---+
| id|   name|age|
+---+-------+---+
|  1|  Jacob| 48|
|  2|Jessica| 45|
|  3| Andrew| 25|
|  4|   Ryan| 53|
|  5|  Emily| 22|
|  6|   Lily| 52|
+---+-------+---+


scala> graph.edges.show()
+---+---+------------+
|src|dst|relationship|
+---+---+------------+
|  6|  1|      Sister|
|  1|  2|     Husband|
|  2|  1|        Wife|
|  5|  1|    Daughter|
|  5|  2|    Daughter|
|  3|  1|         Son|
|  3|  2|         Son|
|  4|  1|      Friend|
|  1|  5|      Father|
|  1|  3|      Father|
|  2|  5|      Mother|
|  2|  3|      Mother|
+---+---+------------+


scala> graph.vertices.groupBy().min("age").show()
```

```
+--------+
|min(age)|
+--------+
|      22|
+--------+
```

Motif finding

The motif finding algorithm is used to search for structural patterns in a graph. GraphFrame-based motif finding uses DataFrame-based DSL for finding structural patterns. The following example, `graph.find("(a)-[e]->(b); (b)-[e2]->(a)")`, will search for pairs of vertices a, and b, connected by edges in both directions. It will return a DataFrame of all such structures in the graph with columns for each of the named elements (vertices or edges) in the motif. In this case, the returned columns will be a, b, e, and e2:

```
scala> val motifs = graph.find("(a)-[e]->(b); (b)-[e2]->(a)")
scala> motifs.show()
```

e	a	b	e2
[1,2,Husband]	[1,Jacob,48]	[2,Jessica,45]	[2,1,Wife]
[2,1,Wife]	[2,Jessica,45]	[1,Jacob,48]	[1,2,Husband]
[5,1,Daughter]	[5,Emily,22]	[1,Jacob,48]	[1,5,Father]
[5,2,Daughter]	[5,Emily,22]	[2,Jessica,45]	[2,5,Mother]
[3,1,Son]	[3,Andrew,25]	[1,Jacob,48]	[1,3,Father]
[3,2,Son]	[3,Andrew,25]	[2,Jessica,45]	[2,3,Mother]
[1,5,Father]	[1,Jacob,48]	[5,Emily,22]	[5,1,Daughter]
[1,3,Father]	[1,Jacob,48]	[3,Andrew,25]	[3,1,Son]
[2,5,Mother]	[2,Jessica,45]	[5,Emily,22]	[5,2,Daughter]
[2,3,Mother]	[2,Jessica,45]	[3,Andrew,25]	[3,2,Son]

Now, let's filter the results as follows:

```scala
scala> motifs.filter("b.age > 30").show()
```

e	a	b	e2
[1,2,Husband]	[1,Jacob,48]	[2,Jessica,45]	[2,1,Wife]
[2,1,Wife]	[2,Jessica,45]	[1,Jacob,48]	[1,2,Husband]
[5,1,Daughter]	[5,Emily,22]	[1,Jacob,48]	[1,5,Father]
[5,2,Daughter]	[5,Emily,22]	[2,Jessica,45]	[2,5,Mother]
[3,1,Son]	[3,Andrew,25]	[1,Jacob,48]	[1,3,Father]
[3,2,Son]	[3,Andrew,25]	[2,Jessica,45]	[2,3,Mother]

You can cache the returned DataFrame if you are doing multiple operations. You can convert the GraphFrame to GraphX using `toGraphX` and also you can convert a GraphX graph to GraphFrame using `fromGraphX`.

Loading and saving GraphFrames

Since GraphFrames are built on top of DataFrames, they inherit all DataFrame-supported DataSources. You can write GraphFrames to the Parquet, JSON, and CSV formats. The following example shows how to write a GraphFrame to Parquet and read the same Parquet files to build the graph again:

```scala
scala> graph.vertices.write.parquet("vertices")
scala> graph.edges.write.parquet("edges")

scala> val verticesDF = spark.read.parquet("vertices")
scala> val edgesDF = spark.read.parquet("edges")
scala> val sameGraph = GraphFrame(verticesDF, edgesDF)
```

Summary

As the complexity of data grows, data can be better represented by a graph rather than a collection. Graph databases such as Neo4J or Titan, or graph-processing systems such as Apache Giraph or GraphX are used for graph analytics. Apache Giraph is based on Hadoop, which is stable and can be used for pure graph-related problems. GraphX is a graph processing system on top of Spark and can be used if the graph is part of the problem. GraphX integrates well with other components of Spark to unify ETL, exploratory analytics, and graph processing.

GraphX can be used for various operations such as creating graphs, counting, filtering, degrees, triplets, modifying, joining, transforming attributes, VertexRDD, and EdgeRDD operations. It also provides GraphX algorithms such as triangle counting, connected components, label propagation, PageRank, SVD++, and shortest paths.

GraphFrames is a DataFrame-based external Spark package that provides performance optimizations and also additional functionalities such as motif finding.

The next chapter is aimed at learning SparkR which is the implementation of the R language on top of Apache Spark.

10
Interactive Analytics with SparkR

Apache Spark 1.4 release added SparkR, an R package on top of Spark, which allowed data analysts and data scientists to analyze large datasets and run jobs interactively using R language on Spark platforms.

R is one of the most popular open source statistical programming languages with a huge number (over 7,000) of community-supported packages. R packages help in statistical analysis, machine learning, and visualization of data. Interactive analytics in R is limited by single-threaded processes and memory limitation, which means that R can process data sets that fit in a single computer's memory only. SparkR is an R package developed at the AMPLab of University of California, which provides features of R on distributed computation engines of Spark, which enables us to run large-scale data analytics interactively using R. This chapter is divided into the following topics:

- Introducing R and SparkR
- Getting started with SparkR
- Using DataFrames with SparkR
- Using SparkR with RStudio
- Machine learning with SparkR
- Using SparkR with Zeppelin

Introducing R and SparkR

Let's understand the features and limitations of R and how SparkR helps in overcoming those limitations.

What is R?

R is an open source software package for statistical analysis, machine learning, and visualization of data. R project (https://www.r-project.org/) is a simple programming language, such as S and S-plus. R can be used on multiple platforms such as Windows, Linux, Mac OS, and other Unix flavors. R was originally developed at the University of Auckland by Ross Ihaka and Robert Gentleman, and now it is maintained by the R development team. It is an implementation of S language, which was developed by John Chambers. R is an interpreted programming language, and is one of the most popular open source statistical analysis packages.

The R features are as follows:

- Open source with over 7,000 packages
- Stable statistics, graphics, and general packages
- Manipulates R objects directly in C, C++, and Java
- Command line and IDEs support

Limitations of R, are as follows:

- Single-threaded
- Data has to fit in memory

R is the most preferred tool for data scientists. *Figure 10.1* indicates how R is typically used by data scientists in two example scenarios. Big data is processed to create a subset of data and then processed in R or distributed storage, as HDFS is analyzed with MapReduce tools for R, such as RMR2 and RHive:

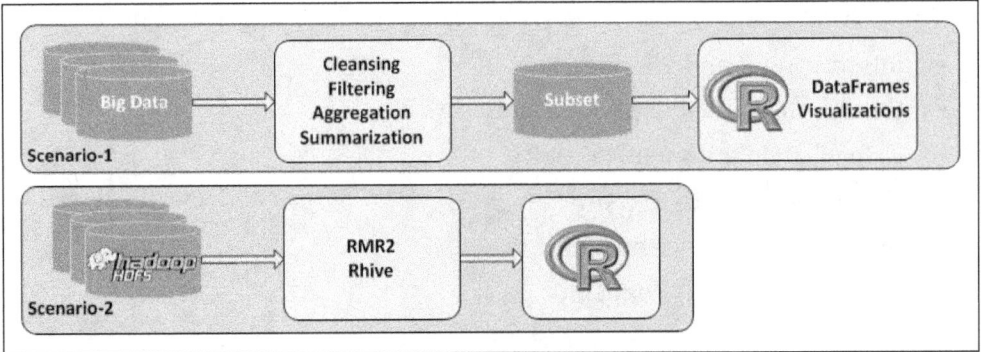

Figure 10.1: Processing patterns using R

Introducing SparkR

SparkR enables users to write R programs on Spark platforms. SparkR was introduced in Spark version 1.4 (June 2015), and currently supports the following features in 2.0:

- Distributed DataFrame based on DataFrame API
- Distributed machine learning using MLLib

SparkR removes additional layers for creating subsets of data or using MapReduce-based frameworks, as shown in *Figure 10.2*:

Figure 10.2: SparkR processing

SparkR provides an easy to use API, and also provides the following benefits:

- **DataSources API**: Spark SQL's DataSources API enables SparkR to read data from a variety of in-built sources such as JSON, Parquet, JDBC, and external sources such as Hive tables, CSV files, XML files, and so on.

- **DataFrame optimizations**: Spark SQL's Catalyst provides optimization for DataFrames such as code generation and memory management. *Figure 10.3* shows that Spark computation engine optimizations make SparkR performance similar to that of Scala and Python. Refer to `https://databricks.com/blog/2015/06/09/announcing-sparkr-r-on-spark.html`:

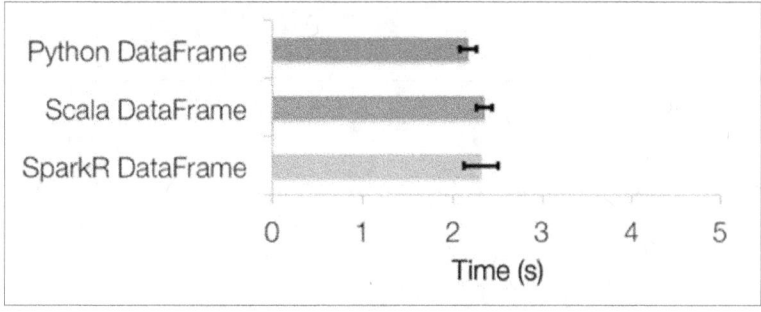

Figure 10.3: SparkR performance with Scala and Python

- **Higher scalability**: Distributed DataFrames created on SparkR will be distributed across all nodes in the Spark cluster. This enables SparkR DataFrames to process terabytes of data.

R integration with Hadoop is supported using many packages and tools. RHadoop, RHive, RHipe, and Hadoop Streaming are a few ways to process data on Hadoop using R language. All these tools are based on MapReduce, and they lack performance in iterative algorithms. In most cases, SparkR would be significantly faster than MapReduce-based implementations of R.

Architecture of SparkR

SparkR architecture is similar to PySpark architecture. Typically, users launch SparkR from a shell, IDE, or RStudio and then load the SparkR package. This will create SparkContext using the R-JVM bridge, and then spawns executor JVMs on workers. Tasks are then shipped from driver to executors, which are forked on R for execution. Executors directly deal with DataSources API to create and process DataFrames. This is depicted in *Figure 10.4*:

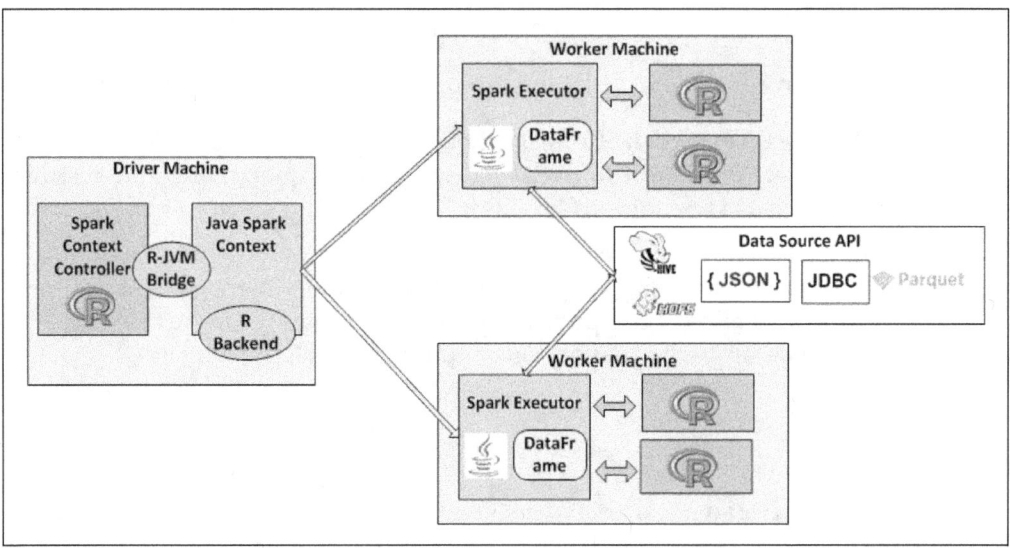

Figure 10.4: SparkR architecture

Getting started with SparkR

Now, let's explore the options to work with SparkR including shell, scripts, RStudio, and Zeppelin.

 All programs in this chapter are executed on CDH 5.8 VM. For other environments, file paths might change. But the concepts are the same in any environment.

Installing and configuring R

The following steps will explain how to install and configure R, and the latest version of Spark:

1. As a first step, we need to install R on all machines in the cluster. The following exercises are tested on CDH 5.7 Quick start VM, which has the CentOS 6.5 operating system. We need to add the latest **Extra Packages for Enterprise Linux** (**EPEL**) repository to the VM, which enables you to install R. EPEL is a community-based repository project from the Fedora team, which provides add-on packages for Red Hat and CentOS. Use the following command to install R on the VM:

   ```
   wget http://download.fedoraproject.org/pub/epel/6/x86_64/epel-
   release-6-8.noarch.rpm

   sudo rpm -ivh epel-release-6-8.noarch.rpm

   sudo yum -y install R
   ```

2. You can test the installation by starting the R shell. Just type *R* on the command line to get into the R shell. CDH 5.7 uses Spark version 1.6. But, we want to use the latest version of Spark (2.0) to work with all the new features of R. So, follow the following procedure to install Spark 2.0. If you have already installed Spark 2.0, skip the following installation steps:

   ```
   wget http://apache.mirrors.tds.net/spark/spark-2.0.0/spark-2.0.0-
   bin-hadoop2.7.tgz

   tar xzvf spark-2.0.0-bin-hadoop2.7.tgz

   cd spark-2.0.0-bin-hadoop2.7
   ```

3. Add the SPARK_HOME and PATH variables to the profile script so that these environment variables will be set every time a new session is started:

   ```
   [cloudera@quickstart ~]$ cat /etc/profile.d/spark20.sh

   export SPARK_HOME=/home/cloudera/spark-2.0.0-bin-hadoop2.7

   export PATH=$PATH:/home/cloudera/spark-2.0.0-bin-hadoop2.7/bin
   ```

4. Let Spark know about the Hadoop configuration directory and Java home by adding environment variables to `spark-env.sh`. Copy the template files to the `conf` directory, as follows:

```
cp conf/spark-env.sh.template conf/spark-env.sh
cp conf/spark-defaults.conf.template conf/spark-defaults.conf
cp /etc/hive/conf/hive-site.xml conf/

vi conf/spark-env.sh
export HADOOP_CONF_DIR=/etc/hadoop/conf
export JAVA_HOME=/usr/java/jdk1.7.0_67-cloudera
```

5. Change the log level to ERROR in the `conf/log4j.properties` file after copying the template file.

Using SparkR shell

Let's learn how to use the SparkR shell in local, standalone, and yarn mode.

Local mode

Now, enter the SparkR shell in local mode with the following command. By default, it will get into local mode with all the cores (`local[*]`) allocated. You can change the number of cores using `master[n]`, as follows:

```
[cloudera@quickstart spark-2.0.0-bin-hadoop2.7]$ bin/sparkR
[cloudera@quickstart spark-2.0.0-bin-hadoop2.7]$ bin/sparkR --master local[2]
```

You will get the following output. Notice that SparkContext is not available, and the only SparkSession is available as `'spark'`:

```
Launching java with spark-submit command /home/cloudera/spark-2.0.0-bin-hadoop2.7/bin/spar
k-submit    "--master" "local[2]" "sparkr-shell" /tmp/RtmpQ6DC4T/backend_port50fe71dbe06d
Setting default log level to "WARN".
To adjust logging level use sc.setLogLevel(newLevel).

Welcome to
    ____              __
   / __/__  ___ _____/ /__
  _\ \/ _ \/ _ `/ __/  '_/
 /___/ .__/\_,_/_/ /_/\_\   version  2.0.0
    /_/

SparkSession available as 'spark'.
>
```

Figure 10.5: SparkR shell in local mode

Use the q() command to quit from the shell.

Standalone mode

Start the standalone master and worker with the following commands, and then start SparkR by passing the standalone master URL:

```
[cloudera@quickstart spark-2.0.0-bin-hadoop2.7]$ cd sbin/
```

```
[cloudera@quickstart sbin]$ sudo ./start-all.sh
```

```
[cloudera@quickstart spark-2.0.0-bin-hadoop2.7]$ bin/sparkR --master
spark://quickstart.cloudera:7077
```

The output will be as follows:

```
Launching java with spark-submit command /home/cloudera/spark-2.0.0-bin-hadoop2.7/bin/spar
k-submit    "--master" "spark://quickstart.cloudera:7077" "sparkr-shell" /tmp/RtmpRknKgY/ba
ckend_port566f765d5f12
Setting default log level to "WARN".
To adjust logging level use sc.setLogLevel(newLevel).

 Welcome to
      ____              __
     / __/__  ___ _____/ /__
    _\ \/ _ \/ _ `/ __/  '_/
   /___/ .__/\_,_/_/ /_/\_\   version  2.0.0
      /_/

SparkSession available as 'spark'.
>
```

Figure 10.6: SparkR shell with the Standalone Resource Manager

Check the Spark UI at http://quickstart.cloudera:8080/.

Yarn mode

If you are still in the Spark standalone shell, exit from it using the q() command. If you don't exit, Yarn will not be able to allocate resources. Make sure Yarn is up and running on the cluster and then pass the yarn-client to the master when starting up the SparkR shell. Also, make sure that the yarn configuration file yarn-site.xml is in /etc/hadoop/conf:

```
[cloudera@quickstart spark-2.0.0-bin-hadoop2.7]$ bin/sparkR --master yarn
```

The output is as follows:

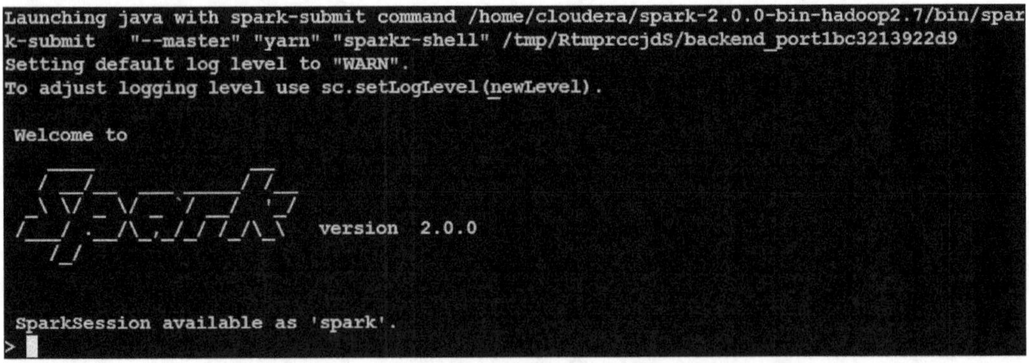

```
Launching java with spark-submit command /home/cloudera/spark-2.0.0-bin-hadoop2.7/bin/spar
k-submit   "--master" "yarn" "sparkr-shell" /tmp/RtmprccjdS/backend_port1bc3213922d9
Setting default log level to "WARN".
To adjust logging level use sc.setLogLevel(newLevel).

Welcome to
      ____              __
     / __/__  ___ _____/ /__
    _\ \/ _ \/ _ `/ __/  '_/
   /___/ .__/\_,_/_/ /_/\_\   version  2.0.0
      /_/

SparkSession available as 'spark'.
>
```

Figure 10.7: SparkR shell with the YARN Resource Manager

The SparkR --help command will show you all the available options such as driver memory, executor memory, and number of cores.

While you are in the SparkR shell, if you are looking for help, type help() or help(lapply) as an example. Use help.start() for an HTML browser interface to help.data() for all available datasets shipped with R installation.

Creating a local DataFrame

Use the following commands to create a local DataFrame in R and convert it to SparkR DataFrame:

```
> localDF <- data.frame(name=c("Jacob", "Jessica", "Andrew"), age=c(48,
45, 25))
> df1 <- as.DataFrame(localDF)
> df2 <- createDataFrame(localDF)
> collect(df1)
```

Otherwise use the following command:

```
> head(df1)
```

Or use the following command:

```
> head(df2)
     name age
1   Jacob  48
2 Jessica  45
3  Andrew  25
```

Creating a DataFrame from a DataSources API

To create a DataFrame from a JSON file stored on a local filesystem, use the following command:

```
> people_json <- read.df("file:///home/cloudera/spark-2.0.0-bin-
hadoop2.7/examples/src/main/resources/people.json", "json")
```

```
> people_json
```

```
DataFrame[age:bigint, name:string]
```

```
> head(people_json)
```

```
  age    name
1  NA Michael
2  30    Andy
3  19  Justin
```

To write the `people` DataFrame as a Parquet file, use the following command. This will create the `people-parq` directory on HDFS, and will create a Parquet file with snappy compression:

```
> write.df(people_json, path = "people-parq", source = "parquet", mode =
"overwrite")
```

Creating a DataFrame from Hive

Copy the `hive-site.xml` to the `conf` directory to let SparkR know about the Hive configuration:

```
cp /etc/hive/conf/hive-site.xml /home/cloudera/spark-2.0.0-bin-hadoop2.7/
conf/
```

If not done already, go to Hue's UI, from quick start menu, click on **Step2: Examples** and then click on on **Hive** to install example tables in Hive quickly.

In Spark 1.6 and below, create the `hiveContext` and use it to fire **Hive query language (HiveQL)**, as follows:

```
> hiveContext <- sparkRHive.init(sc)
> results <- sql(hiveContext, "SELECT * from sample_07 limit 10")
```

In Spark 2.0 and above, create a SparkSession, which is the entry point for R to a Spark cluster. In the SparkR shell, you get a pre-configured SparkSession called `'spark'`. If the `sample_07` table does not exist in Hive, install the Hive examples in Hue's Quick Start Wizard:

```
> results <- sql("SELECT * from sample_07 limit 10")
> results
DataFrame[code:string, description:string, total_emp:int, salary:int]
> head(results)
```

	code	description	total_emp	salary
1	00-0000	All Occupations	134354250	40690
2	11-0000	Management occupations	6003930	96150
3	11-1011	Chief executives	299160	151370
4	11-1021	General and operations managers	1655410	103780
5	11-1031	Legislators	61110	33880
6	11-2011	Advertising and promotions managers	36300	91100

```
> avg <- sql("select avg(salary) as avg_salary from sample_07")
> collect(avg)
  avg_salary
1    47963.63
```

Note that the RDD API is made private in SparkR release 1.4 as it is undergoing major changes. Some of the methods can be accessed using an internal API (via `:::`), as shown in the following snippet. But this is not a recommended method as of this version. For more details, take a look at `https://issues.apache.org/jira/browse/SPARK-7230`:

```
> myRDD <- SparkR:::textFile(sc, "file:///home/cloudera/spark-2.0.0-bin-hadoop2.7/README.md")
> fileCounts <- SparkR:::map(myRDD, nchar)
> SparkR:::take(fileCounts, 10)
```

Using SparkR scripts

When you start the SparkR shell, SparkContext and SqlContext are automatically created. We need to create them explicitly when using scripts. Create a script as shown in the following snippet, and submit it using `spark-submit`:

```
[cloudera@quickstart ~]$ cat sparkrScript.R
library(SparkR)

# Initialize SparkSession
sparkR.session(appName = "SparkR Script")

# Create a local DataFrame in R
localDataFrameinR <- data.frame(name=c("Jacob", "Jessica", "Andrew"),
age=c(48, 45, 25))

# Convert R's local DataFrame to a SparkR's distributed DataFrame
DataFrameSparkR <- createDataFrame(localDataFrameinR)

# Print the SparkR DataFrame schema
printSchema(DataFrameSparkR)

# Print the rows
head(DataFrameSparkR)

# Register the DataFrame as a table
createOrReplaceTempView(DataFrameSparkR, "sparkrtemptable")

# SQL statements on registered table, convert to a local dataframe, and
print
age25above <- sql("SELECT name FROM sparkrtemptable WHERE age > 25")
age25abovelocaldf <- collect(age25above)
print(age25abovelocaldf)

# Write the data out in json format on HDFS:
```

```
write.df(DataFrameSparkR, path="SparkR.json", source="json",
mode="overwrite")
```

```
# Stop the script:
```

```
sparkR.stop()
```

Now, submit the script using the `spark-submit` command and check the result on HDFS:

```
[cloudera@quickstart ~]$ cd spark-2.0.0-bin-hadoop2.7
```

```
[cloudera@quickstart spark-2.0.0-bin-hadoop2.7]$ bin/spark-submit ~/
sparkrScript.R
```

```
root
 |-- name: string (nullable = true)
 |-- age: double (nullable = true)
```

```
      name age
1    Jacob   48
2  Jessica   45
3   Andrew   25
```

```
      name
1    Jacob
2  Jessica
```

```
[cloudera@quickstart spark-2.0.0-bin-hadoop2.7]$ hadoop fs -cat SparkR.
json/part*
```

```
{"name":"Jacob","age":48.0}
```

```
{"name":"Jessica","age":45.0}
```

```
{"name":"Andrew","age":25.0}
```

Use the following command to submit the job using `yarn` as the master and also increase the number of threads used by RBackend to handle RPC calls from the SparkR package from the default number of 2 to 3:

```
[cloudera@quickstart spark-2.0.0-bin-hadoop2.7]$ bin/spark-submit
--master yarn --conf spark.r.numRBackendThreads=3  ~/sparkrScript.R
```

Using DataFrames with SparkR

The following steps will help us to understand more operations with DataFrames on SparkR by analyzing a New York flights dataset:

1. As a first step, let's download the flights data and copy it to HDFS:

   ```
   [cloudera@quickstart ~]$ wget https://s3-us-west-2.amazonaws.com/
   sparkr-data/nycflights13.csv --no-check-certificate
   ```

   ```
   [cloudera@quickstart ~]$ hadoop fs -put nycflights13.csv flights.
   csv
   ```

2. Start the SparkR shell and create a DataFrame using the CSV DataSource. While installing packages, use HTTP locations near you:

   ```
   [cloudera@quickstart ~]$ cd spark-2.0.0-bin-hadoop2.7/
   ```

   ```
   [cloudera@quickstart spark-2.0.0-bin-hadoop2.7]$ bin/sparkR
   ```

   ```
   > install.packages("magrittr", dependencies = TRUE)
   ```

   ```
   > library(magrittr)
   ```

   ```
   > flights <- read.df("flights.csv",source="csv", header="true",
   inferschema="true")
   ```

   ```
   > flights
   ```

   ```
   SparkDataFrame[year:int, month:int, day:int, dep_time:int,
   dep_delay:int, arr_time:int, arr_delay:int, carrier:string,
   tailnum:string, flight:int, origin:string, dest:string, air_
   time:int, distance:int, hour:int, minute:int]
   ```

3. Cache the DataFrame in memory using the following command:

   ```
   > cache(flights)
   ```

4. Count the number of rows in the `flights` DataFrame:

   ```
   > count(flights)
   [1] 336776
   ```

5. Print the first six rows from the DataFrame using the `head` method, or use the `showDF` method to print an SQL-like printout. If you want to print the first two rows only, use the `take` method:

```
> head(flights) or
> showDF(flights)
> take(flights, 2)
```

6. Print the statistics of each column using the `describe` method:

```
> desc <- describe(flights)
> collect(desc)
```

```
    summary                          year                month
day
1    count                          336776               336776
336776
2     mean                          2013.0 6.548509988835309
15.71078699194717
3   stddev 1.1368646858726556E-13 3.414457244678908
8.768607101536823
4      min                           2013                    1
1
5      max                           2013                   12
31
```

7. Filter the columns on a specific condition, and display only the selected columns:

```
> filter <- filter(flights, "dep_delay > 100")
> delay100 <- select(filter, c("origin", "dest", "dep_delay"))
> head(delay100)
  origin dest dep_delay
1    LGA  CLT       101
2    JFK  BWI       853
3    EWR  BOS       144
4    LGA  IAH       134
5    EWR  RIC       115
6    EWR  MCO       105
```

8. Print the number of records grouped by `carrier` in descending order:

```
> carriers <- count(groupBy(flights, "carrier"))
> head(arrange(carriers, desc(carriers$count)))
  carrier count
1      UA 58665
2      B6 54635
3      EV 54173
4      DL 48110
5      AA 32729
6      MQ 26397
```

9. Run a query to print the topmost frequent destinations from JFK airport. Group the flights by destination airport from JFK, aggregate by the number of flights, and then sort by the count column. Print the first six rows:

```
> jfk_origin <- filter(flights, flights$origin == "JFK")

> jfk_dest <- agg(group_by(jfk_origin, jfk_origin$dest), count =
n(jfk_origin$dest))

> head(arrange(jfk_dest, desc(jfk_dest$count)))

  dest count
1  LAX 11262
2  SFO  8204
3  BOS  5898
4  MCO  5464
5  SJU  4752
6  FLL  4254
```

10. Now, register the DataFrame as a temporary table, and query it using SQL:

```
> createOrReplaceTempView(flights, "flightsTable")
> delayDF <- sql("SELECT dest, arr_delay FROM flightsTable")

> head(delayDF)
  dest arr_delay
1  IAH        11
2  IAH        20
```

```
3   MIA         33
4   BQN        -18
5   ATL        -25
6   ORD         12
```

11. Use the following commands to create new columns, delete columns, and rename columns. Check the data before and after deleting the column using the `head` method:

```
> flights$air_time_hr <- flights$air_time / 60
> flights$air_time_hr <- NULL
> newDF <- mutate(flights, air_time_sec = flights$air_time * 60)
> renamecolDF <- withColumnRenamed(flights, " air_time", " air_
time_ren")
```

12. Combine the whole query into two lines using `magrittr`:

```
> jfk_dest <- filter(flights, flights$origin == "JFK") %>%
  group_by(flights$dest) %>%
  summarize(count = n(flights$dest))


> frqnt_dests <- head(arrange(jfk_dest, desc(jfk_dest$count)))


> head(frqnt_dests)
  dest count
1 LAX 11262
2 SFO  8204
3 BOS  5898
4 MCO  5464
5 SJU  4752
6 FLL  4254
```

13. Finally, create a bar plot of frequent destinations. If you are executing this command in a Putty shell, the graph will not be displayed. To display the graph, you need to use a shell session within the VM:

```
> barplot(frqnt_dests$count, names.arg = frqnt_dests$dest,co
l=rainbow(7),main="Top Flight Destinations from JFK", xlab =
"Destination", ylab= "Count", beside=TRUE )
```

The bar plot is shown as follows:

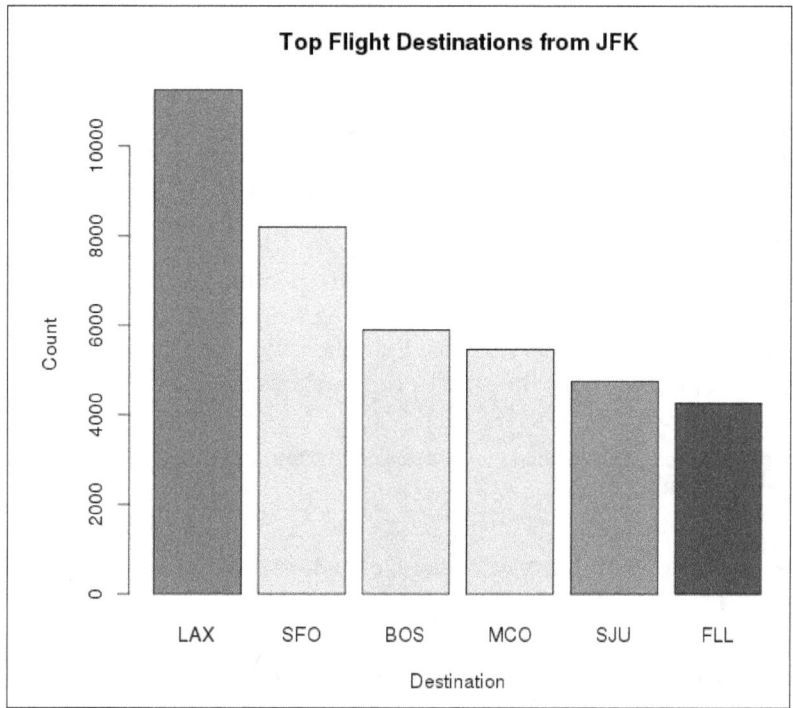

Figure 10.8: Bar plot screenshot from SparkR

14. Though it's not recommended, if you want to convert the SparkR DataFrame to an R local DataFrame, use the following command:

```
> localdf <- collect(jfk_dest)
```

Using SparkR with RStudio

Let's learn how to use RStudio with SparkR in this section. RStudio is an **integrated development environment** (**IDE**) interface for R that provides developer productivity. It is open source and available on multiple platforms including Linux, macOS, and Windows with optional commercial support. It has a familiar R shell, a syntax-highlighting editor that supports direct code execution, tools for plotting, history, debugging, and workspace management. It has a desktop and server version for running from a desktop or centrally from a server. Let's use RStudio Server, which provides a web browser to do analytics, using the following steps:

1. Let's install RStudio Server using the following commands:

   ```
   wget https://download2.rstudio.org/rstudio-server-rhel-
   0.99.903-x86_64.rpm

   sudo yum -y install --nogpgcheck rstudio-server-rhel-
   0.99.903-x86_64.rpm
   ```

2. Open the Firefox browser in the VM and open the page using `http://localhost:8787/auth-sign-in`. Use `cloudera/cloudera` credentials to login to the RStudio server. Paste the following lines in the shell of RStudio and hit *Enter*. Let's use the similar flights dataset we have used earlier for this exercise:

   ```
   .libPaths(c(.libPaths(), '/home/cloudera/spark-2.0.0-bin-
   hadoop2.7/R/lib'))

   Sys.setenv(SPARK_HOME = '/home/cloudera/spark-2.0.0-bin-
   hadoop2.7')

   Sys.setenv('SPARKR_SUBMIT_ARGS'='"--master" "yarn" "--packages"
   "com.databricks:spark-avro_2.11:3.0.0" "sparkr-shell"')

   Sys.setenv(PATH = paste(Sys.getenv(c('PATH')), '/home/cloudera/
   spark-2.0.0-bin-hadoop2.7/bin', sep=':'))

   library(SparkR)
   sparkR.session(appName = "RStudio Application")

   library(magrittr)

   flights <- read.df("flights.csv", source = "csv", header = "true")
   ```

```
# Run a query to print the top most frequent destinations from JFK
airport

jfk_dest <- filter(flights, flights$origin == "JFK") %>%
  group_by(flights$dest) %>%
  summarize(count = n(flights$dest))


top_dests <- head(arrange(jfk_dest, desc(jfk_dest$count)))


# Finally, create a bar plot of top destinations.
barplot(top_dests$count, names.arg = top_dests$dest,col=rainbow(7
),main="Top Flight Destinations from JFK", xlab = "Destination",
ylab= "Count", beside=TRUE )
```

A bar plot shows up in the plots area, as follows:

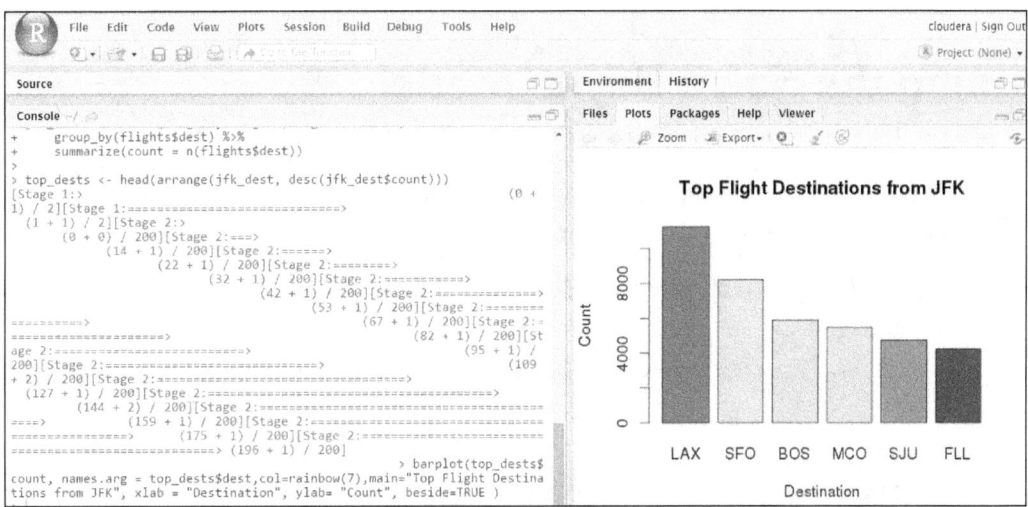

Figure 10.9: RStudio screenshot

3. Write the DataFrame to HDFS in the avro format:

    ```
    write.df(flights, path = "flights.avro", source = "com.databricks.
    spark.avro", mode = "overwrite")
    ```

    Check the output on Hadoop as shown here:

    ```
    [cloudera@quickstart ~]$ hadoop fs -ls flights.avro | awk '{print
    $8}'

    flights.avro/_SUCCESS
    ```

```
flights.avro/part-r-00000-1a6133bd-0039-4dfd-972f-f1ba6b1d0385.
avro
```

```
flights.avro/part-r-00001-1a6133bd-0039-4dfd-972f-f1ba6b1d0385.
avro
```

Check the job status in the Yarn Resource Manager and Spark UI while executing these commands in RStudio.

Machine learning with SparkR

Spark version 1.5 added support for machine learning over DataFrames created in SparkR. SparkR currently supports the Generalized Linear Model, **Accelerated Failure Time (AFT)**, Survival Regression Model, Naive Bayes Model, and K-Means algorithms in version 2.0.

Let's go through a couple of examples to understand how machine learning is implemented in SparkR.

Using the Naive Bayes model

Based on the Titanic survival dataset, let's analyze what sorts of people are likely to survive. The Titanic dataset is summarized according to economic status (class), sex, age, and survival. spark.naiveBayes() fits a Bernoulli Naive Bayes model against a Spark DataFrame. The steps to do so are as follows:

1. Create a local DataFrame and convert it to a Spark DataFrame:

   ```
   > localDF <- as.data.frame(Titanic)
   > DF <- createDataFrame(localDF[localDF$Freq > 0, -5])
   ```

   ```
   > head(DF)
     Class    Sex    Age Survived
   1   3rd   Male  Child       No
   2   3rd Female  Child       No
   3   1st   Male  Adult       No
   4   2nd   Male  Adult       No
   5   3rd   Male  Adult       No
   6  Crew   Male  Adult       No
   ```

   ```
   > count(DF)
   [1] 24
   ```

2. Create training and test datasets from the DataFrame:

```
> trainingDF <- DF
> testDF <- DF
```

3. Create the model from the training dataset, and then print it:

```
> model <- spark.naiveBayes(trainingDF, Survived ~ Class + Sex +
Age)


> summary(model)
$apriori
          Yes        No
[1,] 0.5769231 0.4230769


$tables
    Class_3rd Class_1st Class_2nd Sex_Male Age_Adult
Yes 0.3125    0.3125    0.3125    0.5      0.5625
No  0.4166667 0.25      0.25      0.5      0.75
```

4. Now, predict survivals using the test dataset:

```
> survivalPredictions <- predict(model, testDF)
> survivalPredictions
SparkDataFrame[Class:string, Sex:string, Age:string,
Survived:string, label:double, rawPrediction:vector,
probability:vector, prediction:string]


> showDF(select(survivalPredictions, "Class", "Survived",
"prediction"))
+-----+--------+----------+
|Class|Survived|prediction|
+-----+--------+----------+
|  3rd|      No|       Yes|
|  3rd|      No|       Yes|
|  1st|      No|       Yes|
|  2nd|      No|       Yes|
|  3rd|      No|        No|
| Crew|      No|       Yes|
|  1st|      No|       Yes|
```

```
|  2nd|      No|     Yes|
|  3rd|      No|      No|
| Crew|      No|     Yes|
|  1st|     Yes|     Yes|
|  2nd|     Yes|     Yes|
|  3rd|     Yes|     Yes|
|  1st|     Yes|     Yes|
|  2nd|     Yes|     Yes|
|  3rd|     Yes|     Yes|
|  1st|     Yes|     Yes|
|  2nd|     Yes|     Yes|
|  3rd|     Yes|      No|
| Crew|     Yes|     Yes|
+-----+--------+----------+
```

Using the k-means model

Let's perform the k-means model on the iris data set, which gives the measurements in centimeters of the variables sepal length and width and petal length and width, respectively, for 50 flowers from each of three species of iris. The species are Iris setosa, versicolor, and virginica. K-means clustering is an unsupervised learning algorithm that tries to cluster data based on its similarity. `spark.kmeans()` fits a k-means clustering algorithm on the SparkR DataFrame. The steps to do so are as follows:

1. Create the SparkR DataFrame and create training and test datasets:

```
> DF <- suppressWarnings(createDataFrame(iris))
> trainingDF <- DF
> testDF <- DF
```

2. Create the model to cluster them based on sepal and petal lengths and widths:

```
> model <- spark.kmeans(trainingDF, ~ Sepal_Length + Sepal_Width +
Petal_Length + Petal_Width,  k = 3)
```

The summary of the model shows three different clusters with their respective lengths and widths:

```
> summary(model)

$coefficients
  Sepal_Length Sepal_Width Petal_Length Petal_Width
```

```
1 5.006        3.428        1.462        0.246
2 6.853846     3.076923     5.715385     2.053846
3 5.883607     2.740984     4.388525     1.434426
```

```
> showDF(fitted(model))
```

3. Now create the clusters using the test dataset:

    ```
    > clusters <- predict(model, testDF)
    ```

4. Now let's print the data from three different clusters:

    ```
    > showDF(clusters, numRows=150)
    ```

    ```
    > head(count(groupBy(clusters, "Species","Prediction")))
          Species Prediction count
    1   virginica          2    14
    2     setosa           0    50
    3   virginica          1    36
    4  versicolor          1     3
    5  versicolor          2    47
    ```

Using SparkR with Zeppelin

The latest Hortonworks Sandbox provides a preconfigured Zeppelin service, which can be used to work with SparkR scripts. For other virtual machines such as Cloudera or MapR, we need to manually install and configure Zeppelin. Follow the steps created in the *The manual method* section under the *Installing Apache Zeppelin* section in *Chapter 6, Notebooks and Dataflows with Spark and Hadoop*.

Open the Zeppelin UI at http://localhost:9999. Create a new notebook and enter the following SparkR code in a paragraph. In the next paragraph, query the data using SQL. DataFrames returned from SparkR will be displayed using Zeppelin's built-in interactive visualizations, as shown in the following charts (bar plot and pie chart).

If you get an error such as interpreter not found, click on the **Interpreter binding** icon in the top-right corner of the notebook, and then click on **Save** to resolve the issue:

```
%r
data(mtcars)
cars <- createDataFrame(mtcars)
createOrReplaceTempView(cars, "carstable")
```

The output of SparkR can be visualized with the following Zeppelin in-built visualizations:

Method 1: Bar plot:

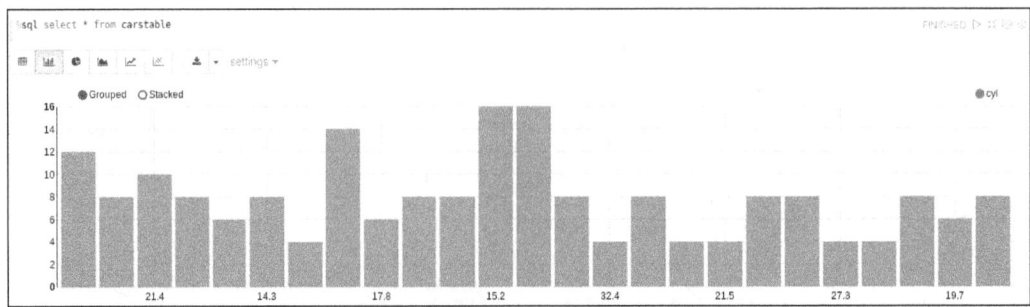

Figure 10.10: Zeppelin SparkR bar plot visualization

Method 2: Pie chart:

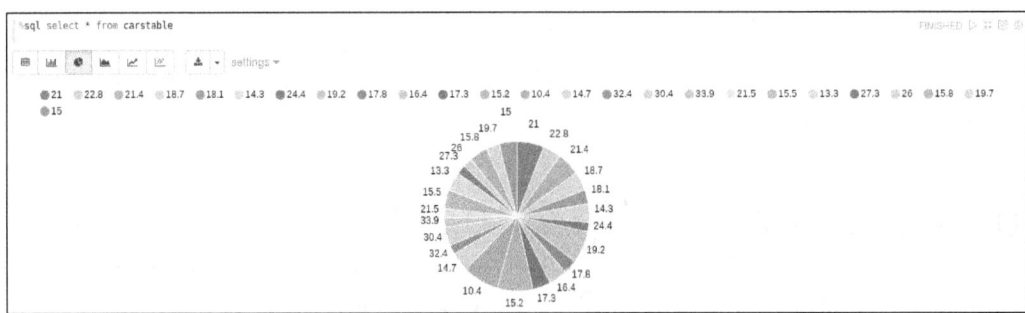

Figure 10.11: Zeppelin SparkR pie chart

R visualizations can be leveraged on Zeppelin notebooks as well.

Summary

SparkR overcomes R's single-threaded process issues and memory limitations with Spark's distributed in-memory processing engine. SparkR provides distributed DataFrame based on DataFrame API and Distributed machine learning using MLlib. SparkR automatically inherits Data Sources API and DataFrame optimizations of Spark engines to provide higher scalability. SparkR is really useful for iterative algorithms instead of using R with Hadoop, which is MapReduce-based.

SparkR can be invoked from shells, scripts, RStudio, as well as Zeppelin notebooks. It can be used with local, standalone, and YARN resource managers. Using the Data Sources API, any external data can be imported to SparkR without any additional coding.

Big Data analytics with Spark and Hadoop is becoming extremely popular and organizations are reaping the benefits of higher scalability and performance with ease of use. While there are plenty of tools available on both Spark and Hadoop, one has to pick the right tool suitable for the use case for optimum performance.

Index

O

Online Analytical Processing (OLAP) 14
optimization algorithms
  about 198
  Limited-memory BFGS (L-BFGS) 198
  Stochastic Gradient Descent 198
Optimized Row Columnar (ORC)
  about 29
  reference 113-115
  working with 113, 114
output operations
  about 138, 139
  foreachRDD(func) 139
  print()/pprint() 138
  saveAsHadoopFile 138
  saveAsNewAPIHadoopDataset 138
  saveAsObjectFiles 138
  saveAsTextFiles 138
  saveToCassandra 138
output stores 139-141

P

packages, Spark
  reference 92
PageRank 249
Pair RDDs 70
Pandas
  working with 118
parallelism, in RDDs 59-63
Parquet
  about 29
  reference 112
  use case 29
  working with 112, 113
partition pruning 114
performance tuning parameters,
      Spark SQL 107
persistence 78
personally identifiable information (PII) 6
pipelining 73, 74
Power Iteration Clustering (PIC) 194
predicate pushdown 114
Pregel API
  implementing 254, 255
Principal Component Analysis (PCA) 194
protocol buffers 28

public movielens data
  URL 217
Python DataFrame operations
  reference 96

R

R
  about 263, 264
  configuring 267
  features 264
  installing 267
  limitations 264
Random Forests 195
RDD operations
  about 106
  actions 57
  transformations 57
RDD
  creating, for recommendation system with
      MLlib 218
  DataFrames, converting to 104
  DataFrames, creating from 100-102
  issues 94
  sharing 181
  using, scenarios 98, 99
RDD transformations
  versus Dataset and DataFrame
      Transformations 95
Read, Evaluate, Print, and Loop (REPL) 163
real-life use cases 15, 16
real-time processing
  about 128
  Spark Streaming, history 130
  Spark Streaming, pros and cons 129
receiver-based approach, Kafka
  about 142-144
  Zookeeper 144, 145
receivers
  reliability 141
  reliable receiver 141
  unreliable receiver 141
recommendation systems
  building 214
  collaborative filtering 214
  content-based filtering 214
  examples 214

User Defined Table Functions (UDTFs) 211